"Cliffie Stone and I received the Academy of Country Music Pioneer Award together in 1972, and our pioneering trails have crossed many times on the Melody Ranch, radio, television, records and music publishing. I am proud to call him my friend and to have had him as a member of my team down through the years. I know that songwriters from all over the world will benefit from his know-how and straight-shooting advice that he shares in this book."

—GENE AUTRY

THE "ORIGINAL" SINGING COWBOY; SONGWRITER; ACTOR; MELODY RANCH
OWNER, CALIFORNIA ANGELS BASEBALL TEAM
SONGWRITER'S HALL OF FAME, 1991
COUNTRY MUSIC ASSOCIATION'S HALL OF FAME, 1969

"So many have written to me over the years wanting to know the answers that are contained in this book — and Cliffie Stone is a name well-respected "across the board" in the music world. He knows whereof he speaks. You'll enjoy reading this informative and amusing book."

—PEGGY LEE

ENTERTAINER/RECORDING STAR — "FEVER," "IS THIS ALL THERE IS?"
ACTRESS/SONGWRITER — "IT'S A GOOD DAY," "MAÑANA,"
"HE'S A TRAMP"
PIED PIPER AWARD — 1990, ASCAP

"Attention: All high schools, universities and colleges with a course in the music business: This is a very important piece of literature for the American songwriter — written by one of the most important and versatile people that I know of in the music business during my lifetime. It should be mandatory reading for anyone who wishes a career in songwriting, publishing or any other phase of the music business. Without being able to tap into the vast knowledge of Cliffie Stone over the past thirty-seven years of my career, my success as a recording artist, songwriter, music publisher and television host would have been very limited. Most important of all, I've also learned how to be a better human being! I love you, Cliffie!"

—BOBBY BARE

RCA RECORDING ARTIST; PUBLISHER, RETURN MUSIC
NASHVILLE NETWORK TELEVISION HOST; SONGWRITER

To STEVE,
ENJOY YOUR
"HALL OF FAME"
CHAIR WHICH CLIFFIE,
NOW WRITE A SONG
Joan Carol Stone
10-18-2008

I

"*Cliffie Stone has been in the business long enough to know all about songwriting and he does!*"
—CHET ATKINS
LEGENDARY GUITARIST; RCA RECORDS PRODUCER
INSTRUMENTALIST OF THE YEAR — COUNTRY MUSIC ASSOCIATION,
1967, 1968, 1969, 1981, 1982, 1983, 1984, 1985
MUSICIAN OF THE YEAR — COUNTRY MUSIC ASSOCIATION, 1988
PIONEER AWARD — 1982, ACADEMY OF COUNTRY MUSIC

"*You don't need to be an aspiring songwriter to enjoy this book. It's fun and entertaining for anyone to read. The way Cliffie weaves his personal experiences throughout the book gives it a sense of country music history.*"
—MINNIE PEARL
COMEDIENNE, GRAND OLE OPRY
COUNTRY MUSIC ASSOCIATION'S HALL OF FAME, 1975

"*Many years ago, I found a home at Central Songs because my buddy, Cliffie, always had an open door and an open ear to my bag of songs. He has worked with great songwriters such as: Tommy Collins, Ned Miller, Freddie Hart, Buck Owens, Jack Rhodes — to name a few. Since he is both a publisher and a songwriter, he understands our needs. Who could be better qualified to write this much needed beginner's songwriting book than Cliffie Stone?*"
—HARLAN HOWARD
SONGWRITER
HALL OF FAME — NASHVILLE SONGWRITERS ASSOCIATION
INTERNATIONAL, 1973

"*Cliffie's new book on songwriting is the closest a new songwriter can get to professional advice from one of the most respected and beloved music men in the business today. The style brings the reader up close and personal with someone who has not merely been an executive, but a doer, deeply involved in the careers of hundreds of successful songwriters. Cliffie combines a practical, down-to-earth, realistic approach to the problems of songwriting with the talents of a master storyteller that will give the reader wonderful glimpses of memorable moments in music industry history as well as career-building advice.*"
—FRANCES W. PRESTON
BMI PRESIDENT AND CEO

"I've written a lot of songs — some were hits and some were misses, and I had to learn the hard way because there wasn't anyone around to help me. I only wish Cliffie had written his book at least twenty years sooner."

—HANK THOMPSON
SINGER/SONGWRITER/GUITAR PLAYER
HALL OF FAME — COUNTRY MUSIC ASSOCIATION, 1989

"Cliffie Stone has created another hit! This one is a most informative book that's a joy to read, but what makes it a truly outstanding addition to music literature is the fact that it's written by someone who thoroughly knows his subject."

—LEE ZHITO
BILLBOARD, VICE PRESIDENT,
EXECUTIVE EDITORIAL DIRECTOR

"Cliffie is a man who has done it all and has been recognized by his peers with almost every conceivable award — including induction into the Country Music Association's Hall of Fame. His book is fun to read but, more importantly, it is informative and guides the beginning songwriter along the right paths."

—JO WALKER-MEADOR
EXECUTIVE DIRECTOR,
COUNTRY MUSIC ASSOCIATION

"Cliffie Stone's book on songwriting puts fun into the fundamentals of this segment of the music industry through personal reminiscence of a life in music. Easy reading and easy learning!"

—SAM TRUST
PRESIDENT, PRIMAT AMERICA
(FORMERLY WITH BMI, CAPITOL RECORDS,
BEECHWOOD MUSIC, ATV MUSIC, LORIMAR)

"I have known and loved Cliffie Stone for many years and I don't know one soul who has more to offer aspiring songwriters. His knowledge of the entire entertainment business qualifies him to be the ideal advisor for those interested in entering the creative world. There is a need to encourage creativity and to lessen the fear of the unknown. Cliffie's book is the definitive answer."

—PAUL CORBIN
DIRECTOR OF PROGRAMMING, THE NASHVILLE NETWORK

III

"Having had major success as a hit songwriter, artist, producer, artist's manager, and being the founder of one of the most successful publishing companies, Central Songs, I should not be surprised that Cliffie Stone would write this book on songwriting. Few people would have the qualifications to undertake a project like this, and I wish I had Cliffie's ability."

—GEORGE RICHEY
SONGWRITER/RECORD PRODUCER
MANAGER, TAMMY WYNETTE

"This one-of-a-kind book from this one-of-a-kind man goes beyond the basic fundamentals of songwriting. After reading it, you will understand why he received the Pioneer Award from the Academy of Country Music in 1972."

—FRED REISER
PRESIDENT, ACADEMY OF COUNTRY MUSIC
DIRECTOR, AWARD-WINNING CRAZY HORSE STEAKHOUSE, SANTA ANA, CA

"Finally — a book chock-full of practical, useful advice for anyone who wants to make a mark in the music business."

—GARY THEROUX
READER'S DIGEST, SR. MUSIC EDITOR
UCLA MUSIC INSTRUCTOR

"In every craft there is nothing more important than fundamentals. I know that Cliffie Stone's book will serve as a valuable resource for all songwriters. I am glad that he took the time to put his wisdom and experience into words, and I'm proud to be his friend."

—DON SCHLITZ
SONG OF THE YEAR, "THE GAMBLER", 1979 — COUNTRY MUSIC ASSOCIATION
SONG OF THE YEAR, "ON THE OTHER HAND" (PAUL OVERSTREET), 1986,
"FOREVER AND EVER AMEN" (PAUL OVERSTREET), 1987 — COUNTRY MUSIC
ASSOCIATION AND ACADEMY OF COUNTRY MUSIC

"Cliffie has been the most important influence on country music that the West Coast has ever had or ever will have. The stars that he has discovered through his radio and television shows and the songwriters that he has helped as a publisher reads like a Who's Who. So read, learn, and write your way to songwriting success with Cliffie as your friend and guide!"

—JOE ALLISON
COUNTRY MUSIC DISC JOCKEY'S HALL OF FAME, 1976
HALL OF FAME — NASHVILLE SONGWRITERS ASSOCIATION INTERNATIONAL, 1978
THE JIM REEVES MEMORIAL AWARD — ACADEMY OF COUNTRY MUSIC, 1969

TOP BOOK REVIEWS AND SOUND BITES

▼

Here's what reviewers had to say about Cliffie's book!

...gives beginners practical advice on everything on the country field from composition to royalties.... Stone's charming, just-folks style helps music business intricacies seem less intimidating to the novice. Clearly no stranger to show business, Stone uses the volume's introductory pages the way a headline act uses a house band — to warm up the audience.
—PUBLISHERS WEEKLY, PENNY KAGANOFF

This wonderfully informative and entertaining book is exploding with tips for beginning and aspiring songwriters, music students, those wanting to put their poetry to music, and inquisitive music fans.... This masterpiece is destined to be a basic tool for musicians.
—LIBRARY JOURNAL, LaDONNE ROBERTS

...A lot of advice here has been offered before in other books, but this time the valuable tips on the process come with the imprimatur of one who's really been there.... Recommended highly for novice songwriters or anyone interested in Country Music lore.
—BOOKLIST, MARTIN BRADY

...His songwriting credentials are formidable.... Stone writes that "Sixteen Tons" had all the elements essential for successful songwriting.
—LOS ANGELES TIMES, MICHAEL ARKUSH

You want to write a song and make a million dollars from it.... Help is here.... Anyone can compose a song by studying Stone's primer.
—THE CHATTANOOGA TIMES, TRAVIS WOLFE

...measures up to the words of praise heaped on it by the likes of the late Tennessee Ernie Ford, Kenny Rogers and Merle Haggard.
—AMARILLO GLOBE-NEWS, MARY K. TRIPP

...highly recommended for everyone who is involved in the creation and appreciation of America's most enduring populist form: country music.
—LOS ANGELES SONGWRITERS SHOWCASE, DAN KIMPEL

...Unlike most music-business books, this one is geared to the absolute beginner, the dreamer who has song thoughts but no knowledge of the song business.
THE TENNESSEAN, ROBERT K. OERMANN

...not only provides a step-by-step guide to songwriting, but also presents anecdotes and observations culled from Stone's 50-plus years in the music business.
TULSA WORLD, JOHN WOOLEY

...It's not just for the songwriter; it's also a guide to the business side of country music and has plenty of anecdotes drawn from Stone's decades in the trade.
THE NEWS-LEADER, EVERETT KENNELL

Aspiring songwriters will love the inside look offered them by Country Music Hall of Famer Cliffie Stone.... Not only are there the nuts-and-bolts tips, but also hundreds of colorful and historical anecdotes about the business.
BILLBOARD MAGAZINE, EDWARD MORRIS

...Stone's book, which gives tips on songwriting, also talks about some of his acquaintances such as Johnny Cash, Willie Nelson and Merle Haggard.
BRANSON BEACON, JIMMY LANCASTER

Songwriting expert, Cliffie Stone, offers industry insight in his book.... No longer is there an excuse for anyone sitting around saying they wish they could write a song. If the interest is there, the method is now there.
THE DENISON HERALD, VICKI LANGDON

...Stone's autobiographical notes and his stories about stars motivated me to read his book, but his practical comments about the songwriting craft, the business of song publishing and the record industry will be of interest to persons longing to enter those fields.
SAVANNAH MORNING NEWS, LARRY POWELL

...his book is worth reading as a historical document as well as a songwriting manual.
COUNTRY CHART ANALYST, NELL LEVIN

EVERYTHING

YOU ALWAYS WANTED TO KNOW

ABOUT

SONGWRITING

BUT DIDN'T KNOW WHO TO ASK

▼

CLIFFIE STONE

WITH JOAN CAROL STONE

SHOWDOWN ENTERPRISES

NORTH HOLLYWOOD, CALIFORNIA

LIBRARY OF CONGRESS CATALOG CARD NUMBER: 91-62145

ISBN 1-880152-00-2

PUBLISHED BY
SHOWDOWN ENTERPRISES
BOX 9275 ▪ N. HOLLYWOOD, CA 91609-1275

FIRST PRINTING JANUARY 1992
SECOND PRINTING JUNE 1992

MANUFACTURED IN THE UNITED STATES OF AMERICA

DISTRIBUTED EXCLUSIVELY BY
MUSIC SALES CORPORATION
225 PARK AVENUE SOUTH ▪ NEW YORK NY 10003
ORDER NO. SD 10000

COVER AND BOOK ART DIRECTION
RIKKI POULOS

COVER PHOTOGRAPHY
HOPE POWELL

BACK COVER PHOTOGRAPHY
PHIL POOL

COPY EDITORS
ASTRID RAMSEY, KATIE KOLPAS

VIII

DEDICATION

This book is dedicated to ALL members of my family who have been and still are the "wind beneath my wings" — with special thanks to:

my mother, Nina Belle Snyder —
whose selfless love and understanding inspired me to be all that I am;

my father, Clifford H. Snyder
(aka Herman, "the Hermit") — who introduced me to the world of music
and encouraged me to become a professional musician;

my late wife, Dorothy —
who gave me roots by standing, lovingly and faithfully, by my side while I
chased "my elusive dreams";

my best friend, Joan Carol Stone —
whose love has brought new meaning and dimension into my life and
without whom this book would never have been written;

my wonderful daughter, Linda —
who has always been there to support all my endeavors and whose
enlightened poetry has only made the bond between us deeper;

my three sons (my buddies) — Steve, Curtis and Jonathan —
who followed in my musical footsteps to find "their place in the sun", and
now I'm learning from them;

my grandchildren —
to whom the "song of life" has been passed on;

and to ALL the songwriters who have ever been, who are now, and who
ever will be — for the special joy that they bring and give to the world
through their songs!

**God respects you when you work,
but he loves you when you sing.**

*But it all begins with a song — for without a song in your heart, you have nothing
to sing.*

Cliffie Stone

CONTENTS

ABOUT THE AUTHOR

Who is more qualified to write about songwriting than Cliffie Stone? As a matter of fact, who is more qualified to write a book on any aspect of both the creative and business side of the music world than he is? This musical jack-of-all-trades has been successful in every musical endeavor imaginable. After reading his achievements, credentials and track record of his fifty years in the entertainment industry which are listed below, you'll know why he's more than qualified and why he was presented with the following awards:

- The **Pioneer** Award from the Academy of Country Music in 1972.

- The Country Music Association's **Hall of Fame** Award presented to him on Nashville's Grand Ole Opry stage October 9, 1989 on CBS-TV.

- The Hollywood Chamber of Commerce presented Cliffie with his own Star on the **Hollywood Walk of Fame** at Sunset & Vine on March 1, 1989.

- The **Walk of Western Stars** was presented on March 24, 1990, in the Santa Clarita-Valencia Valley area.

- The California Country Music Association's **Hall of Fame** was presented to him on November 5, 1990, in Long Beach, California.

- Country Music Disc Jockey's **Hall of Fame** in Nashville, Tennessee, 1979.

- **Silver Spur Humanitarian Award** presented to him at the Gene Autry Western Heritage Museum on November 3, 1989 from College of the Canyons in the Santa Clarita County area.

- Shriners' **Man of the Times** in 1982.

Cliffie Stone is a country music legend whose highly successful "Hometown Jamboree" show was on television and radio from 1946 to 1960. The show originally started at the El Monte American Legion Stadium where for years he "gave them the music they wanted to hear." "Hometown Jamboree" was a launching pad for a multitude of singers that soon became big stars and household names. They include Johnny Cash, Tennessee Ernie Ford, Eddie Arnold, Jim Reeves, Johnny Horton, Merle Travis, Tex Ritter, Liberace, Molly Bee, Lefty Frizzell, Eddie Dean, Tommy Sands, Johnny Bond, Wesley and Marilyn Tuttle, Freddie Hart, and many others too numerous to mention.

Cliffie has worn and still does wear many hats in the music business: bass player; master of ceremonies; singer; comedian, radio disc jockey; songwriter; music publisher; TV, radio and record producer; artist's manager; trustee on the board of directors for the Musicians Union Local 47; and numerous executive positions at recording companies and publishing companies. He has served as vice president of the Country Music Association in Nashville; and in Los Angeles, he's currently serving on the board of directors of the Academy of Country Music. Previously, he has served as its president and vice president.

This master showman still takes his family-oriented "Hometown Jamboree" show out on the road today. They perform at a variety of country/western theme functions such as country clubs, fairs, parks, performing arts centers and nightclubs.

RADIO CREDITS

You don't get in the Country Music Disc Jockey's Hall of Fame for nothing. At one time or another, he was on twenty-eight radio stations in California.

His first radio job was as a musician and comedian on Stuart Hamblen's various radio program shows such as: "Covered Wagon Jubilee," "Lucky Stars," "King Cowboy Revue" and "The Cowboy Church of the Air."

For twenty-two years, Cliffie's "Hometown Jamboree" radio show was rated number one on KXLA radio which was broadcast from the Huntington Hotel in Pasadena.

He was a comedian on "Hollywood Barn Dance" on CBS radio network for eighteen years.

Other radio gigs include: "Pot Luck Party" on CBS, "Radio-Rodeo," "The First Western Quiz Show," "The Cowboy Hit Parade," "Harmony Homestead," "Dinner Bell Roundup," "Country Junction," and the "Cliffie Stone Radio Show" on KLAC.

TELEVISION CREDITS

He produced over 14,000 television and radio shows during his fifty year career in the entertainment industry. He was the producer of "Hometown Jamboree" and the "Molly Bee Show" on TV. He was Tennessee Ernie Ford's manager and the executive producer for the "Tennessee Ernie Ford Show" for five years on NBC television and on CBS radio. For a year, he produced "Gene Autry's Melody Ranch."

Over the years, he worked with talented men like Norman Lear, Bud Yorkin, Jim Hobson, Milt Hoffman, Joe Landis, Selwyn Tauber, and Danny Arnold.

Other producer credits include being one of the executive producers on numerous musical specials for television such as: "Christmas Songs" with Mel Tormé, "Songs for a Lusty Land", "Cross Country" and two "Great American Gospel" shows.

He has appeared on numerous television shows such as the "Tennessee Ernie Ford Show," the "Lawrence Welk Show," "Merv Griffin" and more. His recent television appearances include a half-hour interview on "2 on the Town;" "Nashville Now" with

Ralph Emery; the "Country Music Association's Awards Show" on CBS-TV in 1989; "Tennessee Ernie Ford's 50th Anniversary Show" on the Nashville Network; and Dick Clark's "Academy of Country Music Awards Show" on NBC in 1990.

RECORD COMPANIES

The record companies that he has been associated with include Capitol Records, RCA Records, Warner Bros. Records, Beltone Records, Granite Records, Lariat Records, ARA Records, Newhall Records, Showdown Records, and others.

ALBUM CREDITS

Cliffie's numerous album recording credits include: Tennessee Ernie Ford, Molly Bee, Sons of the Pioneers, Merle Travis, Tex Ritter, Tommy Sands, Stan Freberg, Stuart Hamblen, and the list is endless. Recently, he produced an album with his son, Curtis Stone (Highway 101's bass player) for artist Larry Keyes; other album projects are waiting in the wings.

SONG AND PUBLISHING INFORMATION

Cliffie's award-winning song associations, song-publishing credits and writing credits appear on pages 189 through 192.

In 1946, three of Cliffie's song collaborations reached the Top 5 on *Billboard*'s country charts: "No Vacancy" reached number three (Merle Travis); "New Steel Guitar Rag" went to number five (Bill Boyd and the Cowboy Ramblers); "Divorce Me C.O.D." was number one (Merle Travis); and when the King Sisters recorded it that same year, it went to number five. In 1947, "Divorce Me C.O.D." went to number four (Johnny Bond).

It's also appropriate to mention at this time that one of the special honors bestowed on him several years ago was to have been selected as a national judge by the American Song Festival.

PUBLISHING COMPANIES include American Music, as a writer; Central Songs which he owned for twenty years and eventually sold to Capitol Records; Beechwood Publishing; Bayshore Music; Old Mill Music; Showdown Publishing Group, Inc.; and ATV Music Group (Beatles' catalog). As of the writing of this book (and for the last three years), he is the executive consultant and director of Gene Autry's publishing companies which include Ridgeway Music and Gene Autry Western Music Publishing Co., Inc.

ACKNOWLEDGMENTS

I have been wanting to write a book about songwriting for many years. Everything is timing and I'm glad that I waited until this particular time in my life to write it because a very special person appeared from out of the blue to encourage and inspire me to make my "songwriting book dream" a concrete reality.

As I reread my thoughts and feelings in my chapter about song collaboration, the word "collaboration" has taken on a whole new meaning for me. For without the creative suggestions and concentrated efforts of my best friend and beautiful wife, Joan Carol Stone, a gifted songwriter in her own right, this book would never have materialized.

Joan Carol and I went through a writing process that took a year of dedicated work which basically consisted of me dictating all my thoughts and ideas into my tape recorder for each chapter. After she transcribed and edited the material, we would read it together. We constantly kept adding new ideas and rewriting it until we were both satisfied that the material was presented in the simplest and most logical way in order to help you understand how to write your song(s).

She knows how much I appreciate all her efforts. However, I want to publicly say, "Thank you, darlin', for everything!"

I have been very fortunate and privileged to have been associated with some of the most gifted and talented songwriters who have ever taken pen in hand, either through producing, publishing, and/or writing songs with them. As I look back, I see how the hand of God was at work, for he placed me in the right place at the right time because it wasn't all luck that brought me together with so many of them.

I learned something new, creative and imaginative from every song and every songwriter, and I want to acknowledge and thank them collectively for being a part of my songwriting world, and for contributing to my hopefully important knowledge of songs and the entire spectrum of the music business. One thing is for sure: without them, this book could never have been written. They include: Merle Travis, Tennessee Ernie Ford, Gene Autry, Johnny Mercer, Fred Rose, Stuart Hamblen, Jack Rhodes, Eddie Kirk, Faron Young, Hazel Houser, Gene MacLellan, Bob Roubian, Wynn Stewart, Harlan Howard, Whitey Shafer, Roger Murrah, Bobby Bare, Buck Owens, Merle Haggard, Tex Ritter, Peggy Lee, Bob Wills, Roger Miller, Joe Allison, George Richey, Herman "the Hermit", Stan Freberg, Darol Rice, Porky Freeman, Leon McCalliuffe, Billy Joe Shaver, Barry Mann and Cynthia Weil, Jerry Fuller, Kay Adams, John Hobbs, Tommy Collins, Ned Miller, Charlie Williams, Eddie Dean, Steve Stone, Curtis Stone, Joan Carol Stone, Jonathan Stone, Linda Stone-Hyde, John C. Cunningham, Marc Levine, Vivian Rae, Ginny Peters, Gary Murray, Mark Burnes, Betty Jo Silver, Larry Keyes, and the list is endless. So please forgive me if your name is not mentioned here. You know who you are!

Writing can be a very lonely job because you have to create something out of nothing. You sit there with a blank piece of paper, a pen or a typewriter or computer, and you have to work the wonders of your God-given talent and imagination for long periods of time.

I have often felt that writers in every type of writing field imaginable are not given their due credit, importance or respect for their endeavors. For without the written word, you've got nothing — there wouldn't be a book or newspaper to read, a television show or movie to enjoy, nor a song to sing. Thank goodness BMI, ASCAP, SESAC, the Nashville Songwriters Association International and the country music people know how to honor, appreciate and love their songwriters.

So from the bottom of my heart, I thank ALL you wonderful and talented songwriters for those joyful and golden moments when you have taken me out of my ordinary, everyday life into your "soul world" of song! I love each and every one of you!

I also want to thank ALL the professional people involved in the production of this book, especially Rikki Poulos.

And a special thanks to Melody, our ten-month-old Lhasa Apsos, and Viva, our yellow Lab, for supplying Joan Carol and me with comic relief during the creation of this book.

Cliffie Stone

ACKNOWLEDGMENT AND TESTIMONIAL TO CLIFFIE

I am thankful for the opportunity to be a part of the creation of this book and to share in that experience with my husband, the country music legend, Cliffie Stone. I hope that my contribution will help you to get started writing your own song(s). You never know how far your song idea may take you! So shoot for the stars!

I know firsthand what can happen when you listen to and follow that dream in your heart no matter how long it takes. I am a classic example of being a late bloomer.

I first started writing songs over twenty years ago. To make a long story short, I gave up my dream because I allowed myself to become discouraged by rejections which, in turn, caused me to lose belief in my talents. Then about six years ago, my desire to write again became so strong that I went after it come what may. This time, however, I was armed with belief which produced some magical results.

I was very fortunate to have as my friend and cowriter, Marc Levine, who is a first-class musician (among his numerous musical credits, he was Barry Manilow's bass player for several years). Together, we created some excellent songs.

One song led to another, which invariably led to the "Pied Piper of Music," Cliffie Stone. When he heard our songs, he published them, which only proves how one can have a hobby and how it can turn into a profitable new career.

This prince of a man is so unassuming about his accomplishments, which speak for themselves. What I have learned from him, and what everyone who has been fortunate enough to meet and work with him has learned, is priceless.

He is a "Musical Ambassador of Love and Hope" to aspiring songwriters, singers, musicians and people in general. How he loves to help and encourage people to "let their light shine!" It's no wonder that he's so loved by everybody!

Although our Lord loves all his children equally, I can just imagine how proud he must be of his son, Cliffie, who has truly fulfilled one of his commandments: "You shall love your neighbor as yourself."

Cliffie, thank you for sharing your life and your love with me!

I also want to thank Astrid Ramsey, one of the top executive secretaries in the entertainment industry, for her copy editing suggestions and, more importantly, for her friendship.

Joan Carol Stone

PREFACE

This one-of-a-kind, "how to write a song and have fun while you're doing it" book is a classic. Although many books have been written on the subject, there has never been one quite like this because the author's qualifications transcends the norm and the mediocre.

Three of his most prestigious awards validate this claim: His own star on the Hollywood Walk of Fame presented to him on March 1, 1989; the Country Music Association's Hall of Fame Award presented to him on Nashville's Grand Ole Opry stage October 9, 1989 on CBS-TV; and the Pioneer Award presented to him in 1972 by the Academy of Country Music.

Cliffie wanted his book to have a warm, friendly, and positive "one-on-one" feel to it — as if he were actually having a conversation with the songwriter/reader. His homespun way of saying things and his great sense of humor are interwoven throughout the entire book and make the reading delightful as well as informative.

Through the eyes of one of country music's pioneer legends, you will get a sense of history throughout. Although "disguised" as a "beginning songwriter's book," it has autobiographical tendencies, for he has incorporated many of his personal, song-related experiences from his multifaceted music career to illustrate the validity of the particular songwriting suggestion that he is discussing. This, in itself, makes the book outstanding and entertaining.

Each chapter, with its intriguing title, is interesting and could stand by itself. For example, since there's been considerable controversy about sexually explicit lyrics — to the point of records being banned, which immediately brings into play one of our constitutional rights — Cliffie discusses how far you can go with lyrics in his chapter on sex and songwriting.

The chapter on "The True Story About 'Sixteen Tons'" is worth the "price of admission" alone! While discussing essential music principles, he takes his readers back in time to how one of the great songs, "Sixteen Tons," and his dear friend and associate, Tennessee Ernie Ford, carved a place for themselves in music history.

POETRY

There are millions of people out there who write poetry for themselves. Have you, at one time or another, written a poem to express your innermost feelings? When you follow the simple lyric and melody suggestions, you will be able to write or change your poems into songs.

SONGWRITERS AND MUSIC STUDENTS

Although it's basically a handbook for the beginning and aspiring songwriter, there is something in it for *all* songwriters at *all* levels. Are you a songwriter? If you are, you'll come away from this book with a new perspective and attitude towards songwriting.

INQUISITIVE MUSIC FANS

There are millions of people who are absolutely fascinated about how songs are written, recorded and published. Are you one of them? In simple terms, this book will not only satisfy your curiosity, but may spark a desire in you that you never knew existed which could open up a whole new career of wealth, fame and power.

Regardless, when you are through reading this book, you will know how songs are written and will have an overall picture of the basic, inner workings of the music business. More importantly, you will be delightfully entertained along the way — which is what Cliffie does best!

If it's true that everyone has one book in them, then it's also true that everyone has one song in them!

So welcome to the wonderful world of songwriting and have fun writing your very own song!

Joan Carol Stone

INTRODUCTION

"Everyone has one song in them!"

I have heard it said that everyone has one book in them. Well, it's my belief that everyone has one song in them! This is one of the reasons why I'm writing this book: to inspire and give you a guideline to follow so that you can write that song that's within you just waiting to be written.

Throughout my fifty years in the entertainment and music business, I have had and I am still having a love affair with songs. I have always been a pushover for a good tune and, consequently, this entire subject of songs has always fascinated me!

Apparently, many people also find this subject fascinating, for no matter where I go, when they find out that I'm in the music industry, they start asking me all kinds of questions about songs, how to write them, and the music business in general.

Several years ago, I sent out a questionnaire to approximately one hundred songwriters that I knew — all of them at varying degrees of songwriting abilities and talent. I had twenty blank spaces and I asked them to write in the main questions that they had about songwriting in order of their importance. I was absolutely amazed at the response I got. The majority of writers had asked the same questions and in almost the same order of importance!

Questions like: Which comes first: the lyrics or the melody? What makes up a hit song? How do you get a song title? Why is a song title so important? Is songwriting a gift for the talented few or can it be developed? Am I too old to learn how to write songs? Can poems be made into songs? How do I go about making a demo? How much do demos cost? How do I get my song to a publisher? Should a songwriter also publish his own songs? How do I copyright and register my songs? What is public domain? What's an arrangement? The questions are endless.

Although many books have been written on this subject matter with quite a few of them geared, more or less, to the professional songwriter, I have always felt that the aspiring, beginning songwriter has been sadly neglected. Consequently, I have spent a lot of time discussing what I feel are the basic principles for creating a song for those of you who have never written a song before but who have the desire to write one and would like to know how to go about it.

So I've come up with a book which I hope and feel will be a guideline not only for the aspiring, beginning songwriter but all songwriters at varying degrees. Hopefully, there will be something in it for everybody — even those of you who are just plain curious about the music business! I've tried to make it an interesting, entertaining book, so I have sprinkled a lot of my own personal experiences in it in order to keep it fun because if you ain't having fun reading it or doing it, then don't do it.

I have heard it said that if you want to learn something, then teach it. So I am also writing this book for myself. Why? Because I find that sometimes I forget what I really know to be true about songwriting. Writing this book serves to remind me to stay on track with certain basic principles that have worked for me and for hundreds of songwriters I have known or have worked with in the past, the ones I'm working with today, and the ones I'll be creating with tomorrow.

I consider this book a kind of "musical stew" which is made up of various ingredients and flavors that I'm tossing in — just like I would toss and stir ingredients into a bowl as I followed a recipe of some sort. Please know up front that to my knowledge, there does not exist a tried-and-true recipe for writing a song.

However, one of the main ingredients in any creative endeavor is believing that you can do it! Your belief in yourself can produce magical results for you. Therefore, if any of my suggestions can plant a little seed of hope and belief in your mind or help you to develop your creative abilities as a songwriter in any way, then my book has done its job and has been of value; and for that I will be so thankful, for my efforts will have been worthwhile.

I suggest that you read this book all the way through once, and then reread each chapter individually and spend some time thinking about all the basic songwriting principles that I've presented to you.

Then begin the fun of writing that song I know is within you just waiting to be created! As I said before, it's my belief that everyone has one song in them. If it's the only song that you're ever going to write, then take great pride in the fact that you've done it!

Who knows what the future holds for you? What may start out as a fun and inexpensive hobby could very well bring you recognition and profit! As a matter of fact, there may be a whole new career waiting for you! Isn't that thought exciting? So go for it!

Cliffie Stone

CHAPTER ONE

IS THERE A MAGICAL PROCESS TO WRITING A MONEY-MAKING HIT SONG?

Yes, there is a magical process to writing a money-making hit song. Hit songwriters and all songwriters go through their own individual process of creating a song. Throughout this book, I'll simply refer to it as "the process" which, to me, is magic in itself.

A JOURNEY OF A THOUSAND MILES BEGINS WITH A SINGLE STEP

—Lao-tzu, Chinese philosopher

Throughout my career, many aspiring songwriters have asked me, "What's the first step in writing a song? How do I get started?" I always tell them that when you think about writing a song, you've already taken that first step and you are now in the process of writing it. And they say, "What do you mean by the 'process'?"

Or songwriters, who have moved up a few notches past the beginner's stage, will say to me that they've been writing this song for three months and now they're stuck. They can't seem to get the right words or the right melody to complete the chorus or the second verse, etc. I tell them not to worry, for they are in the process and it will all work out if they patiently take their time. They, too, ask me, "What do you mean by 'the process'?"

The best way that I can explain this is through the following analogy. All my life, I have loved planting and growing things. The garden that I've had on my ranch all these years has always been a place of refuge for me where I could go to get away from the pressures of the music world. It was there that I became aware of how similar the magical process of growing

1

vegetables and plants was to the creative process that one goes through when writing a song.

I would marvel at the miracle of the various steps and stages that corn, for instance, went through from the initial planting of a tiny seed to its final maturity. I remember those times when I was so impatient. When was that corn going to be ripe so that I could have it for dinner? However, there was nothing that I could do to make it grow any faster; I had to constantly remind myself that this corn was growing step by step, day by day and that it was in its own process and would grow and ripen in its own time frame.

I recall going into my garden one time after a particularly stressful day. Not only was I producing and performing on my own television show, but I had a deadline to meet in writing a song for one of my shows and I was in a lyric gridlock. I was frustrated and tried to force myself to come up with lyric lines. I remember looking at an ear of corn, and thinking about how the process of growing corn was like the steps involved in the creation of a song. So I completely relaxed, let go of all my music worries and fiddled around my garden and rosebushes the rest of the evening.

When I woke up the next morning, ideas for lyric lines and melodic rhythm patterns started to formulate. Within a couple of hours, the process of writing this song was completed.

Ever since that experience, I have coined the phrase "in the process" to all the songwriters who have come into my world. I tell them that a song, like a journey of a thousand miles, begins with a firm decision to get started which is the first step. However, the thousand steps that they have to take afterward in order to complete the song are equally important.

When they get stuck in a lyric or melodic gridlock and find that they can't seem to proceed with the song's journey, I tell them to be patient. For once we have given thought to an idea, there is a magical process that our minds unconsciously go through and usually the answers will come if we are patient enough.

Therefore, dear songwriter/reader, this first chapter is entirely devoted to getting you into the proper frame of mind so that you'll be able to naturally, step by step, take the right actions needed in order to write a song or, as I always refer to it, get into the process.

Now, this book isn't about the workings of the conscious and subconscious mind, which I consider a miracle, nor will I discuss the creative versus the logical side of the brain. Quite frankly, I don't know too much about those subjects, and I'm not qualified to write and explain all those fancy theories. I'm just a country boy and I want to keep this book simple by writing about what has worked for me and for other songwriters with whom I have been associated in my life. I am aware that there have been many books written about the mind and how it works and, if you're interested, I highly recommend that you buy one of them.

About as fancy or technical as I'll get is to give you the definition of the word "process" from Webster's Ninth New Collegiate Dictionary which is relative to the way I'll be using the word in this book:....."2 (a) a natural phenomenon marked by gradual changes that lead toward a particular result; (b) a series of actions or operations conducing to an end."

Your desired end or goal is to write a song and you want to go about it in a way that's natural to you. So let's talk about some of the actions that are involved in the process of getting ready to write a song, which are a combination of mental, emotional and physical. However, I don't want you to actually sit down and start writing with pen and paper.

Exactly what kind of a process does a person go through to write a song? If you've ever put pen to paper, then you already have an idea of what I'm talking about because you had to go through some sort of a process if you've written anything at all. People who have written newspaper articles, letters, songs, books, plays, movie scripts, etc. had to have the right words — words that would fit that particular expressive emotion and idea.

I've worked with songwriters at all skill and talent levels: the gifted, the good, the mediocre, the bad and the lucky. All of them went through a process and many didn't even know that they were going through one. They just did it.

One of the world's most natural and gifted songwriters, Merle Travis, who wrote "Sixteen Tons," once said to me, "Cliffie, remember that song we started writing a year ago? Well, I just finished it." It was a very simple song called "Sweet Temptation." (You'll find that most of the great songs are very simple.) We started with a title and several lyric lines, and Merle was in the process of writing that song for one year. (Many singers ended up recording this song, including Tennessee Ernie Ford.)

There are no two snowflakes alike, no two fingerprints alike, no two people alike — not even identical twins — and this goes double for songwriters! All songwriters have different ways of getting mentally, emotionally and physically ready that are unique unto themselves.

I fondly smile as I sit here recalling some of them. I've known writers who can sit through all the distractions of a subway train or a noisy restaurant and write a song. There are those who become so obsessed with writing that they absolutely don't want to be disturbed. It's as if they're in some sort of fantasy world in another galaxy. (I've been accused of this myself more than once.) This obsession with a song idea is an important professional quality to have which you, too, will acquire as you gain experience and confidence in writing.

I had the financial pleasure of publishing Gene MacLellan's songs, "Snowbird" and "Put Your Hand in the Hand," which were recorded by Anne Murray and became two of her biggest all-time hits. Gene certainly had a unique process of writing. He used to go to a little island off Canada called Nova Scotia. Even though there was no one else around, he would still climb up a tree, sit for hours with his guitar and write songs. He was in the process when he climbed up that tree. As a matter of fact, he was in the process when he decided to go to Nova Scotia because he felt like he was going to write and that was the environment his psyche needed to take him off into his fantasy world of songwriting.

I know an airline stewardess who is also a professional songwriter. She writes for a couple of weeks, then she breaks the routine by flying for a few weeks to get her mind on something else. She told me that she has gotten a lot of song ideas while in an airplane. Many times she'll get an idea for lyrics while she's serving her customers. I asked her how she handles that. She said she stops what she's doing, pulls out a pad and pencil and starts writing as if she's taking an order. (I wonder if "Fly Me to the Moon" was written in an airplane.)

So the next time a stewardess stops and starts to write while she is serving you, it could very well be that she's writing a song.

As for me, I like to write when the television or radio is on low. As a matter of fact, I get a lot of song ideas and write them down while I'm driving in my car. I don't know why, but I find that it's one of the most productive times for me. There are no telephones ringing and I feel free to think. (One time I was stopped by a policeman for doing seventy miles an hour; he said to me, "Were you daydreaming or what? Didn't you realize you were going this fast?" I certainly didn't tell him I was in the process of writing a song.)

Merle Travis and I wrote about forty songs together and many of them were created while we were driving in a car to music gigs (jobs). I would drive while he sat there and played different chords on his ukulele. That's how we wrote the song, "No Vacancy." We had driven to Palm Springs and we were looking for a motel; all we saw were "no vacancy" signs. Finally in frustration, I said kind of disgustedly, "No vacancy, no vacancy!" Simultaneously, Merle and I looked at each other and said, "Song title!" And so the process of writing "No Vacancy" began in a car, in the middle of the night in the desert with no place to sleep.

It's important to remember that every song will be completed in its own time frame. Too many songwriters want to rush writing a song. You would think they were rushing to catch an airplane or a train! They get a song title, a few lines and they want to write it in ten minutes because they've heard stories where writers have written songs in a few minutes or an hour and it became a monster hit! It's very rare for that to happen. When it does, it's probably a very gifted or experienced writer. There are always exceptions to the rule.

My buddy, Merle, was that rare and gifted talent who was the exception to the rule. There were those occasions when he would get an idea for a song and write it in a very short period of time. Back in 1946, I produced an album with him called *Folk Songs of the Hills* for Capitol Records. He wrote eight songs the night before the recording session and all of them eventually became hits. (One of those songs was "Sixteen Tons.") By the same token, there were those times when it took him considerably longer to write a song; as I mentioned before, it took him a year to finish "Sweet Temptation."

Although Merle was especially gifted, the length of time that it took him to write the songs I mentioned above are perfect examples of what I'm trying to relate to you here. The process of writing a song has its own time frame — no matter how talented a writer you are!

I can't tell you enough times to think the song out. Let your ideas formulate and take root in your mind before you start writing your song. Again, I go back to the analogy of my beloved garden and the creative process principles that it taught me which I have always applied to writing songs, or anything, for that matter.

A song idea is equivalent to planting a seed of corn. You choose a piece of ground where the sun has access to it most of the day; you properly prepare the ground and plant the seeds. Then you water it for nourishment; you weed it and simply let all the combined essential elements of nature take their course. If you were to dig the seed up at any time to check its stage of growth, it would never take hold and would soon die. If you leave the seed alone, it will go through a step-by-step process until it finally becomes a ripened ear of corn.

And so it goes with planting a song seed idea in your mind, which is the prepared soil. You think about it and lovingly nourish the idea. You may think that the first lyrics you wrote were fantastic. Within the next few days or weeks, you read them over and you might think, I missed it totally. Then as you give it thought, your mind magically comes up with a better lyric line to express your idea. This is all part of the process. You are weeding out the words and phrases that aren't necessary in your song. Your mind, in creating your song, is going through its individual magical process — from the beginning all the way through the various stages that it has to go through until the song is completely written.

The main point that I'm trying to "plant in your mind" is that you have to find your own individual way of getting into the process, and once you are in that process, don't rush writing the song. It's so important for you to give a lot of thought to how and what you are going to write about long before you put it on paper. Let it unfold like a flower, petal by petal, lyric line by lyric line, until your song is in full bloom.

In other words, the magical process of creating a song which could become a potential money-making hit, is what you go through mentally, emotionally and physically from beginning to end.

Here's a cute little poem that Joan Carol and I wrote which may help you to remember:

> Don't ever mess
> With the process
> Take one step at a time
> And soon you'll find
> That the "journey of a thousand miles"
> Only took a little while.

CHAPTER TWO

WHICH COMES FIRST:
THE LYRICS OR
THE MELODY?
THE CHICKEN OR
THE EGG?

I t seems like practically everyone is curious about how a song is put together and created — whether they're an aspiring songwriter or not — because both Joan and I are constantly asked by people from all walks of life, "Which comes first: the lyrics or the melody?" That always reminds me of the cliché, which comes first: the chicken or the egg?

Surprise, surprise! Song titles generally come first, especially in country or pop music. To my way of thinking, they're one of the most important ingredients of a song, and I'll explain why in the next chapter.

All right — let's pretend that you've got your song title. Now which comes first: the lyrics or the melody? The words or the music?

The truth is...it varies. While in the process of creating a song, sometimes the melody comes first and then lyrics are written. Other times, the words come first and music is created for them. In many cases, a writer(s) will create both at the same time — always changing and experimenting with both the music and lyrics to see which sounds better.

Although there are quite a few songwriters who are capable of writing both, more often than not there's a lyric writer and a melody writer. Why? Because one may excel at lyrics with a mediocre melody; the other may have a gift for music with the lyrics being average. This is why song collaboration is so popular and encouraged.

The above is especially true of professional songwriters. Since they make their living writing songs, they want to create the best possible song — lyrically and melodically — which is why collaboration is so prevalent. One writer may write a great melody and send a tape of it to a lyricist who may be in Europe or anywhere in the world. Or another writer may write great lyrics and send them to a melody writer in New York City. Some of your biggest Broadway hits have been written this way.

But let's get back to the aspiring writer who has never written before and has the desire to write — you. I don't think it really matters which comes first. Just do what works for you.

What works for me is to come up with the song title first and maybe that will work for you, too.

So where do you find a song title? Turn the page, dear reader.

CHAPTER THREE

WHY ARE "BUZZ WORDS" SO IMPORTANT IN SONG TITLES AND WHERE DO YOU FIND THEM?

WHY ARE "BUZZ WORDS" SO IMPORTANT IN SONG TITLES?

Have you ever stood in the checkout line at a grocery store and as you casually glanced at the magazine rack, your eyes became riveted to a provocative title on the front cover of some magazine and you ended up putting it in your grocery cart, too? (Very rarely do the contents of these articles ever measure up to their alluring titles, and I always end up saying to myself, Will I ever learn?)

Or have you ever browsed through a library or a bookstore and out of all the books on the shelf, you reached for one whose title was so intriguing that it seemed to stand out among the others and say, "Read me?" I bought a book called *It's Better to Be Over the Hill than Under It* for precisely this reason.

And so it goes with song titles. An interesting song title will simply make you want to listen to it! It has what I call "buzz words," which immediately command your attention just as if someone had "buzzed" you through an intercom system in order to talk to you. This is precisely what happens to me when I look at the multitude of song titles of demo tapes that are sent to my office. I invariably play the ones whose titles have hooked my imagination because they literally seem to say, "Play me." But song titles are more than just an attention-getter. More importantly, it's been my experience that if you come up with a good title, the song will almost write itself. That's usually how a song idea begins and you can build the entire song concept or theme around the title.

Many times, the title is the first and last words that you hear in a song,

9

and the more often a title is repeated, especially in the chorus, the more likely the listener will remember the song. If the listener can go away humming the melody or singing a part of the lyrics, then it has one of the necessary ingredients that makes up a hit song.

WHERE DO WE FIND SONG TITLES?

One of the main purposes of this chapter is to make you aware that sources for titles are omnipresent — they are everywhere imaginable! To me, finding and coming up with titles is probably the most fun and enjoyable part of this entire process of songwriting. I have a field day with my imagination and you can, too!

Everyday conversations: Generally speaking, a song title and its lyrics are made up of ordinary, everyday conversations that have a melodic rhythm pattern to them because that's the way people normally say things (unless, of course, it's heavy metal or rock). So one of the best sources for obtaining titles (and lyric phrases) is from everyday conversations.

Take a look at the list of song titles on your albums, compact discs or tapes. At one time or another, haven't you said or thought those words yourself? Play one of them and listen very carefully to the title lyric phrase and you'll see what I mean.

You are now in the process of taking the first few steps in the journey of creating a song. So in the daily activities and events that comprise your life, start becoming aware of how and what people are saying in ordinary conversations and you'll soon start to hear song titles. Someone will be talking and they'll say something that's catchy and it falls into a rhythm pattern.

In 1986, Randy Travis had a big hit song called "On the Other Hand," which was written by two of Nashville's top songwriters, Don Schlitz and Paul Overstreet; it was chosen Song of the Year by both the Country Music Association and the Academy of Country Music. How many times have you heard that remark in day-to-day conversations? Turn on the television and you'll hear people using that phrase all the time — especially lawyers and politicians discussing various issues.

I'm sure you've heard the great ballad, "I Can't Stop Loving You." Have you ever said that to anyone?

At one time or another, all of us have said, "I Love You" to the people that we care about in our lives. That phrase is used constantly in love songs. Goodness, there are probably hundreds of songs registered with the United States Copyright Office with that title!

Joan Carol heard a casual remark made by a lady at one of the dinner parties we attended recently. When we got back to the ranch that evening, she said to me, "I just got a great song title from one of the comments I heard tonight." She told me and within several days, she had written a country ballad called, "It Was Never a Forever Situation." Say it a few times and you'll feel the rhythm pattern in the phrase. It's a title that immediately hooks your attention, and I feel that this song title is a perfect example of what I've been talking about.

Conversations on Television and Radio Talk Shows: There's a multitude of interesting daily talk shows on both television and radio from which you can get wonderful song titles.

All of us spend a considerable amount of time in our cars, especially driving to and from work. It's the perfect time not only to listen to music, but also to talk shows. It's fun to hear what the average person on the street has to say when they call into the radio station with their opinions. Some of them get pretty emotional and no one knows what they're going to say — not even the caller — and this makes for some very interesting song titles!

The same holds true for the numerous talk shows on television. They are under constant pressure in the ratings battle, so you know they'll always have interesting and current topics that will appeal to the home viewing audience. Here again, listen to the comments of these everyday folks like you and me.

And something else that's very important to remember: These are the people who may be buying your record someday and by using these ordinary phrases and comments, you'll know that the majority of them will be able to identify with your song title.

Soap Operas: I don't have to tell anyone about the popularity of soap operas. Love songs will always be commercial and since soap operas specialize in a constant parade of dramatic love scenes and situations, the potential love song titles that you can get from their conversational dialogues are endless.

So those of you who are soap opera fans, start listening for titles. If your loved ones start to complain that you're spending too much time watching these shows, just tell them the truth — you're listening for a song title!

The important thing is to start listening attentively to how people communicate their feelings about themselves and life in general. Slowly train yourself to become aware and attuned to not only what's being said to you and around you, but also to the rhythm of the sentences as they're being spoken.

After all, songs are basically elongated speech; I like to think of it as a musical conversation. You're just taking a piece of conversation and adding a melodic rhythm to it. Besides, it's quite a conversation piece to be able to say that you got the song's title from a conversation.

Household Items: I'm sure you're thinking to yourself, Cliffie has got to be kidding. No, I'm not! You're going to be surprised at how many song titles you can get with household objects. There are potential song titles all over your house. Just look around.

I don't know about you, but I've got a clock in practically every room of my home. Can you come up with a song title by looking at your clock? Someone sure did a long time ago and came up with a big hit called "My Grandfather's Clock." Just that title alone will conjure up memories of your grandfather. What did he dearly love that reminds you of him? Make a title out of it, file it and someday, you may write a song about it.

At this moment, I'm looking at a red chair in my room. Now if Dolly Parton were here looking at this chair (I can dream, can't I?), she might say, "Cliffie, darlin', let's write a song called, 'The Red Chair Daddy Sat On,' or 'The Red Chair Where Mama Did Her Sewing,' or 'The Red Chair Where I Was Raised on My Daddy's Knee.' " Now all I did was look at a red chair and gave my imagination free rein. Look at the potential list of song titles that I came up with!

Speaking of Dolly Parton, I've always thought her song, "Coat of Many Colors," was one of the best I've ever heard. It's my understanding that it was actually a true part of her life; her mother made it for her from all the pieces of material that she had collected down through the years.

In those days, especially in the rural areas where money is scarce, folks would do everything they could to make the most of what they had, so they saved remnants from clothes and usually quilts were made out of them. Which leads us into the subject of quilts. Do you have one? What kind of a title can you come up with for a quilt? Sit back and think about it for a moment. (Are you having fun doing this? I am! Finding song titles is one of my favorite things to do!)

A long time ago, there was a song called "The Quilting Party." In olden days, women from the surrounding community would meet and spend the day at someone's house when a woman was getting married and they called it a quilting party. (Nowadays, we refer to it as a bridal shower.) Anyway, each one of them would bring a piece of cloth and, together, they would lovingly sew a quilt which they gave the bride-to-be when they finished it at the end of the day. It was their way of wishing her the very best as she started her married life; and down through the years, whenever she touched or looked at it, she could lovingly think of them.

Now let's see what you and I can come up with in our imaginations. Maybe it was the quilt on our honeymoon bed; it was keeping us warm, protecting us, and as long as it was there, we could make it. But the quilt wore out and so did our marriage. How's this for a title: "We Split the Blanket Down the Middle — You Got the Sheets and I Got the Quilt!" Yes, I know it's a little long but I thought I'd throw in a little humor here. I always go for the laugh! Actually, I once published a song called "We Split the Blanket," which was cowritten by Buck Owens and Red Simpson.

I've just laid down on my bed. Now there has to be a lot of song titles here!

My son, Curtis, is with the award-winning group Highway 101, and they had a big hit called "The Bed You Made for Me." It's about a guy who made a headboard and a pillow for the bed that he and his lady shared. Anyway, he ends up sleeping on that same bed with another woman. Naturally, his lady gets upset when she finds out and ends up telling him what he can do with the pillow and the headboard. I don't blame her — what a crass thing for him to do! Right, ladies?

Why don't you put this book down for a few moments and see what kind of titles your imagination can come up with on all the above items that I've just mentioned? You think about it while I take a little nap on this bed, okay?

▼ ▼ ▼

Where were we? Oh yes...beds. Let me stretch for a moment. I'm telling you, folks — there's nothing like a little nap to make a new person out of you! I guess I must have had a wonderful dream by the way I'm holding this pillow. Hey...I just thought about another great song called, "Send Me the Pillow You Dream On."

So here's another household item that we can practice getting a title from. There have been a lot of "pillow" song titles. How about the movie *Pillow Talk* that starred Doris Day? She also had a song in that movie with the same title.

Would you have looked at a pillow and thought of these titles? Someone certainly did and you can do it, too.

Now—I took my little nap on a satin pillowcase and sheets? There's definitely a song title here. In the country field, Jeanne Pruett had a song called "Satin Sheets." This is about a man who has given his lady everything (except himself) that money can buy, including satin sheets. And since he's gone most of the time, making money or whatever, she's lonely and cries herself to sleep on these fancy satin sheets.

And as I visualize this lovely doll on these satin sheets alone, another title immediately comes into my mind: the wonderful sassy, classy pop standard, "Satin Doll." It's about two people who have become attracted to each other in a cabaret, cocktail lounge, or whatever. Apparently, one of them is an extremely cool, smooth and slick person and the other is becoming very enamored with this charmer. How I love this satin-smooth tune!

The above two songs are perfect examples of how totally different titles and themes can be derived from the same word.

I've just walked into my kitchen and I'm sitting on a bar stool while I enjoy a cup of coffee. A lot of people have a bar in their kitchen for eating. As a matter of fact, many folks have a bar in their living room as well, and the word "bar" is no stranger in country songs.

I recently produced an album for artist Larry Keyes, and one of the songs was "Barroom Romeos." Now, isn't that a visual title which depicts the scene at almost any bar or nightclub you might walk into? If you say it a few times, you'll feel how easy the syllables flow and fall into a rhythm pattern.

Bar equals whiskey and whiskey is a household item to a lot of people.

"Whiskey, If You Were a Woman" was one of the biggest hits that my son, Curtis, and his Highway 101 group ever had. I'm sure at one time or another you've heard or danced to the Mexican hat dance song, "Tequila." Quite a few folks out there identify with alcohol and the number of songs that have been written about it are too numerous to mention.

What comes to my mind at this moment are all the Western movies that I've seen where some cowboy gulps down a shot of whiskey while he's playing cards. So the word whiskey has automatically led me into another word association: cards.

Almost everyone has a deck of cards in their home. Do you? Let's use cards and I'll show you how many songs have been inspired by them.

One of the most touching songs I've ever heard, which I recently recorded for my album, was called "A Deck of Cards" (originally recorded by T. Texas Tyler). It's about a soldier boy who attends a chapel with his unit after being out in battle for some time. All the soldiers are asked to open their Bibles for prayer study; and since he doesn't have one, he pulls out a deck of cards instead. Naturally, the commanding officer becomes upset because he thinks the young man is being sacrilegious. Consequently, he gets called before the provost marshal to explain himself. The young soldier then proceeds to go through an entire deck of cards and explain how he relates each card to his religious beliefs.

One of my favorite country newcomers, Ricky Van Shelton, revived Ned Miller's wonderful old standard called "From a Jack to a King," which became a big hit for him. Janie Frickie recorded a song called "The Queen of Hearts." My buddy and fellow Hall-of-Famer Hank Thompson had a song called "You Turned My Whole Card Upside Down." The song "Don't Let the Deal Go Down" was recorded by the wonderful Bob Wills. "Seven of Clubs" was another big hit card song that came out about fifteen years ago. Kenny Rogers starred in a television movie called *The Gambler* and had a single by the same name. "Jack of Diamonds" was recorded by Tex Ritter. The pop field has had its share of card songs, too. Many years ago, Brook Benton had a big hit called "It's All in the Game."

My Dad, Herman "the Hermit," used to sing a song about the gamblers and the ladies of the night and how all of them had to have an "Ace in the Hole" no matter how bad things might get. Now, that's an old title, and, recently, George Strait had a new hit song with that same title.

However, both songs are totally different from each other in song concept and direction.

I wonder if there have ever been songs written about a "Stacked Deck" or "The Deck Was Stacked Against Me" or "It Wasn't in the Cards for Us to Be Together"? These are clichés that people say all the time and would make wonderful song titles.

See how all the above titles and potential song titles originated from a deck of cards? There's always room for more card tunes, so let the magical process of your mind have its way, dear songwriter/reader.

Spinoffs: I'm sure that you've heard the term "spinoff" with regard to a new television show usually created from an episode in a popular TV series. This is exactly what you and I have been doing here. I've shown you how one word can lead into another word through association — they "spin off" one another. We went from clocks to quilts, beds, pillows, bars, whiskey and then to cards. (I hope someone doesn't try to analyze me from my word associations! It's only my active imagination. I'm just a nice, quiet, lovable, homebody-type of Pisces!)

Let's continue having fun by "spinning off" new song title ideas from cards. As an example, let's take the king of hearts. The word "king" is an important word and lots of songs have been written with "king" in them. Roger Miller had a big hit called "King of the Road" which is song I never get tired of hearing. Then there's the wonderful Broadway play which starred Yul Brynner called *The King and I*.

What can you come up with? I just thought of one: "You Make Me Feel Like a King When You Love Me!" That one has a lot of possibilities! I think maybe Joan Carol and I should get together and give it some thought as soon as this chapter is finished. Folks, this is what happens when you go on a song title treasure hunt!

You shuffle a deck of cards, don't you? Well, Red Foley had a song out called "Saturday Night Shuffle." There was also a song called "From Hand to Hand." I can think of several song concepts and ideas from that title alone.

I'm sure you've either been asked or you've heard the expression, what have you got up your sleeve? That term was originally coined by gamblers when they referred to someone who was cheating at card games by putting cards up the sleeves of their coats. Here's another cliché that comes to mind: She wears her heart on her sleeve. Have you ever said that about yourself or about someone?

Isn't it amazing how many titles and song idea spinoffs you can come up with from everyday items in your life?

Billboards: Although there don't seem to be as many billboards as there used to be (mainly because the land space is being used for new buildings of some sort), they are still around and you'll still find plenty of potential song titles on them. (A word of caution: before you use any commercial slogans for your song, I suggest you check to make sure they haven't been trademarked.)

Merle Travis and I once wrote a song built entirely around billboard advertisements called "So Round, So Firm, So Fully Packed." We got the idea for the title from a cigarette billboard. One of the lyric lines was "so complete from front to back" which was from an automobile ad. Another line was "toasted in the sun" and that, too, was from a cigarette billboard slogan. Then we put in a line, "I'm a sun-of-a-gun if she don't make my five o'clock shadow come around at one." The "five o'clock shadow" phrase was from a razor blade advertising slogan.

Why don't you and I try coming up with a title that's billboard related? What comes to your mind? As I sit here and think about it, I remember seeing Tom Selleck's face on billboards long before he became famous. (Maybe this billboard ad was the springboard for his future TV and movie success.) Romance is always in, so maybe our title could be, "I'm in Love with the Man on the Billboard"; or "I Dream of the Billboard Man Outside My Bedroom Window"; or "If Only My Billboard Man Could Hold Me." I'm sure a lot of women have had those kind of thoughts whenever they saw that handsome face on billboards wherever they went.

Once again, have some fun with this; take time out and think about a title. I'm sure I don't have to coax you ladies into giving Tom Selleck a few moments of your time!

Newspaper, Magazine Ads and/or Television Commercials: Another good source for song titles would be cute and catchy captions from the abundant ads or articles that are in magazines and newspapers.

The sports section of a newspaper is always a good source for song titles. Since I work for Gene Autry, I follow baseball to see how his Angels are doing against the other teams. One time I remember seeing the headline

"The Losing Blues," which described how another team (who shall remain nameless) had played an important game in the pennant race. I remember thinking, What a great song title! and I immediately wrote it down so that I could refer to it later.

You can even get titles from newspaper cartoons. Two very popular cartoon strips, "Barney Google," and "Popeye, the Sailor Man," both had songs written about them. Even more up-to-date is the theme song written about "Batman."

With television taking up a considerable amount of time in our daily lives, you'll find that there's a commercial every fifteen minutes advertising something. You'll hear catchy lines and all you have to do is change one or two of the words which will then give a different meaning to the line.

Clichés: So many times I've read articles in newspapers and magazines in which someone criticizes a song because it has a lot of clichés in it. Well, so what! If a song becomes a hit and makes four hundred thousand dollars, who cares if it's got a hundred clichés in it? One of the new pop artists, Taylor Dane, recorded a song called "I'll Always Love You" which was full of clichés and it went right to the top of the charts!

How many times have you heard or used the cliché: If only I knew then what I know now? Joan cowrote a wonderful country ballad with Marc Levine with that cliché as the title. Since that expression is so widely used, people will remember that song title after they hear it once. As I said before, one of the necessary ingredients that makes up a hit is for someone to go away either humming the melody or singing a part of the lyrics.

Clichés are used all the time in normal conversations. For instance, that's water under the bridge. Now you can either use that term, word for word as your song title or you can change a few words around and come up with a new title. Who knows — maybe that cliché inspired Paul Simon to write "Bridge Over Troubled Water"!

Here's an old expression: You can lead a horse to water but you can't make him drink. Why don't you and I change a few words and see what kind of a title we can come up with? How do you like this one: "You Can Take Me on a Date But You Can't Make Me Love You"? You see folks, it's not what you do, it's the way you do it. Now my last statement is also a cliché and, consequently, a song title. Isn't it fascinating how you can change a few words around in a phrase and give it a completely different meaning? All it takes is a little imagination.

Let's go through another song title exercise here. (Are you still having fun? I am!) Let's take a song that's already been a hit and change the words in the title so that it has a completely different meaning. As an example, let's use Randy Travis's big hit, "On the Other Hand," which I previously mentioned in this chapter.

Our song title could be, "On the Other Hand, I've Got a Michael Jackson Glove." We've used the same title but we've added a few words which have given it an entirely different concept; consequently, it will be a totally different song. If you had the same title with a similar song concept as "On the Other Hand," and it became a hit, you would soon be hearing from the publisher and/or his lawyer.

With the millions of song registrations that the copyright office in Washington, D. C. has received, there are bound to be numerous song title duplications. You cannot copyright names, titles or short phrases (although there might be other theories of law that do). You can copyright an idea and lyrics with a direction.

I'm still amazed at the thousands of different song titles and ideas people come up with even though I've been in the music business a long time. Even today, I may get fifty demo tapes a week with five songs on each tape. Out of all these titles, there are rarely two song titles that are exactly alike.

Start a Song Title File: I started one many years ago because I would get an idea for a title but I wouldn't have the time to follow through with it at that precise moment. Goodness, even as I write this, I must have twenty or thirty titles rattling around in my head; and, consequently, tucked away in my file — hoping that one of them will break away from the pack and say, "Write me."

So many of my meetings with writers have been at breakfast, lunch or dinner and more song ideas have been scribbled on napkins, menus, match covers or check receipts. I usually write down two or three key words which will serve as a reminder.

And that's what I highly recommend you do, too. Whenever you get an idea, write it down and file it away. You may end up with thirty or forty song titles before you're through. And after you have familiarized yourself with the basic songwriting principles which I will continue to discuss with you in the proceeding chapters, you can go over them when you feel like you're in a creative mood. Pick out twenty from that list that appeal to you; then pick ten; then five — until you find one title that cries out to be written!

You might start working on one of them and you just can't seem to go any further with it than the title and that's okay. Don't get discouraged and don't throw it away — file it! You may use that title phrase as part of your lyrics in another song someday. There's a lot of wisdom in the old cliché, there are no wasted words.

Go on a Song Title Treasure Hunt: I know that I've spent a lot of time on song titles, but their importance cannot be underestimated. They are such an essential ingredient in this musical stew that you and I are cooking up here because they have several purposes: not only should a title hook the listener's initial attention and be repeated in the song so that it will be remembered, but, in most cases, it's the very idea or concept of the song itself.

I hope that I've opened up your mind to the infinite number of song title sources which are available to you. So go on a song title treasure hunt until you find those "buzz words" that will make your title stand out from the rest of the crowd. Let your imagination take flight and have fun looking for titles — like a busy bee who buzzes around hunting for nectar, the chief raw material of honey. The orchard of possibilities is all around us — just ripe for the "pickin' and writin'."

And once you pick that honey of a title, stash it away in your song title bag. Don't write it yet. Our songwriting process has only just begun. Just let it cook and simmer inside your head for awhile.

CHAPTER FOUR

SONG CONCEPT AND DIRECTION:

FOLLOW THE YELLOW BRICK ROAD!

A s I said before, song titles are usually the concept, theme or idea of a song. Once an idea has crystallized in your mind, all your lyrics must stay in the direction of that theme — just follow the yellow brick road.

I feel that the process of composing a song is similar to the planning process that you would go through when you decide to build a home. Constructing a house requires a lot of time and thought until you have a relatively complete idea or concept of it in your mind's eye. Among the essential elements that make up this concept is the style of home that you want to construct. Is it a two-story English Tudor style? A Spanish hacienda? A one-story rambling ranch-style home?

Once the concept has formulated in your mind and you've worked out the necessary details of your dream house, only then can you have blueprints drawn up which would encompass all the basic construction elements such as the floor plan, correct room measurements, etc. You could then physically build a firm foundation upon which this home could be constructed from these blueprints, brick by brick, until the thousand and one details were taken care of and your home was finally completed.

And so it goes with the construction process of your "song home." Since the title is usually the idea, theme or concept, this would basically be your song's blueprint. Your lyric lines would be the framework structure built in the direction of the concept in order to hold up your song's theme. These lyrics must never deviate from the direction of this concept.

(This reminds me of a classic song that my dear friend, Stuart Hamblen, wrote called "This Old House." He used it as a yardstick to express his own personal feelings about growing old and compared it to different parts of the house such as the roof, door, shingles, etc. It was recorded by Rosemary

Clooney and became a superhit.)

If you were halfway through constructing a two-story English Tudor home, you wouldn't all of a sudden decide to switch directions and build the other half as a Spanish hacienda, would you?

The same holds true for creating a song. If you were writing a sad love song, you wouldn't deviate from the lyric direction of the concept and begin to write happy lyrics halfway through it.

By the same token, if you did decide to change the theme, then you would have to rewrite it from the beginning so that all the lyrics could be directed toward the revised song concept. (I'll talk more about having a flexible attitude later on in this chapter because there are those instances when it's better to go with a new concept.)

So one of my first suggestions in the process of getting ready to write is that you thoroughly think about the concept and direction. You "frame" your lyrics so that they will support the entire theme, and this is the direction of your song. In other words, you take your idea or concept into a particular lyric direction and you stay in that direction until you've reached the song's conclusion. Just follow the yellow brick road.

If you didn't have a concept and, consequently, a lyric direction, all you would have was a song that rambled all over the place and no one would know what it was about. That's why so many songs are turned down by publishers. (Chapter 10, "Who Cares?" gives additional food for thought relative to your choice of a concept.)

A perfect analogy is a speech that's given by a competent speaker. An audience will usually remember the opening and closing statements that are made. This is why the speaker's first statement has to get their attention and why the closing remarks should be a succinct summation of all the points covered during his speech. The hardest part, of course, is keeping their attention throughout the speech with statements that don't wander too far off course from the subject matter. Otherwise, the audience will start getting restless and look far off into space thinking about the chores they have to do around the old homestead or worse, yawning and falling asleep.

I'll never forget the time when an enthused young man came into my office at the Gene Autry organization with a tape full of songs. As he proceeded to play them for me, he became especially excited about one of them which he felt certain was a hit song. Unfortunately, I fell asleep halfway through it and when the last bar was played, Joan Carol nudged me with her foot and I remember waking up and saying on cue, "Yes, yes. Very interesting." Thank goodness I had my chair turned towards the window so he couldn't see my face. Needless to say, this song was rambling so badly that I became bored and nodded off for a few bars.

Would you buy an airline ticket and fly on an airplane unless you knew exactly where you wanted to go? Basically, this applies to songwriting, too. So whenever you start to write, ask yourself, what is my song all about? What is the basic concept and direction of my song? Then make a decision and go with it.

If you've decided to write a love song, ask yourself, what kind of a love song? Will it be happy or sad? For example, let's take the big hit "I Love You So Much It Hurts Me." That song was about suffering love and if you've heard it and really listened to the lyrics, you'll discover that it stayed in one direction and never faltered from that direction which is one of the reasons why it was a hit!

Don Hecht and Alan Block's hit song "Walkin' After Midnight," which was recorded by Patsy Cline, is another wonderful example of the lyrics staying in the direction of the song title's concept. The basic idea here is about someone who goes "walking after midnight" like they did with their lover in the past. Everything they see reminds them of this person and they hope the other still feels the same way, too. Therefore, maybe they'll meet again while they are both out "walking after midnight." All the lyrics keep "walking" in the direction of the song title's concept over and over again.

Billy Hill wrote one of my very favorite songs of all time; and, in my opinion, it's one of the best-constructed songs ever written — "The Glory of Love." Should you have a copy of the song and/or its lyrics, notice the inner rhymes and how the lyrics stay in the direction of the title concept.

Flexibility in Direction: I know that I've been telling you throughout this entire chapter not to detour from your song concept and its direction. Now, I'm not trying to confuse you, but there are always exceptions to the rule. Therefore, I believe that one of the most important attitudes for a songwriter to have while in the process of writing a song is flexibility.

I am aware of the fact that I equated never deviating from the direction of your song with buying an airline ticket and flying on an airplane once you have chosen your destination. Once you're in an airplane at thirty thousand feet, you don't stop the plane to get out if, all of a sudden, you've decided that you don't want to go unless, of course, you have a parachute on or you want to practice faith and free falling at the same time.

A better way of illustrating the airplane example would be to explain the flexibility that the captain has, since he is in charge of the flight. Let's pretend that he is notified of bad weather ahead. He considers all the options and decides to change directions and take an alternate route because he feels it is safer for everyone concerned. That's the flexibility of attitude that I'm talking about here.

Suppose you, dear songwriter, are in the process of writing a song and your original concept and direction is a slow, sad ballad. However, after you've written five or six lines, you discover that it feels better at a faster tempo with a lighter and more humorous touch to the lyrics. Consequently, you are flexible enough to change your song's concept and direction.

By having an open and flexible mind, you will then have given the very best that is within you to give to the creation of your song. If at all possible, however, stay with your original idea and direction.

The Dominant Chord: I had the pleasure of meeting and hearing a great minister and psychologist, Dr. Fletcher Harding. One Sunday morning, the title of his sermon was "The Dominant Chord." He, of course, was referring to the Lord and spiritual principles. To illustrate his point, he went over to the organist, had him strike a chord and then play musical notes around it which demonstrated how they always led right back to that dominant chord. It was an ingenious musical analogy which he used in conjunction with the message of his sermon.

I can think of no better way to close this chapter than with the above musical and spiritual example. For songwriting is soul stuff and it's an indelible way to remember that your song should always lead back to the dominant theme.

There's an old saying: all roads lead to Rome. Just follow the yellow brick road.

CHAPTER FIVE

▼

"FORM" DOESN'T MEAN "36-26-36" IN MUSICAL TERMS

I don't know about you, but the first thing that comes to my mind when I think of music form is Dolly Parton. However, 36-26-36 is not the type of form to which I'm referring here.

"Form" stands for formula or format and all songs have a basic format, structure or pattern to them. I'm sure you've heard the musical terms "verse," "chorus" and "bridge"; these are the various parts of a song that comprise the structure or formula.

In my previous chapter, "Song Concept and Direction," I used the analogy of building a home to illustrate constructing a song. To expand further on that comparison, form is the foundation and overall structure upon which the song is built.

It's hard to separate all the ingredients which make up a song because they intricately overlap one another. But I suggest that while you are in the process of thinking about the concept and direction of your song, you should simultaneously be thinking about the form or structure in which to present it.

Although there are many different types of song formula structures, the simplest, most conventional and most successful one which has been used in the past and which is still being used today is the 32-bar formula.

The 32-bar song is divided into three parts: A, B, C and then back to A. A opens with the story line of your song and it's usually 8 bars; B continues the story line with different lyrics but with the same melody being repeated for another 8 bars; C is called the bridge, which has a different 8 bar melody and lyrics than A and B; then we go back to A for another 8 bars which can have the same lyrics as the original A or new lyrics may be written depending upon the song's story line.

Since I believe in keeping things simple, let's evaluate a song that has a traditional song formula or pattern which most folks have heard at one time or another, including children.

Many years ago, Johnny Marks wrote a classic Christmas song which became a worldwide hit for Gene Autry called "Rudolph, the Red-Nosed Reindeer." The verse has its own lyrics and melody which set up the scene for the song's story line: "You know Dasher and Dancer and Prancer and Vixen/Comet and Cupid and Donner and Blitzen/But do you recall/The most famous reindeer of all?"

Now we have A which has a different 8-bar melody line and, naturally, new lyrics to continue the story.

(A)   "Rudolph the Red-Nosed Reindeer had a very shiny nose/And if you ever saw it, you would even say it glows."

Part B has the same 8-bar melody as A but different lyrics in order to continue the song's concept.

(B)   "All of the other reindeer used to laugh and call him names/They never let poor Rudolph join in any reindeer games."

The bridge is C, which has a different 8-bar melody and lyrics than the verse or A and B. The bridge does to a song what it does to two pieces of land — it connects them.

(C)   "Then one foggy Christmas Eve Santa came to say/Rudolph with your nose so bright, won't you guide my sleigh tonight?"

The bridge leads back into A, which has the same 8-bar melody as it did at the beginning of the song, but different lyrics in order to complete the song's story line.

(A)   "Then how the reindeer loved him, as they shouted out with glee/Rudolph the Red-Nosed Reindeer, you'll go down in history."

The chorus is a recurring theme. A and B in "Rudolph, the Red-Nosed Reindeer" are actually choruses but with different lyrics. (However, you'll notice that in most songs, the chorus is made of the same melody and lyrics which occur over and over again.)

There are a variety of combinations in which you may use this 32-bar formula, depending on which way you feel is the best structure to express the story line concept of your song. You can even add a 16-bar tag line to it. Today's songwriter is allowed more variations in originality then ever before.

Here is an example of some of the questions that you should ask yourself while you are in the process of thinking about the form structure of the song: Should it have a 16-bar verse and an 8-bar chorus? Or an 8-bar verse and a 16-bar chorus? Should it be a waltz? A two-step? A fox trot? A boogie? Or should the song be an instrumental?

One of my little secrets about selecting a form pattern for a song is looking and listening to other songs, especially hit songs, and seeing what kind of a format the writers have used to express their lyrical and musical feelings. Generally speaking, most of them will fall into the same category of the 32-bar song format or some variation of it.

I have said it before and I'll be repeating it over and over again throughout this book: In order for a song to be a commercial hit, it should have a recurring lyric and melody so that the listener will remember the song when he or she has heard it several times. This is one of the ingredients which makes up a hit.

There was a worldwide hit song in the pop and rock field which I think is an illustrative example of keeping a chorus simple both lyrically and melodically: Bruce Springsteen's "Born in the U.S.A." His song title is his chorus and this chorus is comprised of the title phrase being repeated maybe six or eight times consecutively. I don't recall how many times the chorus is in the song. However, talk about hammering the chorus and title into the listener's brain — you will definitely remember that song after hearing it only once!

One major hit song that certainly crossed over the traditional lines of writing music was "High Noon" which was from the motion picture with the same title starring Gary Cooper. I not only coproduced it with Lee Gillette, but I also played bass on it which is why I am so aware of the additional bars of music that the writers, Ned Washington and Dimitri Tiomkin, had in the song. This was done because they felt it was necessary to punch up the story line.

There are thousands of songs like this that have broken the traditional 32-bar sound barrier. Remember, you are writing for yourself — first and foremost — and you have the freedom and the luxury of using as many bars as you need to do the job.

So go with the flow of your original thoughts, for it's this originality that will make your song stand out. If you need to detour from the traditional song formula to make your point, go ahead. There are very few songs where everything is tied up into a neat little package. After all, it's what's in the package that counts.

You may find that many of your songs end up with different song formats and that's okay; you don't want to get locked into the same format pattern with every tune. Songs can be like puzzles and analyzing how the various pieces of your lyrical and musical puzzle are to be presented is all part of being in the songwriting process. However, I caution you not to get too analytical. It's always best to keep it simple because the great songs are simply written.

There are certain guidelines to follow, and I suggest that you aspiring songwriters keep it simple at first. Then as you gain more experience in creating songs, you will understand better what you are trying to say and can choose the type of format for the particular song you're composing.

HOW LONG OR HOW MANY MINUTES SHOULD A SONG BE?

This is another question that I'm asked so often which is an integral part of the format. It reminds me of a story I heard somewhere about Abraham Lincoln. Since President Lincoln was a tall, long-legged, unassuming, country-type of gentlemen, a city-slicker attorney who thought he was being clever asked him, "How long should a man's legs be?" Lincoln thought about it for a minute and said, "Long enough to reach the ground."

And that's how long your song should be. Long enough to meet the needs of your song's lyrical story and theme. For example, let's say that your story line lyrics call for a song format which is over 32 bars. Maybe your verse is 16 bars (generally speaking, one lyric line is 4 bars); maybe your chorus is also 16 bars; then you wrote another 16-bar verse; and you closed out the song with the same chorus. You have written a 64-bar song but that is what your song needed in order to fulfill the story line. Time-wise, depending on the tempo, this 64 bars could possibly be three minutes or more in length.

As a rule, it's best to keep the length of a song under three minutes, especially in country music. You should never waste words in songs or make them longer than necessary. After all, you are not writing a novel, and you've only got approximately one hundred and eighty seconds to complete your lyrical thought concept.

Think of Your Song As a Commercial: In a way, a song has to be like a commercial. Hey! That's a thought, isn't it? A song has to be a commercial for what you are writing about!

I have great admiration for songwriters who write commercials. Just imagine — they have ten, fifteen or thirty seconds to succinctly get their message across and every second counts. If they have three or four seconds of music at the beginning or end of the commercial, these are not wasted seconds. It must be a luxury for them when they are hired to write a thirty-second commercial.

So if you think in terms of your song as a commercial, then you will be aware of any unnecessary words or phrases which might find their way into your song, because they eat up the seconds that are ticking away in your song's time frame.

In that three minutes, you must keep the song interesting and fresh because it could become boring unless you come up with different, yet simple twists on your lyric ideas and still maintain the direction of the song's concept. You have to hold the listener's attention phrase by phrase; if you don't, you won't sell the song which is the product.

Once again, there are exceptions to the rule. You and I have the total freedom to write a song that could last for as long as five minutes if we wanted. However, it's hard enough to hold the attention span of a listener for three minutes, much less five minutes.

One successful hit song in the country field which did hold the listeners was Marty Robbins's "El Paso" which ran approximately five minutes. Now, I'm basically talking about country songs — not rock 'n' roll songs or pop songs which go anywhere from three to five minutes. That's a whole different subject because you are also dealing with dance music.

Radio Stations: And the most important clincher of all which will make you a believer in keeping your songs as short as possible are the radio stations. They love short songs and three minutes is usually the maximum.

I'll never forget what my clever, country-fox buddy, Buck Owens, did when he first started out. He was aware of the time element on radio stations, so he wrote songs that were approximately two minutes long. Many times, the disc jockey only had two minutes of air time to fill before their commercials would come on. So they would just put on a Buck Owens song because it was shorter in length than the rest. This also applies to the songs radio stations play today. A few months back, I read an article in *Billboard* where they, once again, stressed how songs should be three minutes or less in length.

I know that I'm giving you a lot to think about in this chapter. Just tuck all this information away in your computer brain, and the day will come when you'll be amazed at how your mind will sort it all out and make it come together for you.

I love the old cliché, one of a kind. If your song should turn out to be a maverick that has torn down the rules and regulation fences of traditional song formats, or is longer in length than the established norm, then be my guest and go for it.

How long should a man's legs be? Long enough to not only reach the ground, but to take that first step in a journey of a thousand miles and to complete it as well.

▼

CHAPTER SIX

LYRICS:
TELL THEM WHAT YOU'RE GOING TO SAY, SAY IT, AND THEN TELL THEM WHAT YOU SAID

Which is more important: the lyrics or the melody? In most musical categories, they are joined at the hip and go together like love and marriage.

In pop, contemporary and MOR (middle-of-the-road) songs, the melody and lyrics are equally important with emphasis on musical arrangements that complement both the lyrics and melody. Demographically speaking, the age group to which these three categories of music appeal are anywhere from age twenty to one hundred and twenty. Hit songs in these categories are long-lasting and occupy the enviable position of becoming standard songs.

Generally speaking, the lyrics and the melody in rock 'n' roll are not as important as the rhythm sound and the arrangement, except for the old-time '50s rock 'n' roll. Demographically speaking, the age group to which this category usually appeals is anywhere from seven to twenty-one years of age.

R&b stands for rhythm and blues, one of the oldest forms of music to come out of the South; and most of the melodies and lyrics are flexible for both the musicians and the singers. The r&b sound had a powerful influence on Elvis Presley, the Beatles and many other stars in the music world. This music was the foundation upon which the highly successful Motown sound was built.

Jazz is a free-flowing exhibition of music, entirely optional to the imaginative talents of performing instrumentalists. (I don't know what

I just said, but it sounds good, doesn't it?) Comparatively speaking, it has an enthusiastic but smaller audience than the other musical categories; and it appeals to all age groups worldwide.

Although I have played all types of music and my love for it has no boundaries, my heart belongs to country music. It's what I know and what I have specialized in throughout my entire musical career. Country songs, like folk songs, tell a story, which makes the lyrics the most important thing to consider. So let's spend some time thinking about what makes up a good set of lyrics.

Most of us have some sort of a command of the English language or whatever language to which each of us has been exposed in our various cultures. A big fancy education or a large vocabulary is wonderful but that's not going to make you a great lyricist or insure that you'll have all the necessary words to write a big hit song.

In my chapter on song titles, I spent a lot of time discussing how you can get many titles from ordinary, everyday conversations. Since the song title is a phrase in the lyrics, that's also how you would approach getting the lyrics. I cannot emphasize enough that your lyrics (and song titles) should be as natural as the everyday language which you normally would use in ordinary conversations.

These lyrics have to be so simple and must be constructed in such a way that the average person on the street can understand them without having to think about them or figure out what the song is about.

Over twenty years ago, Joan Carol certainly learned the above lesson of keeping her song material simple when she took her first song to her guitar teacher for his opinion. He was born in Italy and he always expressed himself in typical Italian fashion — directly and emotionally. He listened to it, looked at her and very bluntly said, "What kinda song is this? You gotta enough material in here to write a book! Bring it back to me when it's a song — not a book!"

This is important for all aspiring songwriters to remember with regard to lyrics. You are not writing a novel. The idea for a song and its accompanying lyrics is really just an approximate three-minute thought in time.

One of my brothers-in-law, Dick Zettel, who was a professor at the University of California at Berkeley before he retired, shared with me a simple formula which he used to write speeches. I have successfully applied it when writing songs and I'll pass it on to you: Tell them what you're going to say, say it, and then tell them what you said.

A song, like a speech, has a beginning, a middle and an end. Since country songs have a story line, you must present the lyrics in a logical sequence and keep them in the direction of the song's concept. The trick is to keep it interesting both lyrically and melodically, line by line, or you'll lose the interest of the listener.

One of my first suggestions for you would be to write down your song title and all your thoughts and ideas which pertain to this theme on paper. You may end up with several pages full of ideas. After you have written and gone over your ideas, I would then suggest that you make an outline or a draft of your song's concept — a blueprint, so to speak.

Your beginning lyric line and the ones that follow in the first 16 bars are vitally important because this is what the listener hears first. You not only want to get their attention, but you want to keep them wanting to hear more. Using my adopted formula, you open the song by immediately telling them what you're going to say, or telling them what the song is about. It might be the title itself, which is repeated many times in the song. Or, in many instances, the last lyric line in a verse will be the first lyric line in the chorus, and it's usually the song's title. If it's not, it should be!

Everything that is sandwiched in between the beginning and the ending of a song is the "meat", or substance of that song. As you continue the story line, keep saying it; keep directing your lyrics around the song's theme. There is no such thing as "fill-in" lyric lines in good songs. The great songs have tight lyrics; in other words, there are no wasted words. Each lyric line has to contribute to the song — either it will add or detract from the song; if it detracts, you'll ultimately lose the listener's attention. It's all too easy to start rambling and going off into another direction. Just remember to keep bringing the lyrics back to the main idea of the song.

It's sort of like trying to navigate a sailboat. You have to know the direction in which you are sailing; and although you may be pulled off course by changes in the wind or undercurrents, you keep your eye on the compass and/or your landmark and you adjust the sails and rudder accordingly in order to keep or bring your boat back on course.

And so it goes when you're writing lyrics for a song and keeping it in the direction of your song's "compass-theme."

To end your song, you tell them what you said. You have to wrap up or complete the idea of your song. These are the last words that your listener will be hearing, and you want them to be remembered. Make your lyrics so down-to-earth, so sincere and honest that they strike the "dominant chord" that connects all of us to one another. This will make your listener come back for seconds, so to speak.

"ALL MY SONGS ARE JUST FLOATING AROUND IN SPACE"

Many years ago, I was the head of the A&R Department (Artist and Repertoire) of the Country Music Division at Capitol Records in Hollywood, California. Every few months, Fred Rose (who was Rose of Acuff-Rose) would come from Nashville, Tennessee, to see me and other producers with his bag of songs. (He wrote hundreds of songs which include hits like: "Blue Eyes Crying in the Rain"; "We Live in Two Different Worlds"; "Be Honest with Me" with Gene Autry; "Mansion on the Hill" with Hank Williams, Sr.)

I was so amazed at all the great songs which he constantly kept writing that I once asked him, "How do you continue to write these wonderful songs? What on earth do you do?"

I'll never forget what Freddie said: "All my songs are just floating around in space. The words and the notes are just out there. All I have to do is reach up, grab them and put them together. It's so easy."

Easy for him to say! Not that easy for ordinary folks like you and me. But Freddie, like Merle Travis, was exceptionally gifted.

The main point to remember is the words are out there floating around somewhere. They are not going to hit you in the face. You have to reach out, grab them and pull them in. Write them down on paper and look at them. You might say to yourself, No, these are the wrong words. There must be a better and simpler way of saying this. So keep thinking and searching for appropriate words and phrases to express your feelings.

Each of us can only write what we are, what we've experienced or what we have observed in our individual lives. There are a lot of experiences that have become memories which are stored away in your mind. You'll be drawing from them, for they will be an accumulation of all your life's experiences or observations. And these memories will be expressed through the words, phrases and sentences that have come from your particular background and environment.

People who are born in rural areas are considered country, especially those from the South like Tennessee, Alabama, Arkansas, Texas, etc. They have more of an advantage in writing country songs than those born in the city, for they are raised with country phrases and expressions that are used every day.

Many great songs that have become standards have been written about the South, and it seems to me that it has more of a colorful, romantic aura about it than, for instance, Nebraska, Wisconsin, or North Dakota, whose songs have more of a western theme.

But you don't have to have been born in the South to write country music. Let's take me, for example. I was born and raised in Burbank, California, when it was still considered a rural area. So I have always had the "feel" for country songs.

Bakersfield, California's Cradle of Country Music produced many top songwriter-performers who have made great contributions to "Mother Country Music." To mention a few: Lefty Frizzell, Buck Owens, Merle Haggard, Ferlin Husky, Dallas Frazier, Tommy Collins and, currently, we have Dwight Yoakam.

I quietly chuckle to myself whenever pop writers and singers tell me that they've decided to "go country." Because of the simplicity in country lyrics and music, they think it's a breeze. They put on a pair of jeans, cowboy boots, a Stetson hat, start talking with a phony country accent and they now think that they're country. What they don't realize is that one doesn't *decide* to be country — one *is* country! Country is a state of mind from within, and you have to have a sincere love and feel for it.

I know one excellent musician who has played every type of music in the gigs where he has performed throughout the years. He decided to write country songs because, after all, it's so simple that it's a piece of cake. To this day, as far as I know, he has never had a song published or cut. He doesn't know it, but his patronizing attitude towards country music comes through his lyrics and melodies loud and clear. There's an old saying: He's as country as cornbread. Maybe this guy should have been thinking cornbread instead of cake.

Some time ago, I read an article by a columnist in one of the music magazines in which he gave advice on how to write big country hit songs. I could tell by his statements that he wasn't a songwriter; and his condescending and ridiculing attitude towards country music was self-evident as he stated his unqualified theories on how easy it was to write big country hits. I never mailed the letter that I wrote to him which expressed my opinion of his article. My only solace is that he justified his own ignorance in public by writing about a subject about which he knew nothing.

The country folks who publish country songs, who sing them, who listen to the radio and who buy the records can tell whether or not the song is country-oriented and sincere. You just can't fool the country audience! With all the warm hospitality for which they are known, they will politely smile and say, "Thank you all, it's nice to meet you," and that's the last you'll hear from them.

And as long as I'm on the subject of sincere and true country, it'll make me feel a whole lot better to express some innermost feelings and opinions that I've been carrying around inside my head and heart for a long time. There was a period of time when the traditional values which made country music so unique almost became lost in the shuffle. The urban cowboy phase appeared on the scene and the big-buck people decided to cash in on country. Today, not only is traditional country music back and more popular than ever, but it also embraces a wider variety of sounds that have attracted younger audiences.

And one of these newcomers who is breaking wide open in the country field is Garth Brooks, whose versatile singing style, showmanship and down-to-earth attitude has won him (and country music) a multitude of fans. At the 1990 CMA Awards show in Nashville, Joan Carol and I had the opportunity of talking with him, his delightful parents, T. R. and Colleen Brooks, and several other members of his wonderful family. They epitomize the traditional adage: The family that prays together — stays together.

Although the list is endless, I want to personally thank some of the new crop of country stars such as George Strait, Randy Travis, Reba

McEntire, Kathy Mattea, Garth Brooks, Ricky Skaggs, Alan Jackson, Ricky Van Shelton, Clint Black, Highway 101, to mention a few, who brought back the true country sound — and George Jones who never lost it! Country has never sounded better, and it's good to know that "Mother Country Music" is alive and well!

I've gotten pretty emotional here! I better follow my own advice about staying in the subject matter's direction.

Rhyming Your Lyrics: In many ways, songs and poems have a lot in common, which I will discuss further in this book in Chapter 11, "Can Your Poem Be Made into a Song?" Songs (and the majority of poems) are enhanced by, and have a sequence of, rhymes. This helps the listener or reader to remember them. So you also have to think in terms of rhyming your lyrics while you're creating a song.

This is where songwriting can get kind of tricky. The best rhyming songs are the ones where you don't really notice that they have been rhymed. They just seem to fall into place naturally and flow with the story line. It's so important that you don't get too clever with your rhymes, because you don't want to sacrifice the sincere meaning of your lyrics for the sake of rhyming them.

Above all, don't get a rhyming dictionary and start looking up words that will rhyme. Your songs will come out rhyming but they won't mean a thing because you'll get so caught up in the cleverness of rhymes that you'll lose the natural way you normally would express your feelings and thoughts, which is the very essence of your song's theme. I know, because I went through all that!

So for the beginners, I think it might be a good idea to clarify, in simple terms, how to rhyme the lyrics of your song.

If you have four lyric lines in a verse (which will usually be 16 bars melodically) you have the option of rhyming them in several different ways. Many folks will rhyme the last word in the first lyric line to the last word in the second lyric line, and will also rhyme the last word in the third line to the last word in the fourth lyric line.

Others will rhyme the second lyric line with the fourth lyric line and won't bother rhyming the first or third lines, which is okay. It all depends on your story line and how you hear the lyrics inside you and whether or not they naturally flow together.

Always remember that you have a little freedom of expression called poetic license and you are entitled to take liberties with it. Every word at the end of every line doesn't have to rhyme with the word two lines behind it, etc. If it makes sense, you can go ahead with it.

An example of a song that has a minimum amount of rhymes is "Wind Beneath My Wings" which was written by Jeff Silbar and Larry Henley. It was sung by Bette Midler in the movie *Beaches* and went to number one on the pop charts. The next time you hear it, listen very carefully and you'll see what I mean.

Of course, there are inner rhymes in songs. In Chapter 4, "Song Concept and Direction," I mentioned one of the best-constructed songs ever written, "The Glory of Love." Get a copy of those lyrics and observe how the writer, Billy Hill, rhymed his thoughts and how they all flowed together.

One of the songs I cowrote with Merle Travis, "No Vacancy," had an unusual rhyming formula. Let's take a gander at the lyrics:

No vacancy, no vacancy, all along the line;
It's the same old sign awaitin' for me.

Analyze the rhyming structure of that song. "No vacancy, no vacancy" and then there are three rhymes: "all along the line, it's the same old sign, awaitin' for me." "Me" rhymes with "vacancy."

No vacancy, no vacancy and my heart beat slower
When I read on the door...no vacancy, no vacancy.

We rhymed "slower" and "door" and, if you'll notice, "slower" has two syllables and "door" only has one. There might be those of you who will say that it can't work because of that, but it did work for several reasons. First, we took poetic license liberties with the sound. It's good to remember that rhyming is not always with the proper vowel and syllable format; it can also be the proper sound as you can see with the above example of "slower" and "door."

And the second reason this rhyme worked was the mental picture that the listener got from those words.

38

A PICTURE IS WORTH A THOUSAND WORDS

And now we come to another necessary ingredient for you to think about which makes for successful lyrics. Your listener must get a mental picture from your lyrics. You've got to be visual and pictorial in your use of words because our minds unconsciously create mental images from them. When you dream at night, you dream in images — not words.

Every time I hear the song "Blue Bayou," my mind conjures up the most incredible mental images: I'm lying on the sand...getting a tan...in the noon-day sun...near a blue lagoon with a glass of Blue Nun in my hand; and as I drink my wine...I look up at the blue sky...and watch clouds pass by...while in the distance, sea gulls cry. A breeze dances through palm trees as mermaids beckon to me, "Come on in for a swim." And since I'm an imaginative, romantic Pisces, the water sign of the zodiac, I go in. I'd better stop here if I want to finish this book.

Videos play an important part in presenting new songs and keeping the singers in the public eye; and because of their immense popularity in today's marketplace, you really have to keep the visual aspect of your lyrics at the forefront of your mind. So when you write, always ask yourself whether or not your lyric phrases are painting mental pictures. Who knows? Someday you may write a song that's so lyrically visual, it may be the one chosen to be in a video.

I'm sure you've seen and heard the title songs in motion pictures where the lyrics are not only visual, but they also sum up the story line of the film. A classic example of this is the wonderful movie *The Way We Were* which starred Barbra Streisand and Robert Redford in which Barbra sang the beautiful and unforgettable title song. Consequently, whenever I hear it, I not only remember various scenes from that movie but, simultaneously, my mind seems to personalize those lyrics, for I can visualize scenes from my own life which are relative to the song's theme.

So when you write lyrics, think "picture."

"YOU'VE GOT TO GET THEM IN THE HEART, IN THE HEAD, OR IN THE FEET"

The foregoing words of wisdom were spoken by one of California's legendary singer/songwriters, Merle Haggard, when we were once discussing what made up a hit song. I'm proud to say that I spent a lot of time with Merle during his formative, successful years at Capitol; and it was my pleasure to attend many of his recording sessions. To this day, he still teases me about being his good luck charm, for it seemed as though whenever I was at any of his record dates — the song would become a hit! Merle always wrote and sang from his heart and his style of singing has influenced many of today's top artists. His award-winning songs include: "Fightin' Side of Me," "Hungry Eyes," "Workin' Man Blues," "Mama Tried," "Today, I Started Loving You Again" with Bonnie Owens, "Okie From Muskogee" with Roy Burris, and "Are the Good Times Really Over?"

So from the mental pictures which you've created with your words, come emotions. For instance, if it's a slow romantic ballad like "I'm in the Mood for Love," it actually gets you in the mood for love; if it's a fast dance tune like "Twist and Shout," it makes you feel like getting up, shouting and moving your body and feet to the beat; and don't you feel patriotic and full of pride when you hear someone like Whitney Houston sing our national anthem?

Which brings in another factor with regard to emotional responses from a song — performance. I remember a wonderful Jamaican song that Harry Belafonte sang and recorded which became a worldwide hit called "The Banana Boat Song." Comedian-singer Stan Freberg did a version of that song which was absolutely hilarious. As the old cliché goes, it's not what you say, it's how you say it. Ladies, how do you feel about macho men? Did you ever hear the lyrics to the song, "Macho Man"? Regardless, what kind of mental images come into your mind when you hear this title? Many of you might think of the macho character that actor Sly Stallone has portrayed in many of his one-man war hero movies like *First Blood* and *Rambo*.

Or maybe the meaning of the word macho conjures up the type of man who not only has strength of character but who is also romantic and sensitive like Frank Sinatra, Tom Selleck, or Cliffie Stone. (Since this book is a joint writing venture with my wife, I had nothing to do with adding my name to the list.)

I don't know whether or not you've heard the lyrics to the song "Big Bad John," but even if you haven't, the title alone gives you a whole different feeling than the previous two examples, doesn't it?

Many years ago, there was a worldwide pop hit called "Feelings." The lyrics and melody are hauntingly beautiful and very simple; they hit the mark emotionally. The song's concept was very simply about the feelings someone had for a lost love and who was trying to forget his feelings of love.

And that's basically what songs are all about — the expression of feelings, from sad to happy, which encompass the entire spectrum of the human soul. The more you charge your lyrics with the electricity of uninhibited, intense emotions, the quicker and deeper your listener will be able to relate and respond to them, for this is the umbilical cord or golden thread that connects all of us to each other.

And it's my opinion that when a song brings out a deep emotional response in people, they will be motivated to go to the record store and buy it. And this is what keeps the music business in business.

However, it all begins with you, dear songwriter. With your words and phrases, you have the power to paint incredible pictures and images in the minds of listeners which, in turn, will trigger off an immediate emotional response whether they read the lyric sheet or hear it performed. So think "feelings" when you're writing lyrics.

DO THE SONG LYRICS READ WELL?

I have a theory that I've developed over the years which usually works for me. If there is a lyric sheet (and one should always accompany the demo), I usually read it before I listen to the tape, to see if it reads well. (Now I'm talking about what I know best — country songs; not rock 'n' roll or heavy metal, etc.)

In order to read well, the lyrics have to tell me some kind of story in a logical sequence in an ordinary, everyday type of conversation; if it doesn't, then it's probably a rock 'n' roll hit and that ain't my bag.

Let me leave you with one more suggestion, which is my "lyric homework" assignment for you: I feel there is no better way for anyone to learn how to write or construct lyrics than to listen to them on tapes and/or get lyric sheets of big hit songs. Then observe and analyze how the writer(s) have created and presented their song ideas.

How did they open the song and get your attention? Notice how they phrased the lyrics, line by line, and how they kept your attention as the story line continued. What kind of a rhyming pattern did they have? Observe the mental pictures these lyrics created in your mind and feel the emotions they bring out in you. How did they end the song and will you remember it?

I have joyously listened to and observed songs all my life. Not only does it take me into a carefree world where I can get away from it all but, through osmosis, I have continued to learn more about music. It also keeps me abreast of the current trends taking place in the "now" of the music world. Have you ever had homework which was more fun and enjoyable than this?

Give all my lyric suggestions a lot of thought, and the day will come when all these elements which comprise a good lyric will slowly fall into place as the process of your writing development unfolds the potential that you have within you as a writer. Then, as you create your lyrics, you'll be able to construct them in such a way that they will not only paint vivid pictures in the minds of your listeners, but they'll be colored with the sincere, uninhibited emotions that you're feeling. You'll be using word phrases which are from normal, everyday conversations and simultaneously rhyming them in a very natural way so that it doesn't take away from the feeling that you're trying to convey.

By keeping your lyrics simple and sincere, you will have discovered the golden key to commercial and potential hit songs. And to help you write your potential hit song, let me reiterate the simple writing formula which has been successful for me:

Tell them what you're going to say, say it,
and then tell them what you said.

CHAPTER SEVEN

YOU DON'T NEED A PH.D. IN MUSIC TO WRITE A MELODY

I don't think there is anything sweeter or more powerful to the human ear and soul than a simple, lilting melody that will whisk you away to never-never land.

Who can resist picking up a music box, winding it and listening to its enchanting melody? There are no chords, no arrangement — only the sound of a percussion-like instrument delicately playing a melody one note at a time. Young and old alike fall under its hypnotic spell.

In Webster's Ninth New Collegiate Dictionary, the definition of "melody" is: (1) a sweet or agreeable succession or arrangement of sounds; (2) a rhythmic succession of single tones organized as an aesthetic whole.

WHERE IS THE MELODY?

At one time, Decca Records owned one of the most successful and prestigious recording studios in Hollywood, where I performed as a musician on numerous recording session dates. Every time I walked into the studio, I would look up at a huge picture of a six-foot cigar store Indian with his hand on his forehead to shade his eyes from the sun while he looked far off into the distance. Next to his mouth, encircled in a balloon outline (similar to the ones you see by a cartoon character's head when you read comic strips) were the words, "Where is the melody?"

This prominent display served as a constant reminder to everyone in the recording industry who walked into that studio (producers, arrangers, musicians, singers and engineers) about the importance of melodies and to never lose sight of it, especially by over-producing a record in some manner.

Last New Year's Eve, as Joan and I were listening hypnotically to the musical brilliance of the New York Philharmonic Orchestra performing some of the greatest classical music ever written, it really occurred to me how music itself is one of the most elusive of all the arts. You can only enjoy it as it's being played, for it's as fleeting as the wind — you can't hold on to it. It's here and gone with only one's individual memory to recapture the traces of its incredible sound images.

When an artist such as Van Gogh paints a picture on canvas, it becomes immortalized for centuries for all the world to see; when Michelangelo meticulously sculptured his famous statues, he left behind a concrete form to touch, feel and observe; and when poetry, essays or books are written, they are recorded on paper to be read and conserved for generations to come.

Of course, thank goodness, music can also be written down in musical note form which can also be conserved for centuries, as were the magnificent works of musical geniuses such as Bach and Beethoven. But to the average person who can't read or play a musical instrument, it means nothing until the music is performed through some medium of expression — either through live performances or on any one of a multitude of invented reproduction devices such as a tape or compact disc. And once it's performed, it's here and gone, but the memory lingers on.

Therefore, with music being so elusive, how does one even begin to explain how to create it?

In my previous chapter on lyrics, I told you that a big fancy education or a large vocabulary will not make you a great lyricist. The same holds true for melodies. Although it's not necessary to have a Ph.D. in music from some college or music school, whatever degree of musical knowledge you may have acquired, either through music lessons or being self-taught, is very important and to your advantage when you write a song.

If you're an accomplished musician who can read and write music, that's great. Or if you play an instrument in a band and can't read music (you "fake it" as they say in music lingo), that's wonderful, too. I remember playing on radio shows for years with a highly educated musician. However, he couldn't just sit down and play creatively or fake it. He always had to have sheet music to read and to follow.

Strange as it may seem, sometimes too much knowledge of the rules and regulations of music may inhibit you as a songwriter. In other words, you might say, "You can't add a bar here or there because the music won't be technically correct," and you know it's not right because a music teacher told you so or you read it in a book somewhere. Or you're not supposed to do this or that with a melody; or you can't go up two octaves or down an octave and so forth.

But that's not necessarily true, especially in today's music marketplace. You have the freedom of being flexible and writing it in any way that you want and with any beat or rhythm that you're feeling.

I remember reading a wonderful article, written by Julius Robinson, on Tom Snow (one of the best contemporary songwriters around) in BMI's *Music World* magazine, Winter 1990. (Some of the songs he cowrote were: "Make a Move on Me," with John Farrar, recorded by Olivia Newton-John; "He's So Shy," with Cynthia Weil, recorded by the Pointer Sisters; "Let's Hear It for the Boy" with Dean Pitchford, recorded by Deniece Williams, from the film *Footloose*.) In the article, Tom candidly discussed how his successful songwriting career came to be, and one of the things he touched upon was his musical education. Even though he had attended Berklee College of Music in Boston for a number of years, Tom said something to the effect that through constant rejection of his songs, he learned that he had to let go of all his musical training and had to learn how to write simple songs that were commercial.

Reminds me of an old story: A band leader was asked, "How many musicians are there in your band?" He said, "about half." Then he was asked, "Do they read music? He replied, "Not enough to hurt their playing."

Many of the performers and songwriters in all musical categories, past and present, didn't have a formal musical education; and many of them kept on learning and improving as their careers progressed because they were so motivated by their desire and love for music.

Personally, I know and have known a number of great country writers who have a limited amount of musical knowledge and many of them could only play about four chords on the guitar. They think of a title and some words; then they pick up their guitar, hit a chord and start singing with it. When they feel that the melody needs a different chord, they change it to another one.

Merle Travis certainly didn't have a formal musical education; he was an untrained, self-taught, naturally gifted songwriter with a great ear for music. He would get a song title, maybe one or two lines, then he'd sit down, start playing chords and create some of the greatest songs ever written, one of which was "Sixteen Tons."

As a matter of fact, many times while Merle was writing melodies, he would refer to the syllables "do, ra, me, fa, so, la, te, do" which represent the eight tones in an octave of a musical scale.

The importance of this basic and simple music fundamental was demonstrated in the great Rodgers and Hammerstein musical stage play *The Sound of Music*. Joan Carol and I recently watched the motion picture version on television which starred Julie Andrews and Christopher Plummer. (We were mesmerized — that movie is Entertainment with a capital E — great story line, beautiful scenery, wonderful performances and great songs!) For those of you who may not have seen it, Julie Andrews is the governess to seven children of a retired naval captain whose wife is deceased. Since the children don't know anything about music, she has to think of a way to teach them the fundamentals. I can still recall the wonderful song she sang to help them remember the syllables "do, ra, me, fa," etc.

For those of you who are new to some of the fundamentals of music, there are eight full notes in the musical scale from one C octave note to the beginning of another C octave note. When you count the five half-step notes, it makes a total of thirteen notes. These thirteen notes are all that Beethoven, Bach, Irving Berlin, George Gershwin, Fred Rose, Hank Williams, Sr. and all the songwriters of the world have with which to work when composing a song; it's what each one of them did with these notes. As the cliché goes: It's what you do with what you've got that counts.

As long as we're talking about musical educations and using simple musical techniques, I'd like to share with you how our top-echelon country musicians make up a music chart (arrangement) when they're laying down tracks for a country song in a recording session.

Instead of having all the notes and chords written out, which requires a considerable amount of musical training in sight reading and can be time consuming and complicated, they came up with a simple number system which represents the chords of whatever key the song is in, simplifying matters and saving time and money in the studio.

The following number system would apply to any key that a song would be in; let's take the key of C as an example. The C chord would be #1; D chord would be #2; E chord would be #3; F chord would be #4; G chord would be #5; A chord would be #6; B chord would be #7; and the next C note completes the octave. If there was a D-flat chord (which is a half-step down) it would be referred to as #2 with the musical flat sign; if there was a D-sharp chord (which is a half-step up the scale) it would be referred to as #2 with the musical sharp sign, and these number symbols with either the flat or the sharp sign would apply to all the notes in the octave of that particular key. If you were in the key of A, then the A chord would be #1; B would be #2, C would be #3, etc. And so it would go with whatever key you decided upon for the song.

During the session, if the leader decides to make different chord changes, he will call out different numbers and everyone will then make the appropriate number change on their music sheets.

By using this number system, no notes have to be written or read. If you can count up to eight, you can do it (taking into consideration that you are proficient enough to play the various chords on your particular instrument).

With regard to the melody of the song, all they do is listen to a demo tape once or twice, and they've retained it in their minds — now, I'm talking cream of the crop country musicians. Also, they simply refer to the beginning of a song as the "intro," and the end of a song as the "outtro." All these simple techniques are up-to-date stuff that they are using.

You can also write melodies using a number system where a number would represent each tone in an octave in the same way that the syllables "do, ra, me," did, which I have already discussed. In the past, when I have had limited time and a small piece of paper, I have used a number system when a melody came into my mind, and I wanted it written down in some manner so that I could refer to it later when it could be written out properly in the correct key, chords, musical notes and time values. I also know other songwriters who have done the same.

One of my favorite songwriters and entertainers is Kris Kristofferson, who has written some wonderful country classics such as: "Help Me Make It Through the Night," "For the Good Times," and Janice Joplin's big hit, "Me and Bobby McGee." Did you know that he was a Rhodes Scholar? (You've got to be smart in order to qualify for and receive a two- or three-year scholarship to attend Oxford University in England.) He obviously had his choice of professions but he chose to become a songwriter/entertainer which eventually opened up opportunities for an acting career for him. The next time you hear any of his songs, listen carefully to his lyrics and melodies; they are as simple and down-to-earth as he is, which is why they attained commercial success.

The main point that I'm trying to make is: It's not necessary for you to have a big musical education with all kinds of music certificates or degrees hanging on your wall in order to become a successful songwriter. If others can do it — with or without a formal musical education — so can you!

INVEST IN YOURSELF

Most of us spend a lot of our free time with fun hobbies such as golf, skiing, tennis, oil painting, sewing, etc. and, invariably, we spend money on them which, of course, is certainly worth it for the pleasure and joy it gives us. For the most part, it's money we'll never see again, because very few of us will ever be able to earn a living from our hobbies, but it can happen.

If you chose to have songwriting as an avocation, it has an extra added attraction: it may start out as a fun hobby but it could possibly become a fun business or career. However, you have to be willing to invest your time and a few dollars in it, which could possibly pay off in thousands of dollars, or pay you nothing at all, or it may even end up costing you money. However, that's your decision and the chance you take which is all a part of life. (Since you can't take it with you, why not!)

Regardless of what the future may hold for you, just think of all the fun and pride you'll have in yourself for doing something you've always wanted to do — write your very own song! And if you should become a successful songwriter through this enjoyable musical odyssey, then you'll have the time and money to go play golf, tennis, or pursue whatever hobby your heart desires.

Buy an instrument: If you can play a little piano or if you know some chords on a guitar, that's a big plus and you're ahead of the game. If you don't own a piano, there are some fantastic, inexpensive practice keyboards on the market. These portable little keyboards have one or two octaves which will give you just enough notes with which to play around to compose a melody. As I said before, all the songwriters of the world, past and present, only have these thirteen notes in an octave to create their melodies.

I'm very partial to the guitar, and I feel that it's one of the best songwriting instruments. Although a guitar is so versatile that you can do anything musical on it, it's basically a chord instrument. If you can hit a chord on the guitar, it gives you something with which to work, for it's the beginning step to creating a song.

So, for starters, buy either an inexpensive guitar or a little practice keyboard at a music store. And while you're there, I recommend that you also purchase a beginner's music book to show you a few chords. You are now in the process and it's all a part of getting to know a little bit about music.

If you can write musical notes, that's wonderful. But if you can't, it doesn't mean that you won't be able to write a song. Down through the years, I have known so many successful and talented musician-songwriters who can create songs, and yet cannot write them down in proper musical note form. And that's okay because there are plenty of musicians-for-hire who can write out the music lead sheets properly. Maybe you know a music teacher or you have a musician friend or acquaintance who will do it for you. You could also check with your local musicians' union and they'll be able to give you a few names of musicians who do this for a living.

Purchase a Tape Recorder: I feel that tape recorders are absolutely invaluable for all songwriters, and I highly recommend that you buy a little portable one that is both battery operated and electrical. Get one that is small enough so you can carry it around with you. I don't go anywhere without my tape recorder (or my pipe and tobacco). If it's portable and battery operated, you can put it on the front seat of your car while you're driving and talk into it. At home, you can take this tape recorder with you to any room where you feel inspired to write a song. Or maybe you feel more creative when you're at the beach, mountains or possibly the desert. As I always say, do whatever works for you.

Regardless of the environment in which you chose to create, you can hum or sing the melody into the recorder and also record the lyric phrases and song ideas to which you can refer later. If you don't have the musical know-how to properly write out the melody and chords in technical musical form once you have them, you can take your tape to a qualified musician who will be able to transcribe your song from it. Since a musician's life and employment routine are unpredictable with a lot of nightclub gigs, recording dates, etc., they usually prefer to make up lead sheets from a tape because it's easier for them to work it into their busy schedules. Of course, you could sing it to him which may take a considerable amount of time and may end up costing you more money than if you had initially bought a tape recorder.

BELIEVE IN YOUR OWN MELODY

I would especially like to encourage you aspiring songwriters who have a limited amount of music knowledge to believe in yourself and to try your hand at melody writing. I have worked with many songwriters in the past who, through supportive encouragement and guidance, along with their own desire and determination, have come up with original and commercial melodies.

I remember working with one songwriter who was, and still is, excellent at coming up with unique song titles, concepts and wonderful lyrics, which is the most important and oftentimes the most difficult part in creating country songs. However, she always cowrote with talented musicians because she didn't play an instrument, though she had taken a few guitar lessons many years ago. Because she had a limited musical background, she had developed an inferiority complex about her ability to write melodies. I had a feeling that she had untapped talent in that area so I encouraged her to try writing melodies. By golly, she surprised herself with the melodies that she created. Since that time, she has become self-contained, and has written some wonderful melodies which are very commercial. Although she still prefers to collaborate with musicians, her confidence in her abilities has soared, for she knows and believes within herself that she can write excellent melodies if she chooses to do so.

I know another excellent girl singer/songwriter who also doesn't play an instrument and has very little technical knowledge about music. But her desire to write songs was, and still is, so strong that she came up with an unusual way of creating them. She composes new songs from the tracks of demos that she has recorded. She has the type of tape machine which can cut out the vocal track from a demo, leaving only the chord changes and rhythm tracks, and she creates new lyrics and new melodies from them. Even though the new song has the same chords and arrangement, the new melody and lyrics make it a completely different song. She sings the newly created song into another tape recorder and then takes the tape to a musician friend who makes up a music lead sheet for her. It's really amazing how creative you can be when you have the desire!

There's a wonderful song simply called "Sing," and the lyrics encourage the listener not to worry about whether or not their song is good enough for the world's ears; the important thing is to sing a song. How I love that catchy tune, and the lyric philosophy is right on!

So don't worry about whether or not your melodies (and lyrics) are good enough. The more you write and experience small accomplishments and successes, the more confidence you'll develop in your innate creative abilities. I know it's easier said than done because when one is first venturing out into unknown waters, one can become tentative. However, if you can sing or hum your melody, then it's very possible that someone else can hum or sing it, too.

At one of the many social functions that Joan and I have attended, I remember talking to a young man in his late twenties who made an excellent living by giving guitar lessons and performing at local supper clubs. He had an outgoing and confident personality. During the course of our conversation, I asked him if he ever wrote any songs, and he immediately said no. As I continued talking with him, I discovered that he didn't believe he could write original melodies, and he was fearful they would sound too much like someone else's melodies. I thought to myself, What a shame, for he probably had talent that he was hiding under a bushel and fear prevented him from trying.

Surprisingly, I've talked to a number of songwriters down through the years who were overly concerned that their melody might sound too much like another one which had already been written. Well, you certainly don't want to plagiarize or intentionally steal someone else's melody. It's very possible that you may have the exact same musical bar as another song but, after all, there are only thirteen notes and although you have options, there's only so much you can do with them.

All of us have listened to music in our individual lives and whatever we've been exposed to is filed away somewhere inside our heads. There may be those times when you inadvertently have 16 bars which may also be in a standard or hit song. If you do, then change enough of the notes so that it does have a different melody. You have a variety of melodic options in which to express your lyric phrases. If you didn't change it and your song became a hit, you could be infringing on someone else's material and you would soon be hearing from them.

In the final analysis, you never know what you can do until you've tried. Nothing ventured, nothing gained. Believe that you can do it, and chances are you'll do it!

GET IN THE POCKET

When you're composing a melody, think in terms of getting into a "pocket." Now, a pocket is an elusive inside musical term. It's a strain in the music and/or words which seem to fit together and have a natural rhythmic flow. You're holding it all in one place — it's there, it's in the pocket. It's a feeling musicians and/or singers get and it's very difficult to describe. It either happens or it doesn't.

51

When I was producing an album a few months ago, the musicians were not meshing or coming together as a unit while laying down the tracks for one particular tune. So the drummer said, "Fellas, we're not in the pocket. Let's lay back and swing with it." In a matter of minutes, they soon got in the pocket. Once again, it either happens or it doesn't and in this case, it happened.

DOES YOUR MELODY CREATE A MOOD OR PICTURE?

I talked about the importance of mental pictures that lyrics should automatically create in the mind of the listener in my previous chapter. This principle also applies to melodies, for it's a two-way street. A good melody will fit the mood or theme of your song's lyrics and its musical sound should create images in the listener's mind.

An example of this would be the mood and images that instrumental tunes create with their melodies in motion pictures. Every time I hear the theme song from the movie *Chariots of Fire*, I want to put on a jogging suit and start running. For those of you who didn't see the film, the movie opens with the instrumental theme song as European track athletes are jogging on the beach. Throughout the picture, this theme plays in the background whenever they're running.

Did you ever see the movie *Jaws*? It was a very successful film about a shark that was attacking people in the water near a public beach in a resort town, and it scared the audiences out of their socks! If you did see it, do you remember the first time that you saw Jaws? The background music which accompanied the shark's presence and which started with ominous bass tones was frightening and unsettling to the nervous system to say the least. Whenever those bass notes recurred in the picture, you would automatically feel and visualize Jaws lurking nearby, ready to attack, even before he came into view. Goodness, I haven't felt the same about playing my bass ever since I saw that movie years ago!

It's the rare person who hasn't seen the classic movie *Love Story*, starring Ryan O'Neal and Ali MacGraw. Naturally, it was a love story about a young couple and during the course of their relationship, the woman finds out she has a terminal illness. Throughout the film, the beautiful melody theme recurs, especially during the tender moments between them. It is particularly effective, emotionally, during the last scene of the movie. After she dies, he returns to where they first met, which was on an athletic field. As he sits in the bleachers with his head in his hands and with the camera slowly pulling away from him, you hear the "Love Story" theme. I don't know of anyone who didn't cry, and it's my opinion that without this music, that scene would not have been as effective.

As a matter of fact, if you aren't aware of the true importance of music in a film, turn the sound off the next time you're watching a movie video or television show, and you'll see that it loses half its impact. The background music (known as a musical score) in the various scenes of a movie, unconsciously brings out emotional feelings within us.

I will reiterate what I have recommended in previous chapters: one of the best and most enjoyable ways to learn how to construct the various elements that make up a song is to take the time to listen to hit songs in the music category to which you are attracted. This is especially true for melodies which are elusive in themselves. By consciously listening, analyzing and observing, you will automatically absorb the numerous musical nuances which are inherent in melody construction; and this is something that can't be taught or learned from a book.

Of course, nothing can take the place of taking a simple course in the basic principles of musical composition or taking piano or guitar lessons, which will give you a fundamental foundation in all areas of musical construction. In fact, I recommend that you do so if you are highly motivated.

I have tried to give you a brief outline of the necessary ingredients and/or tools which you'll need to create a melody. Now the rest is up to you. With your God-given talent, your guitar, keyboard or your own physical ability to whistle, hum and tap your feet, go within and listen to the music you hear inside you; then bring it out into the outer world for the rest of us to enjoy.

Regardless of the degree of your musical knowledge, I hope the above suggestions will inspire you to try creating your own original melody; and, more importantly, to believe and follow the beat of your own drum.

However, if you should find that creating a melody isn't your cup of tea and your best suite is lyrics, it's okay. I would then recommend that you find a musician who can write melodies and cowrite a song with him or her. Besides, it's more fun to do it in twos, which I elaborate on in Chapter 9, "Song Collaboration."

Lyrics and melodies should always complement and be in harmony with each other. The lyrics to Roy Rogers's and Dale Evans's theme song "Happy Trails to You" wouldn't have had a trail to follow unless they had a melody.

To paraphrase the old cliché, a journey of a thousand miles begins with a single step. For lyrics to take a journey of a thousand miles, they need a melody to carry them along their way.

As the captioned picture of the six-foot Indian at the old Decca Records' recording studio so aptly stated, "Where is the melody?"

▼

CHAPTER EIGHT

PUTTING THIS MUSICAL JIGSAW PUZZLE TOGETHER

Have you ever tried putting a jigsaw puzzle together? Wasn't it fun and challenging? Yet so many times just downright frustrating! You would spend hours going through hundreds of pieces in order to find one piece which would fit one particular spot, and you would do this over and over again until the day finally came when you inserted the last piece to complete the picture. Do you remember how good you felt when you finished it? As with any creative endeavor that anyone starts and completes, one gets a sense of pride and self-esteem that money can't buy and which no one can ever take away.

And so it goes with trying to put together all the elements that make up a song. It can be very puzzling sometimes, so don't make any unnecessary demands on yourself which are impossible to meet. After all, it's your first attempt at writing a song and you're not competing for some out-of-reach, award-winning prize. However, it could be the first of many songs which someday could be published, recorded and, consequently, have the potential of making you money and giving you recognition.

In my previous chapters, I've discussed the various ingredients which make up this "musical stew" that you and I are cooking together. In some instances, I may repeat some of these principles from those chapters, since they are intricately interwoven like a colorful tapestry. And repetition is a good idea, for it will help you to remember, which, as you know by now, is one of the main ingredients for writing lyrics and melodies to a hit song.

Although there doesn't exist a tried-and-true recipe for writing a hit song, how do we put together all these flavored ingredients and how long do we let it cook, simmer, and cool before it's ready for the dinner table?

Let's quickly review the foregoing chapters: I talked about the magical process of creating, which should give you the patience to write a song and have fun doing it during its creative journey; a lot of time was spent on how and where to find titles which are everywhere imaginable; I spoke at length about the importance of song concept and lyric direction, and how this concept must have a form or song format that serves as the foundation upon which your song home is built. Then I discussed the importance of both the lyrics and melodies in separate chapters which, together, line by line, must hold the listener's attention.

Now, how do we put all these ingredients together? I'll try to keep it simple, although there are many factors involved in writing a song which can vary, sometimes radically, from one person to another. Much will depend upon the degree of your innate talent and ear for music, along with whatever musical knowledge you may have acquired. (Having a good ear for music basically means having the ability to distinguish one note from another and being able to duplicate that note when you actually hear it or imagine it in your mind.)

Although I feel all aspiring songwriters at various writing skill levels will be able to learn something from this book, it's basically geared for the beginning songwriter. Let me give you a perfect example of how one songwriter I know began her writing career which first started as a hobby. She had a considerable amount of innate musical talent and a good ear for music. Although she had taken piano and singing lessons for about a year when she was younger, her technical knowledge and skills in music were limited.

As she shared her story with me, I was amazed at how she instinctively followed many of the songwriting principles I've talked about in this book, which only proves how your mind will find the way for you if you have the desire, motivation, patience and are willing to use a little elbow grease.

She always started with an interesting song title and then she would write down everything she could think of that related to the title, which was usually the song concept itself. After she did this, she would outline a skeleton sketch of the beginning, middle and ending from those notes. She would mull it over awhile, and then start writing first-draft lyric lines for the first verse just as one would do when writing a poem.

Since Hank Williams, Sr. had always been her favorite songwriter, she observed and familiarized herself with the form he had used in creating his songs, which was the 32-bar formula. (That ain't a bad songwriting hero to emulate, folks!) With regard to the melody, she bought one of those inexpensive portable, two-octave keyboards that I previously mentioned to you in another chapter. This keyboard had several unique features in it; one of them was the ability to program a rhythm pattern and beat to any tempo she desired. Since her first song was a ballad, she set up a slow, waltz tempo with emphasis, naturally, on the first beat. Then she would refer to her first-draft lyric lines and start composing her "working" melody, one line at a time.

She did something else which was unique in order to help herself create lyrics and melodies. Although she didn't make her living as a professional singer, she always loved to sing, so she pretended she was performing in front of an audience and had to "sell that song emotionally" to them. Consequently, she would "speak-sing" these lyrics as she felt them, holding the note value of one word longer where she felt it should be emphasized and going up and down the scale in a flowing manner.

After she completed the first four lyric and melody lines in the first verse, she would record it on her portable tape recorder. Then she would create each lyric line of the second verse so that it would fit the melody and rhythm pattern of each line in the first verse. This is also the creative technique she used to write her chorus and her bridge.

After she created the first draft of her lyrics and melody, she collaborated with a musician who created a better melody for the lyrics than the one she had composed. Naturally, they spent the necessary time together revising both the words and music until they were satisfied that it was the best they had to offer.

Here's the point I'm trying to make: By having this "working" melody in which her lyrics had a rhythm and melodic pattern, she made her cowriter's job a lot easier when he created a melody for them. By working together in which one excelled in lyrics and the other in music, they wrote a song that was so good lyrically and melodically, it was eventually published along with others they had written. I know because I'm their publisher.

Her songwriting skills improved with every song she wrote; and to this day, she still follows that same creative process and routine.

Now let's talk about you. As I stated before, a lot will depend on your musical ear, natural talent and whatever technical knowledge in music you may have acquired. Since we're basically talking about songwriting from the beginning, let's pretend you have a limited amount of musical knowledge but have a good ear and feel for it like the lady I've just mentioned. Let's say that you've come up with an interesting song title and have given the concept and direction of your song a lot of consideration. So when do you sit down and actually start to put it all together?

First of all, I would suggest that you find a relaxed environment where you won't be disturbed and can feel free to be creative. Maybe it's your living room where you have a piano, or maybe it's down by the beach where you can look at the sea and strum chords on your guitar or whatever.

Since you've got your song title and several lyric lines, start "speak-singing" the words as if you were in a normal, everyday conversation. Snap your fingers or tap your feet to the beat and rhythm you feel inside you. Does that lyric phrase sound like a question? Then go up the scale. When you begin the next phrase, start on a lower note in the scale. Experiment by making the lyric phrase melodically go one way and then try it another way. Which one sounds better to you? As you speak-sing, let the ham in you come out and put feeling into the lyric phrases; hold some of the important words that you want to emphasize as your melody flows along. Keep on playing around with it; however, keep it simple and don't get too fancy. Hum or sing it to yourself and have fun doing it! After all, you are now in the process of creating a song and all creative people have poetic license to be a little eccentric.

Maybe you can play a little piano or guitar. If you know a few chords, play them and get a rhythm going. Try to find the notes and if you can write them down in musical form, do so. Here again, it all depends on your musical abilities and knowledge.

If you have one of those portable keyboards which has the ability to program the rhythm pattern, set up the beat that you're feeling for your song. Once a melody starts forming inside your head, hum or sing it into a tape recorder so you'll remember it and will be able to refer to it at a later time.

As I said at the beginning of this chapter, creating a song is like putting together a jigsaw puzzle. You try a piece here but it doesn't fit. You may become frustrated but you're determined and so you keep on searching for the right piece. You try another one and it fits.

And so it goes with creating a song. You write a lyric phrase for the second verse; then you discover it fits the story line better in the first verse; or maybe you decide it's more appropriate in the chorus or the bridge. This flexible creative attitude also applies to piecing together the melody so that it's balanced and flows.

It's important that the lyrics and melody are in sync and complement each other, since they are joined at the hip, so to speak. You would not write romantic lyrics to a fast four-beat melody; it would either be a waltz or have a slow, lilting kind of melodic feel to it. By the same token, if you had a waltz, you wouldn't write some wild and crazy lyrics which wouldn't fit the music. Once again, let me reiterate an important, creative attitude: You must always be flexible enough to rewrite the lyrics to fit a melody or change the melody to fit the lyrics, no matter how many times you have to do this and no matter how long it takes. Keep doing it until the song "feels" good to you, for it's been my experience that inner instincts are usually on target. Don't be surprised if you end up with a completely different song lyrically and/or melodically; you may also find that another song title will be more appropriate than the original one that gave you the idea for the song in the first place. That's the fascinating and fun part of creating a song — you make something out of nothing; and although you may start with a certain idea, you never quite know how the end result will turn out until it's finished. It's as challenging and intriguing as putting together a puzzle.

And should you cowrite with someone, I would suggest you follow the same creative pattern, which is primarily based on both of you having a flexible attitude while collaborating together. Remember, nothing is etched in granite and what both of you should keep uppermost in your minds is to create the best possible song lyrically and melodically so they both become inseparably one.

As you become song-wise by writing more songs and developing your skills, you'll leave the beginner's level behind and start making your way towards the intermediate level. With patience and continued effort, you will eventually become an advanced writer; and the day may come when all your time and effort pay off — you could become a professional songwriter!

But in order to advance to higher songwriting levels, I suggest that you, as a beginning songwriter, start now to develop a creative writing process and routine which will become a positive habit that will help you to attain optimum results.

Many professional writers have their own routine and process of writing a song, and one of them is Harlan Howard, who is revered by many as the songwriter's songwriter. When you have written between seventy to seventy-five songs which have been in the Top 10 country charts, I think it's probably an understatement to say that he's one the most talented and successful country songwriters in our business.

I first met Harlan many years ago when he brought his songs to me and cut demos at my publishing company, Central Songs. Since then, his songwriter's journey of a thousand miles has led him to the golden streets of the Nashville Songwriters Association International's Hall of Fame.

I would like to mention several of his songs that are my favorites: "Busted" which was recorded by Johnny Cash and Ray Charles; Patsy Cline had a big hit with "I Fall to Pieces," which he cowrote with Hank Cochran. Harlan is a master at composing ageless and commercial lyrics, which is an elusive songwriting technique. "Heartaches by the Number" is his biggest copyright, which is still making money for him today as it did thirty-two years ago when he wrote it. Another one is "Life Turned Her That Way," which was revived by Ricky Van Shelton in 1988 and became one of the nominated songs in the Country Music Association's Song of the Year category. However, life turned "80's Ladies" into the winner's circle that year.

In some of our past conversations, he has shared with me how he usually writes a song. He'll wake up in the morning and have a cup of coffee. After the caffeine has recharged his creative juices, he'll go into his office, sit down in his favorite chair, gather his thoughts and doodle. Maybe he'll write down one of the hundreds of song titles which he has been carrying around inside his head or one that he might have heard somewhere the day before.

When he feels the indefinable creative process take hold of him, he'll go into his special writing room where he gets down to the serious but fun business of creating. He proceeds to write all his thoughts about the song title he's currently working on. After he writes a verse or chorus about this particular song idea, he'll put it away in his files for another time.

He follows the same routine the next morning. Maybe he'll continue working on the song that he started the day before or possibly come up with another song title and write a few verses or chorus about that idea. He may end up with thirty or forty half-written songs in his file.

In a couple of days or weeks, he'll go through and review some of his unfinished songs. He'll pull one out, look at it and, suddenly, more lyric and melody ideas will come to him. At this stage of the game, he'll usually finish writing the song, since he's so talented and experienced.

Here's the main point that I'm trying to convey to you: After Harlan gets an idea, he lets it brew inside his head and heart awhile before he continues the process of writing it. And after the incubation period is over, he goes into his special writing room and completes the job. Once he's satisfied that he's given the very best to this song which is within him to give, he'll have a demo made and he'll submit it to producers or artists who will be recording in the near future.

I think his creative writing process is a wonderful example for all of us to think about, learn from and possibly incorporate into our own individual songwriting routine. What better songwriter is there to emulate? Maybe his magical creative process and routine will inspire and rub off on you to the point that you, too, may someday end up in the Songwriters Hall of Fame.

I'm going through a process right now as I write this book. I, too, am in my special room, sitting in my favorite chair. As I stop and light my pipe, I'm simultaneously thinking about what I'm going to say and I make notes. Then I dictate them into a tape recorder, and after Joan Carol has transcribed and edited my notes, I review them. We discuss them, make additions and deletions, and edit the material page by page, chapter by chapter. They are reread and rewritten many times until both of us are satisfied that whatever it is we are trying to convey to you will be the best possible way to say it in order to help you write your song.

LET YOUR SONG BAKE IN THE OVEN FOR AWHILE

Sometimes I'll hear a remark or get an idea and I want to rush home and immediately write a song about it. However, there have been so many times when I've become frustrated because I found the words just weren't there at that precise moment. I have to constantly remind myself that songwriting is a process and this song will be written in its own time frame which I keep referring to as the process. It doesn't matter whether it takes two weeks, two months or a year to write a song. It's been my experience that my mind has been magically working on the song when I wasn't consciously thinking about it; and right out of the blue, words and melodies will flow into my mind.

And this will also happen to you if you let it happen. I guess what I'm trying to get across to you is to think about your song without rushing or putting a time limit on its completion. Let your imagination, uninhibitedly, be free to try its wings. It will be worth all your time and effort if you persevere.

IS IT A HIT OR A MISS?

Many years ago, there was a very successful television show called "Juke

Box Jury," with Peter Potter as the host. Each week, he would spotlight about five new single releases on his show. After playing and listening to each song, he would say the singer's name, the song title and, like a judge holding court, he would rap his gavel on his desk and ask, "Is it a hit or a miss?" Each celebrity on his jury panel would then give his opinion on whether or not that song was a hit or a miss.

This is the first thought, consciously or unconsciously, that publishers, A&R people, producers and singers have when they listen to a song: Is it a hit song?

WHAT MAKES UP A HIT SONG?

One of the questions that I'm constantly asked is: What makes up a hit song? And as I sit here organizing my thoughts, I realize there must be hundreds of books and articles written on the subject matter.

I've been in the music and publishing business for over fifty years, and I can honestly tell you that I don't know whether or not a song will be a hit. In fact, I don't think anyone in the record business can consistently pick hit songs 100 percent of the time! If they did, they would be president of their own record company and would be making millions of dollars a year. You could just go to them and they would say, "It's a hit or it's a miss."

However, we might have a gut feeling about a song if we have "ears", as they say in the music business, but none of us really knows for sure. ("Ears" used in this context means having the ability to recognize a potential hit song.)

Is it the lyrics or the melody? Is it the way the singer sings or interprets the lyrics? Is it the way the arranger arranged it? Is it the way the musicians played, or the way the engineer and producer mixed the song in the recording studio? Is it the record company? Is it the promotion man who calls on the radio stations for the record company which he represents? Is it the program direc-tor at the radio station where the record company sends the new promo singles? Is it the disc jockey who has the freedom to play any one of a number of records which are on the radio station's play list? Or is it a combination of several or all the above components?

I've discovered that one of the most important and yet baffling ingredients of a hit song is the timing of when the record has been released for the public to hear. For example, "Sixteen Tons" was a worldwide hit for Tennessee Ernie Ford back in 1955. Why wasn't it a hit when it was first recorded by Merle

Travis and released by Capitol Records in 1946? (I discuss this further in Chapter 21, "The True Story About 'Sixteen Tons.'")

First of all, you have to realize that hundreds of new singles are being released each week and there are only so many minutes in a day. Therefore, only so many songs can be exposed to the public's ear. That's why we have song charts in music magazines such as *Billboard*. Radio stations all over the country refer to these charts and generally play the ones that are on them.

When I was talking with Harlan Howard about my forthcoming songwriting book, I asked him how many of his songs made it to number one. He didn't know for sure, but he did know that he's had between seventy and seventy-five in the Top 10. It's been his experience (wouldn't you love to experience this just once in your life?) that oftentimes a song can make more money by being in the Top 10 than by being number one. Therefore, as far as he was concerned, when a song makes it into the Top 10, it's a hit! In other words, it's better to have a record that stays in the Top 10 for awhile (which means there must be a public demand for this record) than to have a song go quickly to number one and then drop out of the Top 10 just as fast.

So, if you should ever have a song that hits the Top 20 chart in *Billboard*, you can start feeling excited. Should it make the Top 10, you may break out in a cold sweat and experience dizziness because it's a potential hit and, according to Harlan Howard — who knows better than anyone — it can make just as much money and sometimes more than a number one song. If it gets into the Top 5, it's almost a hit, so have a little brown bag ready just in case hyperventilation sets in. And should it become number one, you can pass out cigars, because it's safe to assume it's a hit.

But even if it reaches the number-one spot on the charts, it's not a guarantee that your song is a hit. Why? Because it could be a "turntable hit." In other words, the song may have been played many times on the air all over the country, but the public didn't buy it. (Speaking in terms of dollars and cents, this means that you wouldn't make much money for "mechanicals", which are royalties due you from record companies for the sale of tapes, CDs, etc.; however, you would receive "performance" royalties which are certainly something to write home about!)

So timing is a big factor, and the simple fact is it's the public who decides what song is a hit because they are the ones who shell out their hard-earned bucks to purchase it!

I've been actively involved in all aspects of the music business for over fifty years, and it's my belief that the bottom line to having a potential hit begins and ends with a well-written song. May I reiterate what Merle Haggard once said to me when we discussed this subject: "You've got to get them in the heart, in the head, or in the feet."

I'll never forget the day this one songwriter came into my office and told me he knew his song was a hit because it met all the requirements on some hit song checklist that someone had given him, which he proceeded to pull out and show me. I just shook my head as I read about fifty or so questions on whether or not a song had this or that in it so the "steel doors" of a publisher, producer and record company could be broken down and, consequently, get played on radio stations.

Now, I have not only been writing songs for years, but I have also published thousands of songs throughout my career. If I had to answer "yes" to all those questions, I would never have written or published a single song. This "checklist" was enough to boggle and stymie the minds of the best songwriters! Do you think that David Allan Coe, who wrote the hit song "Take This Job and Shove It" bothered to look at a song checklist to see if it met all the requirements?

On the other hand, I have previously discussed various ingredients that you should be aware of which comprise an excellent song. There are some basic guideline questions that you should be asking yourself while you're in the process of creating which will help to keep you on the right track of writing a potential hit song.

Since I like to keep everything simple, let's break it down into three main categories: song title, lyrics and melody:

1. **Song Title:** Is the song title unique and interesting enough to make a publisher, producer, artist or any listener want to hear it? Does it form mental images or pictures in the listener's mind? Is the title repeated enough times in the song so the listener will remember it?

2. **Lyrics:** Did you tell them what you're going to say? Did you say it? Did you tell them what you said? Are your lyric phrases visual? Are you writing your lyrics with feeling so the listener will be able to feel your emotions and, thereby, relate to the song? Are your lyric phrases written in a normal, everyday

conversational way? Do they "read well"? In other words, did you stay in the story line direction of your song's concept? Are the song lyrics tight? Remember, there are no wasted words in a well-written song.

3. **Melody:** Is your melody catchy and easy to remember? Is there a lot of melodic repetition? Do the lyrics and melody complement each other and fit together like the pieces in a jigsaw puzzle? Does your melody put them in the mood to dance, cry, or sing along?

GO FOR THE SONGWRITER'S BRASS RING!

One of the best ways to learn from a book is to read it all the way through once; then take each chapter one at a time, reread it and think about it. Remember, easy does it. Take one day and one step at a time and the pieces to your musical jigsaw puzzle will eventually fall into place, depending on your desire and whether or not you persevere long enough.

I wish I could be there with you to share in all the joy that creating a song can be. However, the next best thing is this do it yourself and have fun while you're doing it songbook; and I hope it will be very instrumental in guiding you through all the fundamentals of songwriting.

I read somewhere that if you try to please everybody, nobody gets pleased; but if you please yourself, then at least someone gets pleased. You are the chief cook, and as you add and stir the various ingredients into your musical stew, you have to "season to taste". Hopefully, folks will come back for seconds. And if they do, that's great! If they don't, so what! At least you'll be pleased with it and that's what counts, because after all is said and done (like with everything else in this life), we have to go through it and do it ourselves. Therefore, we might as well enjoy the journey. After all, happiness is not at the end of the trail but along the way.

My dear reader, even though you are a beginning, aspiring songwriter, you have as much chance to write a hit song as anyone else on this musical carousel that we call planet earth — so go for the songwriter's brass ring!

▼

CHAPTER NINE

SONG COLLABORATION:
It's More Fun
To Do It In Twos!

I've heard that writing can be a very lonely occupation. So I've always thought, Why not be lonely with someone? Some of my happiest moments have been collaborating on a song, which I have always preferred because it's more fun to do it in twos.

Collaboration is sort of a citified New York term for writing together. In country, it could be referred to as two mules pulling a load in the same harness — otherwise known as teamwork.

I've already mentioned collaboration in several of my previous chapters because it's commonplace among songwriters, especially the professionals.

Over the years, however, I've talked with thousands of songwriters and would-be songwriters, and surprisingly, quite a few of them confided in me that the very thought of writing with someone — for one reason or another — turns them off.

If you feel this way, too, then I hope this chapter will open your mind to all the good reasons why cowriting is such a positive thing to do and would benefit you in so many ways.

TWO HEADS ARE BETTER THAN ONE

There are many songwriters who are capable of writing both the lyrics and melody. Generally speaking, however, one will excel at lyrics with a mediocre melody while the other has more talent for creating music than lyrics. By putting two talented heads together — one who excels in each area — they have the opportunity of composing an excellent song which has a chance of being published and recorded in the commercial marketplace.

There's another factor which I consider to be very important: No matter how secure anyone appears to be, we all need encouragement; when you collaborate, you have a built-in support system. You have a buddy with whom you can have a cup of coffee or call on the telephone, and who will have a sympathetic ear, since both of you are striving for the same goal and can face it together.

By writing with someone, you have the input of another person's talent, ideas, abilities and whatever they may have experienced or observed in life — and vice versa. This will stretch your talent, which will simply make you write better and it will be a growing and learning experience that will benefit both of you. Many times, your idea input and lyric suggestions will automatically stimulate the other person, and they'll come up with phrases and/or rhymes you wouldn't have thought of yourself — and vice versa. Or you might have a feel for how the melody should be in a certain lyric phrase, and as you sing or hum it, your cowriter gets another idea which will help improve upon the one you had — and vice versa.

Attitude is everything as you share this musical adventure together. Respect for each other's talent is essential, so have a flexible attitude when creating; be willing to change either the lyrics or the melody. Don't hold back — communicate your ideas and thoughts with each other. Even if you don't agree, accept their suggestions temporarily, for you can always change it later if both of you discover it doesn't work. This is why they have erasers on pencils — nothing is etched in stone (excuse the pun).

Above all, don't be so serious! Always keep your sense of humor in your hip pocket — ready to be pulled out and used at a moment's notice! Laughter has a dual purpose here: you'll not only be having fun, but it will relax both of you. When you're relaxed, more creative ideas will flow through you. If you don't have these attitudes, why bother collaborating in the first place?

Most publishing companies have a writing room, and I have fond memories of working in them with so many different writers down through the years. We would spend the whole day bouncing ideas off each other and have fun doing it! But a writing room can be any environment of your choosing. It should be a special place where you won't be interrupted and one that your mind associates with the freedom of creative thinking and writing.

By the same token, when those creative juices start to flow, one usually becomes oblivious to one's surroundings. It all depends on the intensity of your concentration. You never know when an idea will come to you — in a noisy restaurant or while you're driving a car. This gives you the wonderful option of being able to write anytime, anywhere.

I'll never forget when Tennessee Ernie Ford's late wife, Betty, told him she was pregnant with their first child. He was so happy and excited about it! We were talking and laughing about how he'd react to being a father — getting up at midnight to feed the baby, changing diapers and so on. We decided to write a song about it that night. So in the little town of Monterey Park, "Anticipation Blues" was born in Ernie's garage where he had his piano.

At that time, as far as I knew (this was over thirty years ago), there had never been a song written about pregnancy. In fact, the word was rarely spoken in public, so we were writing about a very delicate subject. However, the song turned out so cute and was so well done. It ended with a tribute to love, marriage and family. I'm happy to say it was well received by the public, and I'm even happier to say that I'm still getting royalty checks to this day. (Through the mail this week, I received a brand-new CD on Rhino Records entitled, "The Best of Tennessee Ernie Ford — Sixteen Tons of Boogie," which gave me a big thrill because two of the songs that I had written with Ernie, "Anticipation Blues" and "Smokey Mountain Boogie," were included in this classic collection.)

"Anticipation Blues" was one of our best collaboration efforts, not to mention all the fun we had writing it together. If any of you have ever heard or seen Ernie perform on radio, television or a concert stage, then you know how irresistible his country-boy sense of humor can be, which, in my opinion, made him a great entertainer and a big star.

I want to seemingly digress for a moment and talk about what makes a great entertainer. Since artists are always fighting for their musical lives with every record release, it will show the importance of creating the best possible song, which is one of the main reasons why you collaborate in the first place.

Anyone can sing and enjoy popularity while they are in their "hit song" cycle. Yes, the singers will have standing room only crowds while they're hot. However, these artists should develop a show along the way because, unfortunately, there comes a time when the hits don't come that often; in fact, they may even stop coming altogether! And when they stop coming, record companies will lose interest and will start promoting the new kid on the block.

Therefore, speaking from years of experience, if singers want to continue to earn a living after "the dance" is over, they need to develop as entertainers. I believe it's what they do and say in between songs that will give them longevity on the stages around the world.

My dear buddy, Bobby Bare, is a perfect example of a singer who developed showmanship along the way, which is why he continues to enjoy immense popularity and his legion of fans continues to grow. A few years back, he was the Randy Travis of his era. I recently saw his sell-out show at the Crazy Horse Steakhouse in Santa Ana, California, and what a performance he puts on! He sings all his old hits like "Five Hundred Miles," "Detroit City," "Sheila," "The Winner" and "Marie Lavaux." Between songs, he tells humorous stories to his audience as only Bobby can! He, like Ernie Ford, has that country-boy charm which endears him to audiences all over the world. This is what makes him a great entertainer, for it keeps his faithful fans wanting more! Record companies — where are you? This guy is still hot!

And it was on a hot but fun-filled, nostalgic August 1990 evening in Nashville, Tennessee, at the National Songwriters Guild dinner, that Bobby was presented with the prestigious Aggie Award. Among the speakers were two of my longtime buddies and business associates, Charlie Williams and Joe Allison.

Charlie, one of the writers on Bobby's award-winning song "Five Hundred Miles," ran my Central Songs office in Nashville until he left to become Willie Nelson's manager. His songs have been recorded by top recording artists such as Johnny Cash, Roy Clark, Willie Nelson, Bobby Bare and Randy Travis. Down through the years, he and his lovely wife, Diane Dickerson, have been my personal security blanket in Nashville's music circles.

Joe Allison is not only an award-winning songwriter ("He'll Have to Go," "Live Fast, Love Hard, Die Young," "Teen Age Crush"), but also an excellent executive. He managed my Central Songs office in Los Angeles while I was Tennessee Ernie Ford's manager. I was influenced by and learned so much from this knowledgeable music man. He deserves a great deal of credit for building Central Song's great catalog. My personal 21-gun salute to both Charlie and Joe.

Speaking of collaborating with humorous people, have you ever heard any of Stan Freberg's big hit records? I wrote several songs with him and one of them was the worldwide hit "John and Marsha," which I discuss in Chapter 20, "Sex and the Songwriter." Not only was it fun collaborating with Stan, but I also laughed all the way to the bank, which leads into one of the best reasons for song collaboration:

IT'S BETTER TO HAVE 50% OF SOMETHING
THAN 100% OF NOTHING!

If this isn't a good reason for cowriting, I don't know what else is! Isn't it better to collaborate and have a 50 percent share of writer's credit on a well-written, commercial song which has a shot at being published and recorded someday than to have a 100 percent share of writer's credit on a mediocre song that doesn't have a chance whatsoever? Think about it, because having a song recorded gives you the potential of making money.

I can just imagine how much money Jeffrey Silbar and Larry Henley, the two writers of "Wind Beneath My Wings," must be making from the performance royalties of their song alone — not to mention synchronization rights, mechanicals and print sales (see Chapter 16, "How Do I Make Money from a Song?"). Usually, every song has its own story, and although I don't know how these two got together to write this song or the inspiration which caused them to do so, I feel the combined talents and experiences of both writers made this magnificent song unique which contributed to its worldwide popularity. Here again, two heads are better than one.

About a year ago, a talented young writer brought me a song whose theme was touchingly sensitive. Although I knew this song had something special, it fell short of the mark. The story line was incomplete; it was one of those songs that was only 60 percent finished.

I had Joan listen to it and after she gave it some thought, she saw what had to be done in order to complete the story line. So the two of them collaborated, and if it ever gets recorded, released and the public has the opportunity to hear it, I believe it will be a super hit.

"INSIDE-OUTSIDE" THEORY

While I was in the process of writing this book for you, I had to think about how I would explain some of my songwriting suggestions. This is how I became aware of my "inside-outside" theory, which only goes to prove that if you want to learn something — teach it.

When you are in the throes of creating a song — either by yourself or with someone — you are "inside" the song; you are struggling and giving birth to it, so to speak. You have so many ideas, words and musical notes at your disposal and decisions must be made as to which ones you'll use. This is why I constantly stress that you take your time when you're in the process of creating a song. Put it aside for a few weeks or a month after you've written one. Then when you review it, you will approach it with a fresh mind and can look at it objectively from the "outside", as if you were seeing it through the eyes of another person. By viewing it from the outside, you will see how and where it should be changed if, in fact, it needs to be changed at all.

I know it's not easy to be objective about something you've created. However, I suggest you try to develop your own inside-outside ability, which is basically an unbiased point of view.

This inside-outside theory is certainly applicable to the aforementioned song revision and collaboration example. The writer was so inside his song that he couldn't see the forest because of the trees. He had a great idea but he could only take it so far by himself. It took another writer (in this case, Joan) to view it from the outside in order to turn it into a finished product. The point I'm trying to make is many times it takes the ideas and talents of another person's objective point of view in order to make the creation of a song as perfect as possible so that it can be a contender in the commercial marketplace.

As I've mentioned before, collaboration is prevalent in the professional world of songwriting. Examples include Rodgers and Hammerstein; George and Ira Gershwin; and Rodgers and Hart. Although great writers in the pop and country fields have written by themselves, you'll find that many of them have collaborated. As a matter of fact, some of their biggest hits were songs which were written with other writers. Why? Because this is how they earn their living and they want to create the best possible song — lyrically and melodically — so it will have a good chance of being recorded. They know firsthand that it's better to have 50 percent of something than 100 percent of nothing.

One time, in the wee hours of the morning, I saw Sammy Cahn being interviewed by Charlie Rose on CBS-TV's "Night Watch." Sammy talked about his highly successful songwriting career and the various collaborators who helped him create hit songs and the stories behind many of them. The interview with this mega-talented and fun-loving man was delightful! What an inspirational example he is for all songwriters worldwide!

If you do collaborate with someone and finish writing a song, there's a possibility that you'll either end up loving or hating one another. It's an intimate thing to participate in because both of you are reaching deep inside and you're sharing the creative element that is alive in each of you. It's similar to being married because you need the same attitudes to make it a successful relationship, which I discussed earlier in this chapter.

As you know by now, I'm collaborating on this book with my wife, Joan Carol, who is also an excellent songwriter. We have so much fun writing as a team and the creative sharing — which is "soul stuff" — only serves to bring us closer together. No matter where we go or what we do, when we hear a buzz word or a catchy remark, we'll look at each other and simultaneously say, "Song title!" Then we're off and running with another song idea, and we spend days having fun by exchanging thoughts and lyric lines. Naturally, there were those times when we had to exercise patience and control our enthusiasm because we had moments when our harmonious writing attitudes were challenged. She now knows never to ask me anything about songs before breakfast and I, in turn, learned never to approach her when she has her head in her computer.

As I told you at the beginning of this chapter, if you collaborate with someone, you will continue to develop your songwriting skills. The same holds true for me, too. Even though I've been in this business for fifty years, I continue to learn from every songwriter with whom I write. For the past few years, I've been collaborating on songs with Ginny Peters, a top country recording star in New Zealand. I call her from Los Angeles, give her a song title and we discuss the song's concept, mood and direction. In a couple of weeks, she calls me long distance from Auckland, New Zealand, and sings me the chorus and maybe a verse. We discuss it; I change a few lines, give her more melody ideas, and so on. We go back and forth like this until we're both satisfied with it. Then she makes and sends me the demo. This is a perfect example of international songwriting collaboration and what fun we have doing it together!

I've also learned a lot from Vivian Rae, a talented Texas songwriter from San Antonio, whom I've known for the past five years. She is a remarkable source of authentic country song titles and ideas. This down-to-earth Texas lady has me laughing the entire time we're on the phone writing our songs.

Since I have the pioneering spirit, I'm experiencing something entirely new in the way of songwriting: fax collaboration. For my birthday, Joan bought me a fax machine. Recently we had to fax a letter to George Richey and Tammy Wynette, who live in Nashville. (One of George's songs, which he cowrote with Norris Wilson, "A Picture of Me (Without You)," was recorded by the legendary George Jones, and it knocks my socks off every time I hear it. Once again, a great song and a great artist equal dynamite.) Anyway, I casually mentioned in the fax how much fun we were having with our "new fax toy." George sent a reply saying that he couldn't wait until he wrote his first song with a cowriter by fax. That was all I needed to hear and we were off and running with our new fax song collaboration adventure. (I think I'll start a company called Fax Publishing.)

I'm sure there are those of you who may say that you know quite a few hit songs which were written by only one writer. You may even cite a few of the songs that I've already mentioned in this book. For instance, Harlan Howard was the only writer on "Life Turned Her That Way" and "Heartaches by the Number"; and Gene MacLellan was the only writer on "Snowbird" and "Put Your Hand in the Hand."

As I said at the beginning of this book, these are only my personal thoughts which I have accumulated down through the years from my observations in the music business. Everything this Stone says is not etched in stone. However, if you want to satisfy your curiosity, I would imagine there are statistical lists of published hit songs for the past fifty years (which would include song collaboration) that are available to the public. You could probably get this information at a library, a bookstore, or from organizations such as *Billboard* magazine and performing rights societies. Regardless of where you obtain this information, I think you'll find that many of them had two or more writers.

TOO MANY COOKS SPOIL THE BROTH

On the other hand, maybe you're the type of person who prefers to write alone and that's okay. Most of us have our own mental vision of our song concept, title, lyrics and melody. Sometimes it's difficult to have an open, flexible mind to another person's ideas and thoughts, especially if you feel your ideas are better than theirs. Should this be the case, there's really no reason to collaborate.

There are other positive reasons for writing alone if you choose to do so. If you are good at both lyrics and melody, you are then self-contained and self-reliant. Therefore, you can make your own decisions about everything with regard to your song. And when you feel in the mood to write, whether it's day or night, you can do so. You won't need to call someone or coordinate a time in order to have a writing session or music meeting.

And here's one of the best reasons of all: if your song should be recorded and become a hit, you'll have 100 percent of the writer's credits, which equals more money and recognition.

Since many of you reading this book are beginning, aspiring songwriters, you may be hesitant and shy about asking someone to cowrite with you, especially if they have more musical know-how and experience than you do. After all, you are venturing into new waters and you may want to experiment by writing alone to see what kind of lyrics and melodies you can create.

Generally speaking, all confidence is acquired; and after you've experienced small successes with writing, this will give you the necessary encouragement and confidence to ask someone to collaborate with you.

Dear reader, if you've never collaborated on a song before, try it! You just might like it! However, if you should find that collaboration isn't for you, then you can always go solo. Or you may end up, intermittently, doing both.

Regardless of whether you write alone or with someone, it should be an enjoyable experience. As for me, I feel it's more fun to do it in twos. Besides, it's better to have 50 percent of something than 100 percent of nothing!

CHAPTER TEN

▼

WHO CARES?

W ho cares? Outside of your mother, father, family members, friends, and yourself, who is going to care about your song(s)?

My very dear friend and business associate, Dale Sheets, who is the manager of the multitalented Mel Tormé, recently gave me a copy of Mel's autobiography, *It Wasn't All Velvet.* For those of you who aren't familiar with his name, he is probably the foremost male jazz vocalist in the world — not to mention his talents as a great songwriter and musician. (He cowrote one of my favorite holiday songs, "The Christmas Song" with Robert Wells.) They always refer to his voice as "the velvet fog" which explains the interesting and appropriate title of his book.

I enjoyed reading the preface where he tells his readers how he happened to make the decision to write about his life. As he mulled over the prospect, he remembered the critique he had once read on one of his previous books which had been given by the publishing company's president; and although this top executive had liked Mel's work, he ended his critique with, "Who cares?"

So Mel gave a lot of thought to "who cares?" Who would care about reading his autobiography?

Who cares? I got kind of hooked on the meaning of this simple, perceptive statement. And the more I thought about it, the more I realized it's one of the most important questions that anyone can ask themselves when they start to write anything creative — whether it's a book, song, whatever. In other words, who will care enough to listen to your song or read your book, especially to go out and spend their money to buy it?

Who cares? Think about it for a moment. Who is really going to care about your song(s)?

Who cares? The publisher? He hears thousands of songs. What's going to make him care enough about yours to publish it? Is your song commercial enough for him to possibly get it recorded and, thereby, make money for both of you? Does it fit his particular catalog? You wouldn't take a country song to a publishing company that publishes pop or rock, would you?

Who cares? The producer? The entire recording session which your song is on is the producer's personal project. He has to care enough to invest, sometimes thousands of dollars, in recording costs which include musicians, studio, engineer, mix down and final distribution. Therefore, he has to feel that your song is hit material and will appeal to the larger portion of the record-buying public; he also has to decide whether or not it's the type of material his artist can perform. If he likes your song, he'll have the artist listen to it.

Who cares? The artist? When the artist hears a song, he has to be able to relate to it emotionally so that he can interpret the lyrics and, thereby, care enough to cut it. He, too, is looking for a song which will be a hit and one that he feels will appeal to his fans. If your song was a country ballad, you certainly wouldn't take it to a rock 'n' roll artist because he couldn't relate to it and, therefore, wouldn't care about recording it.

Who cares? The record company? They are in business to make money so they promote artists and songs which they believe will sell records. Do they feel that your song is a potential hit which would, therefore, make them care enough to record it and spend the necessary money promoting it?

Who cares? The program director? The disc jockey? As you know, there are radio stations which are formatted to play all types of music such as pop, country, gospel, rhythm & blues, rock 'n' roll, jazz, etc. A pop station won't care about playing a country tune. Stations generally schedule their radio play from songs that are on the national record charts. The disc jockey will care enough about his job to play whatever the program director has scheduled for air play. But it doesn't hurt if he cares enough about your song to say nice things about it on the air for the public to hear, does it?

Who cares? The public? After a song goes through all the different people and committees in the music system, it finally gets to the public. What sector of the population will care about it when they hear it? The pop field? The country field? The rock field? And when they hear it on the radio, television or at concerts, will they care enough to get in their cars, drive to their local record store, walk in and lay down their hard-earned bucks for a tape cassette, CD or home video?

After all is said and done, it's the public who makes the final decision on the commercial success of your song. They are the ones who buy it and keep the music business people in business. This is the bottom line.

What it all boils down to is a well-written song. For openers, it means that you must be very selective of a song title; you must have a title which is so original and intriguing that it causes the potential listener to unconsciously say, "I want to hear this song!"

And after the title has caught their attention, you've got to hook them with the song's theme, its lyrics and its music so they care enough to include this song in their own musical collection.

Let me give you a few examples of public sectors who would care enough to buy a song because of its theme. Since millions of people are animal lovers, let's start with a dog's unconditional love as the song's subject matter. Several years ago, Joan wrote the lyrics to a song that she collaborated on with George Landress which, in essence, was a tribute to all the faithful little dogs that she has had and has loved in her life, called "Little Guy." While attending numerous social functions, we've found that the subject so often turns to animals since we both love dogs; and it seems like practically everyone we meet also has one which has become a member of their family, too. When she tells them about her song, they all want to hear it and request a copy for themselves — for the simple reason that dog owners care and relate to this song. (I only wish I had a dollar for every cassette that we've freely given of "Little Guy.")

Recently, I read a magazine article which stated there were approximately twenty-four million dog owners in the United States. With the kind of response we've experienced, it's safe to assume that this vast majority of people would care about the song, too.

Since love is the greatest and most important emotion that we can feel and experience, love-oriented songs, from sad to happy, have been and always will be in season with their universal appeal. At one time or another, all of us have experienced the variety of emotions which only love can take us through and, therefore, we relate to that song's particular love theme. When we're in love, we only care about happy love songs. On the other hand, when the blue skies of love have turned to gray, we relate to sad love songs.

Why did the magnificent love song "Wind Beneath My Wings" have such worldwide appeal? I feel its lyrics uniquely pay tribute to the unsung hero or heroine in everyone's life who, seemingly and unassumingly, walks in the shadow of their beloved while they, in turn, shine and fly high in the sky. Yet, they could not have done so without the other person's support and true love. As the cliché goes, behind every great man, there's a great woman — and vice versa.

In 1955, people all over the world cared about "Sixteen Tons," and, today, they can still relate to its theme about working hard and never being able to get out of debt. Just the other night, Joan and I watched a wonderful movie, *Joe Versus the Volcano* — starring the delightful Tom Hanks, whose depth and versatility as an actor have only just begun to be explored. In the opening scene, people were unhappily trudging into this one particular business establishment to go to work; and as the movie credits were rolling, "Sixteen Tons" dominated the entire scene and set the mood for the film's theme. The writer/director, John Patrick Shanley, ingeniously used humor to deal with this thing called life. In between the comedy, there are some dramatic moments and dialogue that hit the mark. I will never forget the scene in which Tom Hanks realizes God and gives thanks for his life. If it sounds as though I care about this film, it's because I do.

Who cares? This question goes right to the heart of the matter, so always keep this thought in the forefront of your mind when choosing the concept or theme of your song. "Who cares about this book?" I cared enough about songwriting and you, the beginning songwriter, to write a book about it. You cared enough about songwriting to buy it and spend your time reading it. By the same token, the people who are not interested in the music business won't care enough to purchase it.

With regard to your songs, this is also the bottom line. It's that simple.

By the way, thank you for caring.

CHAPTER ELEVEN

CAN YOUR POEM BE MADE INTO A SONG?

I f you have written poetry and have always wondered whether or not your poem could be made into a song, stop wondering and start reading. The answer is in these next few pages.

A few years ago, I remember reading an excellent article that pertained to poems and the millions of ordinary, everyday people who wrote them in order to express their innermost feelings. It went on to say what a wonderful, creative outlet it was for them emotionally. This article certainly confirmed why so many people have asked me whether or not their poems could be made into songs down through the years. Even when I sent out my songwriting survey questionnaire to a number of writers in which I requested that they write down any questions they may have that were song-related, I was surprised at how many of them brought up the subject of poems.

Occasionally, I've received letters at my office asking me if I knew of someone they could pay to write music to their poems. I've always told them that to pay someone to write music for such a personal thing as a poem, somehow, just doesn't set well with me; also, their poem would probably be better off with their original thoughts being spoken because it wouldn't be that easy putting music to it without making considerable changes.

One of the most memorable letters I've ever received was from my own daughter, Linda, who has been writing poetry to express herself ever since she was a little girl. My three sons, Steve, Curtis and Jonathan, wrote songs and pursued their interest in music, laying the foundation for each of their highly successful careers in the business today. During one of the conversations Linda and I had while I was in the process of writing this chapter, I requested that she send me one of her poems that had always been a favorite of mine (which is the closing paragraph in the last chapter of this book). With her permission, I'm going to share with you a greater portion of the letter she wrote me — for I believe her thoughts universally represent what many people may be feeling who have also written poems. Otherwise, why all the interest in whether or not poems can be turned into songs?

Dear Daddy,

Enclosed, please find the poem you asked for. How I have wished, over time, that I knew how to put together a song as opposed to a poem. I do know there is a definite difference.

In terms of impact and importance, I know that music accompanying words has so much more to say to people. Somehow, except in conversation and personal contact, songs offer a broader and more universal avenue for communication than poems.

So many ordinary, everyday people have that need and inspiration and wish they had the necessary knowledge to write a song which would inspire, entertain, or send others a message; this is the magic of good songs and music. We can relate to them because we all have a song in our hearts, and there are those times when all of us wish that we had written or sung a particular song ourselves.

Music is (or can be) passive participation. We sit, we listen and we relate. We respond from our radios, our tapes and our records. The rhythm of the melodies and the musical arrangement that surrounds the words add another dimension to whatever message is intended by the writer.

Actually, if I knew how, I would be trying to write songs instead of poems; but I know that I don't know how, so I don't — but if I thought I did, I would!

So your book should have an audience for people who know that they don't know but would like to know how.

I am a 'wanna-be songwriter' like all the rest!

Love, Linda

So for all of you poets out there, including my daughter, I hope that what I have to say in this chapter will inspire you to try your hand at songwriting.

Can your poem be made into a song? The answer is yes, no and sometimes. Sometimes it can be done successfully, but it would all depend on the poem's cadence and structure; for the most part, however, it's not that easily done. Poems have a different form and cadence than a song. They are written in a verbal rhythm pattern that you can change with every breath; and when you write and/or read a poem, you can establish any kind of rhythm that you are feeling at that precise moment.

With music, however, you are locked into a certain amount of notes to each bar. Although there is more freedom and flexibility in the rules and regulations of today's music than ever before, there are some basic musical principles to which you must adhere when writing a song, which I have already discussed in previous chapters. If you've been inspired to write a poem, then there's no reason why you can't take that basic idea and use it as your song's concept which, oftentimes, is the title itself. You might also be able to use your poem's title for your song or it could trigger off a word association that could lead to a title which is more interesting and commercial.

Although there is no musical order in the lines of your poem, they do have a rhythm pattern which could be the basis of your melody. So pick out one or two lines from each one of your verses which are relevant to your theme, and use them as an outline sketch of the song's story line even though you may have to rearrange them or create a different set of words.

Poems have a tendency to wander, which is another reason why it's difficult to make a song out of your poem in the exact same way in which it was written. I've already talked with you about the importance of a song having a direction and how you must not deviate from that direction if you want to write a good song. When you write a song, especially in country, you are telling a story and you must always come back to the main theme and direction of the song. As I've said before, the mark of writing a good song is to repeat certain lyric phrases and melodies over and over again.

Joan Carol wrote poems long before she started writing songs. She, like so many others, asked me how to put music to some of her favorite poems that she had written many years ago. One of them was a daily prayer/poem and together we created a beautiful spiritual song from it by using the guidelines I've given you above and throughout this entire book.

Let's compare the "before" and "after" by first reading the prayer/poem in its original form.

"Thank You, God"

Thank you, God, for giving me today.
Let your will guide me along the way.
Show me what to do,

Just how can I serve you?
And if I should get concerned,
Let me lean back on all I've learned.
To stand in the center of your light,
Whenever things don't go quite right.
For it's there I'll find...inside of me,
the power of all eternity.

Here are the lyrics to our song after we rewrote it by using the theme of her poem as the inspiration. Notice how we started each verse with the song's title, which is the concept.

"Lord, I Thank You"

Lord, I thank you for giving me this day.
Please lead me along my way.
How can I serve you, please show me what to do.
Lord, I just can't make it without you.

Lord, I thank you for making me aware
That your love is always there.
When I get concerned, when nothing's going right,
Lord, I just go to your guiding light.

(Bridge)
My Lord...do with me what you will.
My Child...be still...be still.

Lord, I thank you for all you've given me;
For my friends and family.
And when you take me home, I'll be with you I know.
Lord, I love you...more than I can show.

(repeat first verse) ©1989

We took the basic prayer/poem concept, rearranged many of its lines, added new ones and, using a standard song format, we composed a simple melody.

Now let's take a look at one of her philosophical poems to further illustrate how you can take your poem's basic idea and through your imagination, create a commercial love song from it.

"Love's Freedom"

I let the butterfly go…
Tears clouding my eyes…
As I say goodbye…
As I let go of love.

Into the sun it flies…
Testing its wings…it tries
A new way of living
Not hearing my cries or goodbyes.

"Let go," the butterfly says
As he struggles to be free.
"Free to live…
Such a short time," says he.

And when we struggle and strive
And finally are set free,
There's so little time to enjoy
The flight's reality.

Although I loved her basic poem concept, it did not have a song format and, therefore, it would have been very difficult to put a repetitive melody to it, especially since there was no repetition in the words. It was definitely a poem that would have to be completely rewritten in order to make a commercial song out of it. I suggested she think about it, and about a month later, she came up with one of the most hauntingly beautiful but sad love songs I've ever heard.

"Blue Butterfly"

Blue butterfly, blue butterfly...dancing in the sky.
You've landed on my sleeve, can you tell me why?
Why did my love leave me for someone new?
Blue butterfly, blue butterfly, I'm just as blue as you.

Blue butterfly, blue butterfly...tell me why you're here.
Do you see my heartache flowing in my tears?
Tell me why he needed somebody new.
Blue butterfly, blue butterfly, I've never felt so blue.

Our love came to be...'cause we loved so free,
And it's hard to believe it's a memory.
Blue butterfly...you're bluer than the sky.
Or are teardrops clouding my eyes?

Blue butterfly, blue butterfly...are you leaving too?
Are you getting ready to try something new?
Are you here to tell me...love must be free?
Blue butterfly, blue butterfly...thanks for your company.
Blue butterfly, blue butterfly...fly away free.

©1989

You will notice that she used the butterfly concept as a comparison to letting go of love in both her poem and in her song. Notice her visual and intriguing song title. It makes people immediately wonder if there is such a thing as a blue butterfly, and note how many times she repeats it in the song. Several of the poem's phrases were rewritten and rearranged in order to fit the song format and the story line which constantly stays in the direction of the song's theme.

The above poems with their song counterparts are wonderful examples which will show how you, too, can take your poems and make songs out of them. You might have to stretch your imagination a little but, after all, that's what your imagination is for.

No matter who you ask, I'll bet they'll tell you they've written a poem at one time or another. Looks can be deceiving and I am constantly amazed at some of the most unlikely people who write poetry. For example, who would have thought that Joan Carol's big, burly, ex-football-playing brother, Ronald Kiczenski (University of Southern California) loved to write poems? After he read the first draft of this book, he shyly told Joan that he thought he had one song in him, so he gave her a poem that he had written some time ago. She took his poem's concept, rearranged some of his lines, wrote additional lyrics, and then music was created for it by Mark Burnes. The result: "(You're My Goddess of Love) My Venus DeMilo," a sensitive love song that is now being held by one of our top romantic male crooners for recording considerations.

But whether or not it's ever recorded or an income is ever earned from it, is not the point here. We started out with Ronald's poem, which was the basis of a wonderful song, and this was something he had always wanted to do but he didn't know how to go about doing it. Today, he's very proud of his one and only song, which he gave his fiancée, Cory, on Valentine's Day and, naturally, she was flattered. What could be more romantic than to have your loved one write a song about you? It's better than flowers or candy!

I wish I knew more about the great poets and their poetry than what I do. However, I'm sure many great poems have been successfully put to music. One of the most outstanding ones that I know is "The Night Before Christmas." Since the poem is public domain, anyone can write an arrangement and register it with the Library of Congress in Washington, D. C. I've heard about ten musical versions of it and the one I liked best was Gordon Jenkins's beautiful arrangement.

The number of gospel songs that have Biblical passages and verses, especially from various Psalms, are too numerous to mention. At one time or another, I think everyone has heard "How Great Thou Art," which is pure scripture. Although "The Lord's Prayer" isn't a poem, the melody that was composed for this universal masterpiece has added an inspirational dimension to all who hear it.

My dear, departed friend and associate, Stuart Hamblen, wrote hundreds of songs about every subject imaginable. He has a large catalog of gospel songs that are known worldwide which he composed incorporating Biblical verses; they had inspired him to write them. One that immediately comes to mind is "Teach Me, Lord, to Wait." His chorus is from Isaiah 40:31 which is one of my favorite Biblical verses, and I refer to it constantly.

> *But those who wait on the Lord, shall renew their strength;*
> *They shall mount up with wings as eagles,*
> *They shall run and not be weary,*
> *They shall walk and not faint.*

I have always encouraged people to participate in life, especially when it comes to self-expression. We human beings have all these emotions inside us and sometimes it's hard to put them into words. Here is where creative writing, especially poetry or songs, comes into play.

Although poems are an intimate and personal thing, I have a hard time understanding why so many people are hesitant about sharing them with their families, friends and the world. Maybe they're afraid someone will laugh at them; if they did, then they're not that good a friend, to my way of thinking.

It's important to remember that you never know when any of your words will inspire, encourage or help someone. I remember one sad occasion when family and friends gathered together after my sister-in-law, Charlotte, passed on. Everyone got up and talked about some of their feelings and experiences about her. I'll never forget the poem that my nephew, Michael Adams, shared, which spoke of the thoughts and feelings of love that he had for his mother. As he was reading it, his words helped each one of us to get in touch with our own emotions about her which, in turn, helped all of us to get through a very difficult time.

I know of no better way to close this chapter than with the inspirational example of Rod McKuen, one of the most commercially successful poets that I know, which should encourage you to do something with your poems. Quite some time ago, Rod had written a number of poems which he consolidated into a book. Eventually, he recorded many of these poems with original music behind them, which became extremely popular. It only goes to show you that anything is possible.

So write your poems and maybe someday you, too, can publish them in a book or add music to some of them. If you decide to do the latter and discover the structure and cadence prohibits you from doing so, try creating a song from the basic concept and incorporate all the songwriting suggestions that I've shared with you throughout this book — especially in the first eight chapters.

However, for those of you who love to write poems, the most important thing to do is to keep writing them, simply because it's your own individual mode of self-expression, even if you never put music to them. Write what you feel from behind your kneecaps, and don't be afraid to share them with your friends or the world.

For this is what life is all about — the sharing of our love, thoughts and feelings with others. After all, we're all in this thing called life together!

CHAPTER TWELVE

AGE IS ONLY A NUMBER:
You're Never Too
Old To Learn!

D id I just hear someone say, "I'm too old to start learning how to write songs?" No way, Jose! As a matter of fact, you're never too old to learn anything. Age is only a number!

If you are in the prime of your life and have always had an interest in or a desire to write songs, what better time to pursue it than now? The most wonderful thing about the magic of believing is that it has no age boundaries, simply because our miraculous minds are ageless!

When you have an interest (whatever it may be), it will keep you young, excited and enthused about life. I firmly believe that if you lose this essential zest for living, you lose the joy and that's when you stop participating and retire from life.

I have a pretty vigorous work schedule for being over sixty-five years young — even though I'm supposed to be semiretired! I'm still writing songs and producing albums for artists. I still perform as master of ceremonies at various social functions or when I take my "Hometown Jamboree" show out on the road.

And for the last several years, I've been the executive consultant and director of Gene Autry's music publishing companies — thanks to my ageless buddy, Pat Buttram, who suggested that I give Mr. and Mrs. Gene Autry a call because they were looking for young blood to oversee their publishing company. (Pat was Gene Autry's sidekick in his Western movies and has enjoyed immense popularity in his own right as a comedian and actor. You might also remember him as Mr. Haney in the television series "Green Acres.")

Naturally, to meet the demands of my busy schedule which I so dearly love, I pace myself in all areas of my life. I take my afternoon nap or lie down for a quick snooze whenever I feel the need. I take all my pills on a regular basis, including vitamin pills. I have freshly squeezed juices such as carrot, apple, orange and pineapple every day in conjunction with a health-oriented diet.

I make sure not to overdo my physical fitness activities, which I do on a regular basis; and I'm proud to say that I constantly receive compliments on my youthful vitality and appearance.

I am happily married for the second time to Joan Carol, who makes doubly sure that I do all the above health stuff! Melody, our Lhasa Apsos puppy, keeps me laughing with her antics. I see my beloved grown-up children and grandchildren on a regular basis, and it ain't a boring family, folks — there's always something happening!

In the midst of all my daily activities, I live one moment at a time and I "stop to smell the roses" every chance I get. I'm healthy, life is good and I am so thankful. I believe that one of the main ingredients in my "fountain of youth" secret is my interest in all aspects of my musical career, especially the love affair I have always had with songs. So now that I've got you interested, enthused and believing that it's never too late to start writing songs, what have you got to offer at your age? Everything! Your subject matter is unlimited!

For a song to be believable, to ring true and hit the common chord that binds all of us to one another, it has to have substance. Look at all the memories and wisdom you have to draw upon from every time period in your life: your youth, teens, mid-twenties, middle age and the golden years. You are seasoned in life and your songs will have substance and quality in them that many of the younger writers don't have, simply because they haven't lived as long as you. Consequently, they can't write about the variety of subjects that you have experienced or observed in life.

What makes country music so wonderful and endearing is that it is life itself; its subjects encompass every phase and emotional aspect of our human condition. You can write songs about your childhood, parents, children, grandparents, or grandchildren. A perfect example of this is the big hit the Judds had a few years ago called "Grandpa (Tell Me About the Good Old Days)." The title tells you exactly what this wonderful country song is all about.

The subject of love is perennial. Write about the first time you fell in love or the different seasons your marriage brought you and how love sustained you through all of them. Or if you've never been married, write about your love affairs. In my chapter on sex and songwriting, I mention that quite a few older people have come into my office and many of their songs were pretty romantic, to say the least, which only goes to prove there's still a fire burning even though there's snow on the rooftop.

I am very aware of how many senior citizens live on fixed incomes, and staying within a budget can be extremely difficult because taxes, rent, food, utilities, medical costs, etc. all seem to be steadily increasing. So give your songwriting desire and interest a whirl. This is a relatively inexpensive thing to do, and has the potential of making you money, as I've already mentioned in previous chapters.

Some of you may be feeling lonely; the kids have gone or maybe you're a widow or widower and there you are — filled with all these emotions inside you and no one with whom to talk or share quality time. I think it's important to note that songwriting is a free health benefit for you! Songs deal with feelings and emotions. Medical facts and articles have proven that anyone can become physically sick when emotions are left unexpressed for long periods of time. When you have a positive and healthy outlet such as writing, you'll feel better mentally, physically and emotionally. Besides, it's downright fun and enjoyable!

To start this exciting adventure, all you need to do is sit back and relax in your favorite chair, read all the songwriting suggestions that I've given you in this book and give them some thought. When you feel you're ready to write a song, have a pencil and paper handy and write down all your ideas simultaneously, applying the songwriting guidelines that I've shared with you. By making your memories come alive through the medium of song, they will stay forever in the "now" of today.

Dear "prime-lifers" — I'm one of you! At this stage of my life, I'm totally thrilled to be doing something I've always wanted to do: write a beginner's songwriting book, which now makes me an author.

So I speak from experience when I say, "Don't let your age stop or limit you from trying to develop your untapped writing talent." You are never too old to learn how to write songs and there's no reason why you can't keep writing them for the rest of your life. The fountain of youth is within you — so don't be ashamed of your age! After all, age is only a number!

CHAPTER THIRTEEN

SHOWCASING YOUR SONG

Next to writing your song, "showcasing" it, known in the music trade as making a demo (demonstration recording), is probably the most important thing you will ever do. You are now about to embark on one of the most wonderful and sometimes agonizing areas connected with the ecstasy of writing a song — the creative planning which goes into the production of your demo. So absorb and think about all the demo suggestions that I'm about to give you.

Whether you're making a demo for your own sense of accomplishment or whether you're planning on submitting it to publishers, producers, or an artist, it should appeal to the imagination of the potential listener. Try to keep it simple and yet interesting — sort of like dangling a carrot in front of a rabbit or a teaser in front of a baby.

Realize that the product you're trying to sell is your lyrics and melody, and this is precisely what you should be showcasing — not the talented singer's voice, not the genius of the musicians, arranger, producer or studio engineer. You want to keep your listener's attention focused on the lyrics and the melody, and if there is too much of a musical production in any one of the areas that I've just mentioned, it can take away from them.

Understand, however, that your demo will need all the abilities of these talented people to present your song in an interesting way. Sometimes there might be friction when you have musicians because they all like to hear themselves play on a record, so they might "overplay." Or the arranger might "over-arrange" or in the mix, the engineer might get the music too loud and drown out the vocal, and so forth.

Since your lyrics and melody will be creating mental images, think of them as a painting; likewise, think of the wonderful talents of the musicians, singer, producer and engineer as the framework that will enhance your song painting in such a way as not to distract from it.

One of the most important things to consider is: Who will care about this song? (See Chapter 10, "Who Cares?") Is it the country market? Is it the pop or middle-of-the-road (MOR) marketplace? Maybe you've written a tune that falls into the rhythm & blues (r&b) or gospel category.

Regardless of your song genre, it has to have the appropriate musical arrangement. For example, if you've written a country tune, then you'll need to have a country arrangement, and so on.

HOW MUCH DOES A DEMO COST?

It's difficult to put an exact dollar amount on it, since there are so many variables. Basically, you should spend enough money to do the job, which is simply presenting your lyrics and melody to the listener without a lot of unnecessary fanfare. I've known people who have spent hundreds, even thousands of dollars on a demo; others have spent as little as thirty dollars.

Home Recordings: Since this book basically deals with the beginning songwriter, I would suggest that you start out in the least expensive way, which is singing your song into your portable tape recorder with a piano or guitar accompaniment. Or you could find a musician/singer and pay him twenty-five dollars to do it for you. That way, you'll have the song in a fixed mechanical form (which, in essence, is your copyright); and if you should decide later on that you want to spend more money on your song to make a better demo, you can present this tape to the musician and/or engineer who can then use it as a guideline when he lays down the new tracks for your song.

Professional Recordings: Now, I don't want to scare you off, but if you choose to take it a step further than your home recording, there are many costs to consider: rates for a sixteen- or twenty-four-track recording studio vary anywhere from fifty to one hundred dollars an hour plus the recording tape costs. This hourly rate may include the services of the engineer; if it doesn't, their fee is usually around twenty-five dollars an hour.

Generally speaking, musicians charge fifty dollars per song and usually you'll need a drummer, bass, piano and guitar. You can hire a professional singer in the neighborhood of fifty dollars or more. If vocal harmonies are required on your song and your lead singer can't do them, you may have to hire another singer. However, I would recommend hiring one who is capable of doing both.

Therefore, as of the writing of this book, I would estimate that making a good demo will cost you approximately five hundred dollars. This is what we base our demo budget on per song in the publishing world.

Professional four-track or eight-track demos: There's a less expensive way of making demos which will adequately do the job, and it certainly would simplify the above considerations, which can be mind-boggling, especially for demo newcomers.

With the electronic and computer age affecting all industries, including the music world, four-track and eight-track recording systems are commonplace among musicians, and many have them set up in their homes or garages. This electronic computer age has also brought with it high-tech synthesizer keyboards which can be hooked up to these four- or eight-track recording systems (or to any recording system, for that matter). Consequently, one talented musician can reproduce any musical sound on these keyboards, which means money doesn't have to be spent hiring a lot of musicians.

Therefore, depending on the musician's talent and skills, he's a unique combination of engineer, producer, musician and arranger. The costs would be considerably less than if you used a big-time sixteen- or twenty-four-track studio, which you really don't need to do when making a demo.

I would estimate the approximate cost to be anywhere from one hundred to four hundred dollars — depending on location. In smaller towns and rural areas, the cost should be less than in cities like Los Angeles or Nashville. So if you're planning on sending your song out into the music marketplace and want more of a professional demo, I would suggest you go this route.

If you don't know of anyone offhand who has a four- or eight-track recording studio in their home, you can always call your local musicians' union. Also, many of them will advertise in music magazines, so look in there. Inquire at places where music is happening, such as local nightclubs or music stores. "Seek and ye shall find," and eventually, you'll connect with a talented musician who makes his living or supplements his income in this way.

Once you have found your jack-of-all-trades musician whose production fee is within your budget, ask to hear some of the demos that he's produced in your song's category. And even though you may not have much experience in recording a demo, use the simple guidelines that I've shared with you at the beginning of this chapter and follow your innate instinct when listening to his previous demo productions.

If you feel he can do the job, hire him. Although you'll be relying heavily on his musical and recording skills, don't be shy about your opinion when you hear the finished product of your song. You are now aware that demos should be simply done with the main focus on lyrics and melody with the proper arrangement to enhance them (unless, of course, it's rock or heavy metal). If you think the instruments are too loud and you have a hard time hearing or understanding the lyrics, tactfully tell him to remix it and put the voice out in front more. After all, you are his client and he'll want to do his best to make you happy, for he's interested in repeat business. If he doesn't use a keyboard synthesizer for all the instruments, then he'll take care of hiring the musicians and also the singer, since they all network with each other.

A lot of writers bring me their songs on four- or eight-track demo recordings which are certainly good enough for me to make a decision on whether or not I want to publish them. If I feel the demos have been well done, then I'll use them for submission to producers; if I don't feel they're professional enough, then I'll make another one at my expense.

And when I do, it's been my habit to take the songwriter into the studio and have him or her sing their own song, even if they're not great singers. I do this because I know they will put their feelings into their song, which professional singers might not be feeling, simply because they are the ones who wrote it in the first place.

If their performance is not good enough on the demo to send to producers, then I'll hire a professional to come in and overdub the song. (Overdub means to either sing over the track that the previous singer sang on or sing on another track simultaneously using the same music track.) As a matter of fact, I usually have the professional singer listen to the songwriter's interpretation, for they will get a better feel for the song and the melody line.

And although I don't use the songwriter's version as the final product to be sent out for submission, I'll have Brian Friedman, who has been my engineer for over twenty years (and one of the best in the business), make up a special tape of them singing their song for their own personal collection. How I love to see the look of pride and joy on their faces when I hand them their tape!

I've published songs which were recorded that never had a demo. A number of years ago, our company heard through the music grapevine that Kenny Rogers needed one more song to complete his album. So Roger Bowling, one of our staff writers, was sent over to the office of Larry Butler, who was Kenny's producer at that time. Armed with only his guitar, Roger sang, "You Took the Wrong Time to Leave Me, Lucille" (which he cowrote with Hal Bynum), to Kenny and Larry. With his great ear for song material, Kenny had the courage to record this unusual song with its dynamic lyrics and it became a huge hit for him! In 1977, the Country Music Association and the Academy of Country

Music both chose "Lucille" as the Single of the Year. Kenny is the perfect example of the perseverance and courage it takes to not only make the dream in his heart come true, but to constantly strive for and reach the heights of superstardom which are known to very few. And what a wonderful friend he is to songwriters!

Many of you may be wondering what I meant by that last statement, and I'll be more than happy to tell you. Some of today's recording artists attempt to write all their own songs. They may write one hit, but no one can consistently write enough quality songs to keep them in the winner's circle. The true recording artists, who stay at the top of their game, are the ones who have an open mind and an open door to all the talented songwriters in Nashville, or anywhere, for that matter. They only look for a hit song—no matter who wrote or published it!

The classic example of this type of artist is George Strait, who, like Kenny Rogers, is a wonderful friend to songwriters. Down through the years, George has consistently had more number-one records than any of the other artists who try to write their own material. How can he and fellow superstar Kenny Rogers miss when they let the best writers supply them with their songs?

In 1989, I attended the Nashville Songwriters Association International's Hall of Fame Award dinner which honored Sanger D. ("Whitey") Shafer that year. Since George Strait is friends with Whitey and had two big hit songs that Whitey had written, "Does Fort Worth Ever Cross Your Mind?" and "All My Ex's Live in Texas," he took time from his busy schedule to freely give of his singing talents to honor him that night. At that time, George also made a few heartfelt comments about how he appreciates and respects the writing abilities of songwriters. I was one of the writers and publishers in the audience that night who stood up and gave him a standing ovation for those wonderful words which were music to our ears. I speak for all the songwriters and music publishers of America when I say, "Thank you, George Strait and Kenny Rogers."

Here's something else for all songwriters at every level to know and think about. Let's say you've made a great demo. Maybe the producer likes your production so much that when he records it with an artist, he'll have the same feel, chords, and arrangement identical to your demo. Or maybe the producer and/or artist will change everything about your song's tempo, feel and arrangement because they need to tailor it to fit the artist's particular talents.

You, the songwriter, have very little control over how your song is arranged and produced once you have given permission for it to be sent out for commercial use in the recording world. As for me, if someone such as George Strait, Conway Twitty, George Jones, Alan Jackson, Garth Brooks, Randy Travis, Tammy Wynette, or any other talented singer has chosen to do one of my tunes, I am more than happy to let them have their way with the arrangement. Quite frankly, I consider myself lucky when one of my songs has been chosen to be recorded.

Once again, let me caution you about your demo being over-produced, since I feel strongly about the subject. In order to properly showcase your lyrics and melody, I suggest you keep it simple. This, in turn, will leave a lot of room for the producer and the artist to create their own arrangement, which they'll probably do anyway. By giving a lot of thought to your song's presentation, it will help you to make the correct producing decisions. You didn't rush the creation of your song — so don't rush the production of your demo.

The thrill you will experience when you hear the demo of your first song is indescribable, and I guarantee you'll never forget it. It makes songwriting worth all the time and effort and will add immeasurably to your sense of creative accomplishment.

Remember, next to writing your song, showcasing it is the most important thing.

▼

CHAPTER FOURTEEN

BASHING THE MYSTERY OUT OF COPYRIGHTS AND REGISTRATION

I know I've been giving you a lot to think about in the creative area of songwriting, but I also feel it would be to your benefit to know something about the important and sometimes mysterious area of copyrights and registration.

Intermittently, I am asked about this subject, since there have been so many revisions and additions to the United States Copyright Act during the past few decades. So I called Washington, D.C. and talked with the lady in the copyright office to verify some of these revisions, and I'll be sharing with you some of the things we discussed.

Now, I certainly don't want to confuse you with all the rules and regulations that encompass all the various scenarios which could occur with regard to copyright and registration. So I'll stick to the basics and keep it relatively simple by discussing what I feel beginning, aspiring songwriters really need to know in order to protect their material.

Basically, "copyright" is simply the "right to copy;" and it's under the aegis of a statute comprised of a group of exclusive rights for authors to protect their creative material or works from being exploited without their permission. The definition of copyright in Webster's Ninth New Collegiate Dictionary succinctly says it all: "The exclusive legal right to reproduce, publish and sell the matter and form of a literary, musical or artistic work."

Since your song has words and a melody, it is considered both a literary and a musical work, and obtaining a copyright is unbelievably simple. Once you have completed both the lyrics and melody of your song, you can do one of two things: you can have a "fixed visual copy" like a lyric/music lead sheet made up which you can read; or you can record your lyrics and melody which would be "fixed" on a "phonorecord." The latter means a mechanical reproduction device such as a cassette tape or record which is perceived through sound. And presto! You have technically copyrighted your song!

Your unregistered copyright is permanent and gives you authorship protection for your song material. In other words, no one is legally permitted to use it for any reason without your expressed consent. (I feel it's always better to have things in writing.)

You are not required to register your unpublished song, but you could do so at any time after you've written it if you so choose. You can also shop or take your song to publishers without it being registered. However, if you're going to be taking your song out into the music marketplace, I suggest you register it with the Library of Congress in Washington, D. C. The choice is yours.

Though I don't believe the whole world is waiting to steal your song from you, I know that many writers get a little paranoid about someone ripping off their songs. Consequently, if you've registered your unpublished song like the music professionals do, then you'll have peace of mind.

Unfortunately, there are those instances when legal disputes of some sort can happen, and I want you to be aware of your rights. If you could prove that any of your copyright's "five specific rights" had been infringed upon, and it couldn't be resolved through negotiation, you could pursue it in a court of law. However, if you didn't have it registered with the Library of Congress, and someone violated your copyright and you took legal action, the courts would not hear your claim until you did register it. Your registered copyright is an official public record that could help you should a copyright dispute arise.

I feel it's to your advantage to be aware of your five specific rights (Section 106 of the Copyright Act): (1) the right to perform copyrighted work publicly; (2) to reproduce the copyrighted work in copies or phonorecords; (3) to display the copyrighted work publicly; (4) to distribute copies or phonorecords of the copyrighted work to the public by sale or other transfer of ownership, or by rental, lease, or lending; (5) to prepare derivative works based upon the copyrighted work.

Speaking as a publisher, if I decide to publish a song that someone has brought me, one of the first things I ask for is the copyright registration certificate. Standard songwriter/publisher agreements include a copyright assignment from the writer to the publisher. If the song hasn't been registered, then my company immediately sends in an application to the Library of Congress in Washington, D. C.

Also, when a song is recorded and released, it is imperative that we have the registration number so that all the legal musical details can be taken care of properly as soon as possible.

HOW DO I REGISTER MY COPYRIGHT?

If you decide to register the copyright of your unpublished song, you can obtain the proper application form by writing and requesting several copies of Form PA (which stands for Performing Arts) at the following address: Register of Copyrights, Library of Congress, Washington, D. C. 20559.

Once you have received and read the form, you'll see that it's pretty much self-explanatory. You simply fill in the necessary information in the proper spaces. If there is more than one songwriter on the song, be sure they do the same, and have each one sign their name on the indicated signature line.

If there is something you don't understand or if you have any questions whatsoever, I recommend that you call the copyright office. As of the writing of this book, their main number is (202) 479-0700. Whenever we have had copyright questions in our publishing office in the past, we have called them and they have been very cordial and helpful.

After you fill out the application and sign it, enclose a check or money order made payable to the "Register of Copyrights" in the amount indicated on the application. (As of January 1991, the fee is twenty dollars.) Don't forget to enclose your deposit material, which can be either a music/lyric lead sheet or a cassette tape with your melody and lyrics on it. (I prefer to send a copy of the music/lyric lead sheet as my deposit material because it's more convenient for filing for both the copyright office and myself.)

Then you mail these items to the address indicated on the form which I have already stated above. Since there are hundreds of thousands of songs being sent to them each year, it will take approximately three months before you receive your registered copyright certificate.

Collection of Songs: There is another way to register your songs, and this type of registration is known as a "collection of songs." However, there are certain requirements and conditions you must meet, and I'll enumerate a few of them for your information.

(1) You have to have two or more songs and, although there isn't a limit to the number of songs you may have in this collection, it's recommended that you have no more than ten. I will briefly discuss this later. (2) You have to be

the author on each song in that specific collection even though you may have a different cowriter on each of the songs; and (3) This collection must be owned by the same entity; that is, it is either owned by you, since you contributed to each song, or by a company. For example, the entity name could be *Jane Doe Collection* or a company name such as *Jane Doe Enterprises*. The entity name that you choose will appear on your registration certificate and on the public records.

The reason they recommend having no more than ten songs in this collection is that it could become complicated if there were ever a legal dispute about the authorship or date of creation on any one song. Each song is a small part of a large collection and they are protected as a whole; the song titles themselves are not listed on this certificate, only the collection title name.

However, if you use the song collection method of registration, I would suggest you take it one step further. After receiving your copyright registration certificate for this specific compilation of songs, you can then fill out a supplemental application called Form CA and thereby list all the song titles in that particular collection. In that way, the copyright office can index these song titles for the public record.

As of the writing of this book, the fee to register the collection of songs is twenty dollars, and the fee for the supplemental registration is another twenty dollars. However, you have only invested forty dollars for ten songs as opposed to paying twenty dollars for each individual song, which is a substantial savings of one hundred and sixty dollars. I know quite a few prolific writers who are constantly writing songs and they register them in this way, since inflation seems to be a way of life and money is tight. I recall one writer who had a song that I decided to publish and he had it registered in a collection of songs. Since I require that every song in my catalog have its own copyright registration number, which is good business policy in music publishing, my company sent in an application for an individual registration.

HOW LONG DOES MY REGISTERED COPYRIGHT PROTECT ME?

This is important for you and your heirs to know. One never knows when a song will become a hit, which could be years after it was originally written.

In 1978, there were major revisions in all areas of the Copyright Act laws. One of the revised areas included the protection time limit of a registered song.

This was basically done because too many writers who knew nothing about copyright or registration laws lost their ownership. For one reason or another, they didn't renew at the proper time. Consequently, once their initial copyright protection time period had terminated, the song went into public domain, which meant the whole world could have at it.

Any song written after 1978 is protected for the lifetime of the writer plus fifty years after the official date that he left for songwriter's heaven. In other words, his heirs would be entitled to the royalties fifty years after his passing, at which time it becomes public domain.

If there were two or more authors on the registered copyright, it is protected until the surviving author has passed on and from that date, there's still a fifty-year protection period for all the heirs before the time limit expires.

Therefore, you only have to apply one time for a copyright registration, which eliminates the renewal procedure required in the past. I think all this will make more sense to you if you know a little about how copyright registration worked before the new laws were enacted in 1978.

The original copyright protection time period on songs that were written before 1978 entailed two consecutive twenty-eight-year periods. The writer, a year before the first twenty-eight-year copyright expiration date ran out, was required to fill out the proper application in order to apply for the second twenty-eight-year renewal period which made for a total of fifty-six years. If he didn't renew it, his works became public domain.

Another law was in force: After this second twenty-eight-year period was over, this same song could be renewed for another nineteen-year extension, which made for a total of seventy-five years. This period of time was considered to be the life span of the average person. After that time period, it became public domain. So with the long interval between renewals, you can see how easy it would be to lose track of the appropriate time period in which to file for renewal and, therefore, you could lose the copyright ownership to your song.

Now, if you had written a song before 1978 which was with a publishing company, it would be their responsibility to file the necessary papers at the appropriate time for renewal. Copyrights are the lifeblood of publishing companies, so they all have their own system of keeping track of the renewal dates in their song catalogs. If they didn't, then both you and the publishing company could lose a lot of revenue. (To be on the safe side, however, it would behoove you to keep track of the renewal dates and call to remind them when it's time for the second extension period.)

The Poor Man's Copyright: I'm sure that many of you have heard about the "poor man's copyright" and, intermittently, aspiring songwriters have asked me about it.

As I have previously stated, the courts require a registered copyright with the Library of Congress before they'll hear a complaint. Although I don't know to what extent a poor man's copyright would benefit you in court, it seems to me that it would be additional evidence as to the proof of your authorship and date of creation. For those of you who want to inquire about it, go to your nearest United States Post Office for the necessary information.

However, as I've said before, I feel it would be a wise decision to follow one of the proper copyright registration procedures at the outset if you believe your song is commercial enough to send out into the music marketplace. By doing so, if there ever was any legal debate on your song whatsoever, you would get the benefits of all the copyright laws which were written on your behalf in the first place.

I have tried to give you all the necessary information and options with regard to copyright and registration as I understand them to be. If you have any questions, I suggest that you, too, call the lady in the copyright office in Washington D. C.

I have been in the music business for over fifty years and, comparatively speaking, any legal disputes that I have encountered over songs have been minimal. When they did occur, they were taken care of easily. Therefore, I believe the chances are more than good that you won't be involved in any type of legal dispute or court action with regard to your song.

However, it's up to you to choose what to do. Once you've made your decision and have done all the necessary things in order to protect your song, bless it and turn it loose for the whole world to enjoy!

CHAPTER FIFTEEN

BREAKING THROUGH THE MUSIC PUBLISHER'S SOUND BARRIER

Hypothetically speaking, let's say you've written a wonderful song and you've made a professional demo to showcase it. Now you're toying with the idea of getting it to a publisher. However, you're a little tentative about it because you don't know anyone in the music business, much less a publisher. So where do you go from here?

Look upon "breaking through the music publisher's sound barrier" as a challenge — just like our jet pilots did when they broke through the sound barrier. You have to believe it can be done simultaneously following the magical ingredients of my "PEP-C" recipe — Positive Energy and Perseverance with a dash of Courage.

There are many ways you can break the sound barrier between you and the publisher. However, you'll have to do some creative thinking and research, but that's something you'll have to do no matter what your area of interest is in life. Realize that songs are the lifeblood of a publishing company, whether they are old standards or new material. Speaking from a publisher's point of view, I have always believed that it's a good idea to keep an open mind and an open door to new songs, because one never knows where or when a great song or a potentially great songwriter will appear on the scene. So always keep this uppermost in your mind during your door-knocking song quest.

Now, if I were a beginning, aspiring songwriter, I believe the first thing I would do is contact BMI, ASCAP or SESAC and ask them for a list of publishing companies with whom they are affiliated. (These are "performing rights societies" and they collect money for performances of songs via radio, TV, and concerts, as well as other music users, for the publishing companies and songwriters who are registered with them.) These three international organizations will be able to give you a complete list of publishing companies that are affiliated with them.

Once you've received the list, pick three or four publishing companies which are located in the vicinity where you live and would, therefore, be the most accessible for you. Of course, most major publishers are located in Los Angeles, Nashville or New York and you may want to send your demo to a publisher in one of those areas. In either case, you can always find out their telephone numbers and call them to get their addresses and the publisher's name. I've received telephone calls, letters and demos from songwriters not only from practically every state in the union, but also internationally.

Before you contact them, however, I want to reiterate an important consideration which I discussed with you in "Showcasing Your Song." In what music category does your song belong? Is it country, pop, rock, bluegrass, etc.? After you've decided, listen to some of the tunes which have been recorded by various artists in that particular category so you'll have a feel for which artist your song would most likely appeal to if they heard it.

Then I suggest you send a personalized letter to the publisher (nothing turns me off more than to get a form letter saying "Dear Publisher") with one little paragraph about yourself. In the second paragraph, write something to the effect that they were recommended to you by BMI, ASCAP or SESAC as an aggressive publishing company. This should impress them. Continue on with the letter by saying you would like to submit the enclosed cassette with one or two of your songs.

You might also mention an artist whose singing style would fit your song. For example, casually state that you heard Kenny Rogers singing a ballad last week and since your song is also a country ballad, this might be good material for him. By doing this, you've given the publisher a direction in which to think as he listens to your song.

Have a folded lyric sheet (preferably typed) wrapped around the cassette with a rubber band (this is how the professionals do it). Then enclose a stamped, self-addressed post card with two short paragraphs on it: one should say, "I like your songs and I'm interested"; the other, "Thank you but at this time, I cannot accept any more songs. Good luck." Most publishers will appreciate your businesslike letter, especially when you supply them with an immediate way to respond to your material.

Another innovative approach would be to look at the song credits which are listed on the jacket covers or inserts of albums, tapes or CDs of the artists that you believe are likely candidates for your song. Publishing companies are among the credits listed after each song. After getting their names, you can then obtain their telephone numbers, addresses and then contact them.

Usually, the name of the artist's manager with a mailing address will also be listed somewhere on the jacket cover or insert, and many of these managers have their own publishing companies. So you might write and send a cassette to them, too.

Through your own creative initiative and motivated research, you've done two important things: not only do you have an idea of what artist(s) you feel would be good for your song, but you've found publishing companies who handle the category in which your song belongs.

The above is a basic beginner's approach to contacting publishers. However, it's a step in the right direction and a journey of a thousand miles begins with a single step.

Since I'm trying to open up your mind to the new and exciting business world of music, which is all a part of your development process, I'd like to talk for a moment about the numerous music magazines available at newspaper stands and through subscription. A few that immediately come to mind are *Billboard*, *Cashbox*, *Radio & Records*, *Country Music-USA*, *Music Row*, and *Bullet* magazines.

There are many reasons why it's beneficial for you to read a few of these publications on a regular basis. You will become more informed about the current events in all areas of the music world. They will have album and single charts of the current hits in all musical categories which will keep you up-to-date, and you'll be aware of the wide variety of artists in your song's category. You can then either listen to these artists on the radio or go buy their records. Consequently, when you write to a publisher or have a one-on-one meeting with him, you'll be able to converse in a knowledgeable manner which will definitely make a good impression on him.

I suggest that you always send a publisher a nonreturnable tape with no more than two songs on it. Understand that publishing companies get several hundred tapes a week, depending on the size and the prominence of the company. Most of the time, they don't return them; if they did, it would cost them the salary of a full-time person and a fortune in postage. (Usually, they will send your demo back if you send them a stamped, self-addressed envelope.)

Many writers have asked me whether or not they should send their songs to the A&R department of a record company. In the old days, that was the way to go. However, things have changed considerably. Quite frankly, I believe it's a waste of time and money, because most of them do not accept unsolicited material. They usually go through established publishing companies that have made sure it's an excellent song, and who have taken care of all the necessary paperwork and legalities.

Now, I hate to bring up the "R" word—rejection! However, you're probably going to face a certain amount of rejection as most of us have, but here is where the ingredients of my PEP-C recipe will help you to keep on keeping on.

Goodness gracious! Do you realize how many times publishing companies get their songs turned down before one of them gets recorded? I would venture to say for every "yes," there are a hundred "no's." It's always been my attitude that when an artist or producer turns down one of my songs (and they have), there are still five hundred more potential people out there in the "musical field of dreams" to whom I can send it.

Actually, I smile every time I hear that word, for I remember the positive attitude of a highly successful salesman I know who told me he thrives on rejection! It's pretty hard to keep saying no to someone who doesn't take no for an answer, especially if they have a charming personality.

So if you do receive a "thanks but no thanks" reply to your letter and demo, then send that same letter format, demo and card to another publisher. Each time you do, however, find out the publisher's name so you can personalize each letter. Just remember the old saying, the squeaky wheel gets the grease. By squeaking a little more than the average writer, you'll get their attention.

There are more sophisticated ways of contacting a publisher where you can eventually establish some kind of a rapport or relationship with them, such as music seminars and songwriters' showcases. In most major cities where music is an important entertainment factor, there should be organizations that promote songwriters and their songs through seminars and listening groups. As a matter of fact, this type of organization is in countries worldwide.

Southern California is my part of the world, and there's an organization here called LASS which stands for Los Angeles Songwriters Showcase. For a fee, you can become a member. They have their own publication called *Songwriters Musepaper* in which they have wonderful articles encompassing all areas of songwriting.

Also in their musepaper, you'll find a variety of ads which are music-related. One of them is for their songwriters showcase schedule, which includes various song listening events such as "Cassette Roulette." Most of you are aware of how the game of roulette is played. Cassette Roulette is actually a listening session wherein they have a music publisher in attendance who will critique your song. They have a roulette wheel which holds approximately seventy-five tapes and throughout the evening, they spin it and where it stops, that's the tape which gets heard and critiqued by the publisher.

For an admission fee, you can bring your tape and lyric sheet and participate in the event, which I feel is a good experience for aspiring songwriters. You get the opportunity of meeting other songwriters who have the same goals, and you'll be exposed to a wide variety of songs that other writers have created. This, in turn, will help you to learn and develop your talent. You may even end up collaborating with someone. We all need a support system and the camaraderie that you'll find in events such as this is wonderful.

I have always enjoyed participating in them as a celebrity publisher whenever the time and opportunity presented itself. If I heard a song that I liked at these events, I would take the tape home. The next week I would listen to it again, and if I still liked it, I would schedule a meeting with the songwriter. If I felt the song had merit but was only 50 percent complete, I would give him suggestions and would have him rewrite it. Should the rewrite turn the song into a commercial one which I felt had a chance of being recorded, I would issue him a Writer/Publisher's Agreement.

By the same token, if I didn't like it after hearing it again, it would be discarded along with other songs that my company couldn't use. (I'm sorry, dear songwriter, but that's the way it is in the music business.)

Should you ever attend one of these song showcases or a music seminar and have the opportunity to talk with a publisher, I would recommend that you use a direct approach. Have your cassette in hand with no more than two or three songs on it, with the lyric sheets wrapped around it with a rubber band and give it to the publisher. Be sure your name, telephone number and return address are on both the cassette and lyric sheet. The publisher has to have a way of contacting you if he likes your song(s).

Regardless of the way you get your demo tapes to publishers, either in person or by mailing them, don't be depressed if you haven't heard from them for awhile. They receive numerous tape cassettes each week and it takes time for a listening session. Realize that their number-one priority is to work the songs they already have in their catalog because this is how they stay in business.

When they are not out pitching their songs to artists, producers, recording companies or taking care of the numerous administrative duties which go with the territory of being a publisher, they are listening to new material.

As of the writing of this book, I am the executive consultant and director of Gene Autry's music publishing companies. I have always had my own personal publisher's routine which I still follow to this day. Usually, I'll set aside one day for listening to songs; another day, I'll have songwriters' appointments. The next day, I'll concentrate on which songs I'm going to pitch for that week; and I'll get on the phone or dictate letters to my assistant, Karen Palmer, who then sends out the demos. On another day, I work on issuing new licenses or synchronization rights.

Now, that's the schedule I like to think I have. More often than not, however, I'll end up incorporating all those tasks in one day. So you can see by my routine how busy the life of a publisher can be; he can only devote so much time to promoting his material and listening to new songs.

The "R" word keeps popping up. However, the road to success is paved with rejection slips. There are hundreds of stories where a publisher has turned down a song and another one likes it and it eventually becomes a hit. Like most music publishers, I am not infallible in my song judgement; and occasionally, with great regret, I recall a song that I've turned down. I remember a young kid by the name of Roger Miller who walked into my Central Songs office; he sat down on the floor, crossed his legs and with his guitar in his lap, he played and sang a song he wrote called "Dang Me." I stopped him halfway through the song and said, "Roger, that song will never sell. Why don't you write one so that I can understand the lyrics!"

Well, further on down the road, another publisher heard it, liked it and the song became a worldwide million-seller. It made Roger a star and made me minus a lot of money I would otherwise have made as a publisher. To this day, whenever I see Roger, he reminds me that I turned down "Dang Me."

I'll never forget some of the statements that songwriter Joe Brooks made on television when he received his Grammy Award for "You Light Up My Life," which won Song of the Year in 1977. (It was recorded by Debby Boone and it was also nominated for Record of the Year and Best Pop Vocal Performance-Female.) As I recall, Joe said something to the effect that his song had been turned down by practically every recording company in town, so it gave him great pleasure to receive this award. (Genius Mike Curb, of Warner-Curb

COURTESY OF SUZY HAMBLEN

I'm singing and playing bass on Stuart Hamblen's "Lucky Stars" radio show on KEHE. I was so proud when Stuart received the Pioneer Award from the Academy of Country Music in 1971. Left to right: Frank Liddell, me, Wesley Tuttle, Stuart Hamblen, Darol Rice, Herman "the Hermit".

Top Row (left to right): Archie Wallace, Skeeter Hubbert, Joe Espitallier, Jerry Hutchison, Rufus "Goofus" Brewster, Darol Rice, and myself. Bottom Row (left to right): Vince Engel, Lyn Dossey, Stuart Hamblen, Sonny Dawson, Herman "the Hermit".

My first job with Stuart Hamblen's "Lucky Stars Cowboy Radio Show" in 1936. The trophies are for the Best Cowboy Band.

A picture is worth a thousand words, and if this picture could talk, it could tell a thousand stories. All these wonderful people were my coworkers and my friends. For over six hundred television shows and thousands of radio shows, we helped each other to sound and look good. Without their individual talent and support, "Hometown Jamboree" would never have happened.

Back Row (left to right): Roy Hart, Billy Liebert, Ray Merrill, Herman "the Hermit", Billy Strange, Speedy West, Les Taylor and Al Williams. Middle Row (left to right): Jimmy Bryant, Bucky Tibbs, Jonell McQuaid, myself, Glenell McQuaid, Joanie O'Brien and Harold Hensley. Bottom Row (left to right): Tennessee Ernie Ford, Molly Bee and Gene O'Quinn.

"Wake Up Ranch" (which was on KFVD from 7 a.m. to 9 a.m., Monday through Friday) was my first disc jockey job, and it opened doors for me in the record business. At one time or another, I was on twenty-eight radio stations in California. These radio shows include: "Lucky Stars," "Cowboy Church of the Air," "Radio-Rodeo," "The Cowboy Hit Parade," "The First Western Quiz Show," "Dinner Bell Roundup," "Country Junction," "Harmony Homestead," "Potluck Party," and "Hollywood Barn Dance" on CBS radio network; "Cliffie Stone Radio Show" on KLAC and "Hometown Jamboree" on KXLA.

PHOTO BY "CHAS" JONES

Here I am with Roy Rogers on the "Hollywood Barn Dance" radio show on CBS. Roy received the Pioneer Award from the Academy of Country Music in 1975. He was inducted into the Country Music Association's Hall of Fame in 1988.

My Capitol Records days as a producer in the mid-1940s. Here I am with Ernest Tubb and Jack Guthrie in Nashville, Tennessee. (I don't know the name of the beautiful young lady in the photo with us.) Ernest was inducted into the Country Music Association's Hall of Fame in 1965.

On vacation in Chicago with Dorothy, my beautiful wife and loving mother of our four children.

PHOTO BY CHICAGO PHOTOGRAPHERS & PHOTOGRAPHIC ILLUSTRATORS

COURTESY OF CAPITOL RECORDS, INC.

My favorite Capitol Records album cover — *The Party's on Me*. Ten popular dance songs, which include the exciting "Hokey Pokey."

When I became Tennessee Ernie Ford's manager, a handshake was our only contract which, I'm proud to say, lasted for twenty years. This particular photo was taken during the "Hometown Jamboree" radio days on KXLA.

Me with my forever friend Molly Bee, at one of the rodeos on my "Rolling Stone Ranch" in California. Molly started on my "Hometown Jamboree" show at the age of eleven, and practically grew up on television shows such as: the "Pinky Lee Show," the "Molly Bee Show," "Swinging Country," the "Tennessee Ernie Ford Show," and the "Jimmy Dean Show."

Tennessee Ernie Ford as he looked when he
first appeared on my "Hometown Jamboree"
television show. A few years later, here we are on
his NBC daytime television show reliving our
first television days together when I was his
straight man.

To
Gibbie
one of the best
friends & associate
I ever knew
Gene Autry

I'm sharing a few laughs with America's first singing cowboy, Gene Autry, on his "Melody Ranch" set at KTLA-TV in Hollywood. It was my great joy and pleasure to be the first producer on this show.

▼

PHOTO BY HOWARD LEVINE

Shaking hands with Gene Autry after signing with him to head up his music publishing division in June 1988. ("Back in the Saddle Again.")

In 1983, the Golden Boot Awards was started by Pat Buttram to honor the great Western stars, cowboys and cowgirls, sidekicks, producers, directors and singers in American history. Here I am with Pat at the ninth annual Golden Boot Awards, which took place August 17, 1991. Pat has enjoyed immense popularity as a comedian and as an actor. He was Gene Autry's sidekick in Gene's Western movies.

Standing (left to right): Jonathan Stone, Steve Stone, Pat Buttram, Eddie Dean, Gene Autry, Linda Stone-Hyde, Curtis Stone. Kneeling (left to right): Johnny Grant, me, Bill Welch.

A very special and memorable day! Me with my Star on the Hollywood Walk of Fame, at Sunset and Vine, surrounded by family and friends. My beloved late wife, Dorothy, was there with me in spirit.

There are no words to describe how I felt when Chet Atkins announced my name on Nashville's Grand Ole Opry stage on October 9, 1989 on CBS-TV, as the recipient of the Country Music Association's Hall of Fame Award. It's my most cherished award, which is equivalent to receiving an Oscar in the motion picture industry.

Me, Frances Preston (BMI's president and CEO), Rick Riccobono (vice president of BMI's West Coast office) and Joan Carol enjoying ourselves at BMI's 50th Anniversary Pop Awards banquet, which was held on May 22, 1990, at the Regent Beverly Wilshire Hotel in Los Angeles, California.

Joan Carol and me with our dear friends, Annette and Jerry Fuller, at the Nashville Songwriters Association International's Hall of Fame dinner in 1989. Jerry's award-winning songs include "Travelin' Man," "Show and Tell," "Over You," "Way Back," and "It's Up To You."

PHOTO BY HOPE POWELL

I'm having a great time at the 1989
ASCAP Awards banquet in
Nashville with Joan Carol Stone, my
wife, collaborator and best friend in
the whole world.

PHOTO BY DAN LOFTIN

Tennessee Ernie Ford and I are together again and having a ball at the 1989 pre-awards party given by the Country Music Association in Nashville. An hour later, I was inducted into the prestigious Hall of Fame. A year later, it was Ernie's turn to be the recipient of this Hall of Fame honor. These awards certainly made our musical careers come full circle.

Visiting with Garth Brooks in his dressing room at the Grand Ole Opry. In 1990, Garth received the Horizon Award from the Country Music Association; and his horizon dramatically came into full view in 1991 when he received six awards from the Academy of Country Music. They include Song of the Year ("The Dance"), Male Vocalist of the Year and Entertainer of the Year.

I'm proudly wearing my Angels jacket while backstage at the Grand Ole Opry in Nashville with one of country music's pioneers, Buck Owens, who hails from Bakersfield, California. His manager, Jack McFadden, is in the background. Buck received the Pioneer Award from the Academy of Country Music in 1988.

I'm reminiscing with my good buddy, Harlan Howard, at the Nashville Songwriters Association International's 1990 Hall of Fame dinner and induction ceremony. It's no wonder that Harlan is a member of this prestigious Hall of Fame group, since he is one of country music's most successful songwriters. I'm so proud to have been a part of his career. (See "Associated BMI/ASCAP Award-Winning Songs.")

Joan Carol, me and Randy Travis at the 1990 ASCAP Awards banquet in Nashville, Tennessee. This talented young man is one of the new crop of country singers to bring back the traditional sounds of Mother Country Music. Thanks, Randy.

Don Schlitz and me at the 1990 BMI Awards banquet in Nashville. It all begins with a song, and it's songwriters like Don who keep Mother Country Music alive and well by supplying country singers with great material. Two of his songs (cowritten with Paul Overstreet and recorded by Randy Travis) won Song of the Year. (In 1986, "On the Other Hand" and in 1987, "Forever and Ever Amen" — Country Music Association and Academy of Country Music.)

Hank Thompson — singer/songwriter/guitar player, whose hits include "Honky Tonk Angel," "Humpty Dumpty Heart" and "Wild Side of Life." Pee Wee King — songwriter/ accordion player, whose writing credits include "Tennessee Waltz" (Redd Stewart), "You Belong to Me" and "Slowpoke" (Redd Stewart and Chilton Price).

Three Country Music Hall of Famers (left to right): Hank Thompson, Pee Wee King and me.

PHOTO BY HOPE POWELL

Me with Roger Miller at the 1989 BMI Awards banquet in Nashville. As you can see by the BMI Awards medal that he's wearing around his neck, he was among those songwriters awarded that night for a million-performance song. Two of his biggest songs were "King of the Road" and "Dang Me." I was so happy for Roger when he received the Pioneer Award from the Academy of Country Music in 1987.

Happy memories with Kathy Mattea. Joan Carol and I were sitting next to her and her husband, Jon Vezner, when both of us won CMA awards in 1989. Kathy won Female Vocalist of the Year and I was inducted into the Hall of Fame.

My dear buddy Bobby Bare, Joan Carol and me at the 1990 National Songwriters Guild dinner in which they honored Bobby with the prestigious Aggie Award in Nashville. Down through the years, this great entertainer/singer/songwriter has had numerous hit songs, which include: "Detroit City," "Five Hundred Miles," "Sheila," "The Winner," and "Marie Lavaux."

I'm so proud of Highway 101 — one of country music's top award-winning groups. (Left to right): my son, Curtis Stone (vocal/bass player), Cactus Moser (vocal/drums) and me, holding hands with the beautiful lead singer, Nikki Nelson. Where is Jack Daniels when you need him? This picture was taken at the Gene Autry Museum in 1991, where they performed on the same bill with Buck Owens and surprise guest Dwight Yoakam.

Backstage at the 1990 CMA Awards show at the Grand Ole Opry with Jo Walker-Meador, the charming and lovely executive director of the Country Music Association, her husband, Bob Meador, and Joan Carol Stone.

Happiness is being hugged by Paige Sober (BMI's senior director, writer-publisher relations of the West Coast office) and the dynamic Fran Boyd (executive secretary of the Academy of Country Music).

Here I am with two of country music's greatest storytellers, Tennessee Ernie Ford and Minnie Pearl. Minnie is country music's most beloved and priceless treasure.

Me with my genius engineer, Brian Friedman, and award-winning musician, John Hobbs, who is king of the keyboards. They are both veterans of thousands of hours in the recording studios of Hollywood and Nashville. I'm lucky to have their friendship and musical expertise.

Enjoying an evening at the Hollywood Bowl with my business associates and dear family friends, Sam and Joan Trust. Sam, one of the top-echelon music publishing executives in the business, is president of his own company, Primat America.

Me with one of the most respected award-winning publishers in all musical categories, Lester Sill, at RP International's "Vision" Benefit dinner on June 29, 1991. On this memorable evening, this organization, which is dedicated to the preservation and restoration of eyesight, honored Lester with the 1991 Humanitarian Award.

Celebrating Christmas with my poet daughter and three musical sons. Left to right: Curtis (Highway 101); Linda (teacher at Oralingua School for the hearing-impaired); me; Steve (Vice President, Creative, Warner/Chappell Music, Inc.); Jonathan (General Manager, Windswept Pacific Entertainment Company).

I'm having fun with Joan Carol's family on Mother's Day. (Left to right): Joan, me, Daisy (her mother), Ron (her brother) and Leo (her father). Wonderful Daisy is in my "Mother-in-Law's Hall of Fame."

PHOTO BY PORKY JOHNSON

The legendary Peggy Lee and Joan Carol at Peggy's backstage party after her sold-out May 10, 1991 performance at the Raymond Theater in Pasadena, California. Miss Lee's versatile singing style was never better or stronger and the standing ovations were at a fever pitch!

"On the Road Again" with "Hometown Jamboree" 's current cast: me, Molly Bee, Eddie Dean and Roberta Linn (Lawrence Welk's champagne lady). Here we are having fun at the Fountain Valley Fiesta in Fountain Valley, California on July 7, 1991.

Records, recognized the hit potential in that wonderful song and believed in it enough to release the record.)

Here's another wonderful rejection story which only goes to prove that my PEP-C recipe (Positive Energy and Perseverance with a dash of Courage) pays off in the long run: Herbie Alpert's band, the Tijuana Brass, was turned down by every major label in town but he didn't let that stop him. He started his own record company. The first release by the Tijuana Brass was "The Lonely Bull," which became a big hit and started A&M Records on the road to success.

So, whenever you're feeling discouraged, just think about these three rejection examples which all had a happy ending.

I guess you might say I'm not your typical everyday type of publisher, since I have and still do wear a lot of musical hats. All my life, I've continued performing and being with people in one way or another, and I expect people to try to give me their demo tapes when I'm in these musical environments. No matter where I go, however, I'm usually approached by someone who just happens to have a demo tape, and many of them have been in the most unusual circumstances.

I remember the time when I had some root canal work done. I was sitting in a dentist's chair, turned halfway upside down with my mouth wide open, full of Novocain with a plastic contraption in my mouth. A dentist, who appeared to have a malicious look on his face, was bent over me with a drill. The only thing that calmed me down, somewhat, was this pretty dental assistant, who smiled sweetly at me. Just by looking at her, I figured I could get through the agony of this experience. Now the last thing I was thinking about was songs; however, the dentist said, "Would you like to hear some music?" Naturally, I assumed it would be soothing and relaxing background music which would help me to forget that I was about to get drilled, so I said, "Yes."

The music turned out to be a tape of six original songs recorded by Betty Jo Silver, the pretty dental assistant. Since I was a captive audience, I listened. Soon I became so concentrated on her voice and her songs that I forgot about the drilling and cutting which goes with dental work of this type.

As it turned out, Betty Jo had a wonderful country voice and had written some really outstanding songs. Since then, I've recorded her and she's appeared on many of my shows.

I guess that's one innovative way to get your songs to a publisher. Generally speaking, I don't recommend that you plug your songs to a publisher when he's in a dentist's chair. He's not going to be mentally or emotionally receptive to listening to them.

As I sit here smoking my pipe, I recall another incident where I was given a demo tape in a very unusual environment. I've tried many ventures in my life, and one of them was the cattle business. Since my late wife, Dorothy, and I had a big family (one girl and three boys), we thought we would save money by raising our own beef and freezing it. Now, there's a process for curing the beef where it's hung in a meat locker for a certain length of time and the nearest one to our ranch was in a little town located about forty miles away.

One cold and rainy Saturday morning, I drove out there to pick up some steaks. As I walked into the freezer compartment, the ten-degrees-below-zero temperature hit me like a ton of bricks. It was so cold that my eyes had frozen open. I couldn't even blink! With the help of the butcher, who was wearing a white blood-stained butcher's coat, white gloves and who was also holding a long menacing knife, I began to select some special cuts. As I reached for them, the butcher shoved a tape of songs that he had written into my hand. Now, I've been approached by people in unusual circumstances before, but this was ridiculous! However, this wasn't the time to say no, so I took them home along with my steaks; and as I listened to the songs that evening, they were so bad that I figured the tape hadn't thawed out yet!

Here's another one of my favorite demo stories which still amuses me whenever I think about it. There was a knock on my front door one day, and as I opened it, I became startled. There stood a six-foot-four California Highway Patrol officer who asked me if I was Cliffie Stone, and I said, "Yes." As he proceeded to serve me with a summons, he said, "Cliffie, here's a tape with some songs that my wife wrote. Will you listen to it?" Well, I won't tell you what I wanted to say to him. Eventually, I did listen to the songs; however, I've got the right to remain silent in my opinion of them.

I could go on and on. I guess all publishers, producers and artists have their "demo" stories.

Here's another important thing for you to consider, whether you're going to mail your tape to him or meet with him in person. Don't take or send him a tape with ten songs. He just doesn't have the time to listen to all of them.

I've already suggested that you pick one or two and certainly no more than three of your best songs which fit that particular publisher's catalog. Stop and think about the psychology of this. If he sees there's only one song on a tape, he'll think, That's only three minutes of my time. Then when he's in between telephone calls or has a few minutes between meetings, he may pop a tape with one song into his machine and it could be yours.

Naturally, I've read music articles all my life, and one of the more recent ones was about how some publishing companies have "song tape piles." They'll have designated piles which have one song, two songs, three songs, etc. Guess which pile they'll usually go to when they have a few extra minutes?

Many years ago when I had my own publishing company, Central Songs, I used to listen to tapes which had anywhere from eight to ten songs on them. Usually, I would like no more than one song out of the entire tape. Actually, a publisher really has to be careful when he listens to a tape which has that many songs on them. He could fall into a trap because if they aren't that good, he may find one that he feels is better than the others and pick that song because it's the best of a bad lot. Then he'll listen to it a week later and wonder why he ever picked that song in the first place.

Under the direction of Sam Trust, president of the ATV Music Group which had the entire Beatles catalog, I was head of the Country Music Division. One time, I remember receiving a demo tape from a Nashville writer named Billy Joe Shaver which had ten songs on it. I didn't especially care for the first nine tunes I heard so I almost didn't listen to the last one. The only reason I did was because the title totally intrigued me. Thank goodness I listened because when I heard "I'm Just an Old Chuck of Coal (But I'll Be a Diamond Someday)," I liked it and we published it immediately. It became a big hit in the country field when John Anderson recorded it.

I'll never forgot the lesson that I learned from this experience. Had I not had the patience to listen to all the songs on that tape, I would never have discovered the last one which turned out to be a hit song, nor would I have discovered the big talent of Billy Joe Shaver who, in my opinion, is one of the great cowboy songwriters of all time.

This also goes to show you that even great writers don't always write one good song after another or, for that matter, write one hit song after another. However, Billy Joe Shaver had more than his share of hit songs. Waylon Jennings loved Billy's songs so much that he recorded a number of them on RCA Victor. The money that was made from the sales of his recorded songs by Waylon more than paid for our investment in purchasing Bobby Bare's publishing company, Return Music.

A good publisher knows that anyone can write one good song, and that ain't bad, folks. However, they are always looking for a writer who is a "source." A source is someone who can write more than one good song and who will continually keep coming up with new song ideas and titles. One of Frank Sinatra's biggest hits, "I'll Never Smile Again," was written by Ruth Lowe. Johnny Mercer believed her to be a source, so he signed her to a songwriting contract. Even though she wrote numerous songs after that, she never wrote another hit. Goodness gracious! How could she ever top that song credit, which has to be the ultimate experience for a songwriter? I'm sure millions of writers (myself included) would be more than satisfied to have one big hit with the great Frank Sinatra. As a matter of fact, they'd be proud to have him record anything they wrote, whether it was a hit or not. I sure would!

Publishers are also always on the lookout for writers who have the ability to be an "assignment writer." In other words, all you have to do is give them a concept or situation and they have the ability to sit down and write a good song. This is how songs are usually written for motion pictures.

Or maybe I'll get a call from Nashville saying that Tammy Wynette is recording in a couple of weeks and they're looking for new songs for her. I'll call several talented writers that I know and ask them to submit any tunes that they feel would fit Tammy or write new ones that do. This is how I've had a lot of songs recorded and these kinds of writers are priceless to publishers.

Now, this may sound strange, but if you have consideration for the publisher then, most likely, he'll consider your songs over and above the others. I've told you some "do's" to do; now I'd like to tell you about two of my pet "don't's" to do:

First of all, don't pressure the publisher. Don't call him every two days or every two weeks to see if he's listened to your tape. Even if you have a song published by him, be careful not to bug him too much. As I told you earlier in this chapter, publishers have other priorities which take a good percentage of their time and, although listening to new songs is one of them, they also have other responsibilities which are equally important. There are only so many hours in a day to do everything they have to do.

However, I do recommend that you either write or call him intermittently so that your songs don't get lost in the shuffle; and in this way, he'll also become familiar with your name.

Secondly, don't con the publisher — I've been hustled by the best. I've had calls from people who say, "I've got one song and I know it's a hit; I'll only take five minutes of your time. Can we have a meeting?" So I schedule a meeting. He'll come in, play the song for me and maybe I don't like it. Then he'll say, "The one I really wanted you to hear is the fourth one on the tape. So we might as well listen to the next two." Well, you've just put me, the publisher, in a bad frame of mind. I consider myself a very tolerant and fair person, but nothing turns me off more than when someone does that to me.

Dear aspiring songwriter: I encourage you to follow through on your songwriting dream. Isn't it better to have a dream or a fantasy which brings you joy and gives you hope for the future than to have none at all? Besides, how are you going to make a dream come true if you don't have one?

You may get your share of "thanks but no thank you" replies but take pride in the fact that you're out there trying. Just give yourself a pep talk and put into action the magical ingredients of my PEP-C recipe (Positive Energy and Perseverance with a dash of Courage).

Although there will be obstacles, it's important to believe that you can break through the music publisher's sound barrier. Along the way, there will be some people who will tell you that it can't be done. However, be like the guy who didn't know it couldn't be done, so he went ahead and did it!

Matthew 7:7: "Ask, and it will be given to you; seek, and you will find; knock, and it will be opened to you."

CHAPTER SIXTEEN

HOW DO I MAKE MONEY FROM MY SONG? HOLD ONTO YOUR DAY JOB!

D own through the years, newcomers to songwriting have asked me basically the same questions with regard to income from songs. Questions like: "How do I make money from my song?" "How do I go about selling my song?" "Do I and can I get advance money on my song?" "How soon and from whom do I receive my royalties once my song has been recorded?"

The aforementioned questions are valid and it rounds out the newcomers' musical education to know something about the various sources of income their songs may generate if any one of them should be recorded.

First of all, you don't sell your song to a publisher. You assign the copyright of your song to the publisher when you sign a Writer/Publisher Agreement. (If you have previously registered the copyright of your song with the Library of Congress in Washington, D. C., then you must grant a copyright assignment to the publisher.) This agreement means that you are in partnership with the publisher; you each have a fifty-fifty share. Then you wait while your song goes through the proper music channels, which takes time, and because it takes time, I recommend that you hold onto your day job.

"Can I get some advance money on my song?" I've been asked this question so many times by writers throughout my career. Publishing companies are not in the loan business. They, like all companies, have a tremendous amount of business overhead, and it's financially difficult for them to give song advances on your potential royalties, especially when you don't have a track record as a writer. As it is, the publishing company will be spending a considerable amount of its own money promoting your song to producers, record companies and artists.

If you're a newcomer and they've advanced you money against your future royalties, they may never recoup their investment if your song isn't recorded. They would soon be out of business if they did this for every songwriter. By the same token, if you have a track record wherein you have had a few songs recorded which have already made money for a publishing company, then it's not uncommon for them to advance money against future royalties.

Naturally, if a publishing company has hired you as a staff writer, you would be receiving a monthly advance which would be deducted from your "earned royalties" on songs that you've already written, are writing or will write while you are under contract to them. They practically own your brain! The terms of these agreements might vary from writer to writer. Once again, if none of the songs you've written during the term of this contract were recorded, the publishing company will never be compensated for the money they've paid you.

But let's get back to the world of the beginning, aspiring songwriter and the question that I'm asked so often: "How soon and from whom do I receive my royalties once my song has been recorded?"

I think the easiest way for me to answer this question would be to give you a couple of hypothetical scenarios which could happen with your song. Then I'll explain the various sources of income, which will simplify and yet give you a comprehensive picture of how, when and from whom you can expect to receive your royalties.

Let's suppose that I liked your song and I've agreed to publish it. Within a period of six months or so, I've sent your song out to three or four producers and/or artists and everyone has turned it down. Since I believe in your song and I take rejections in stride, I continue to spend money promoting it. Then we get lucky! A producer likes it and sends me a letter of intent or calls me on the telephone to put a hold on the song for Kenny Rogers or some other top recording star.

Now, it could be months before they record. Maybe your song was lucky enough to be one of fifteen or twenty songs that have been picked for the final countdown. Let's say that you got luckier and yours has been chosen to be among the ten tunes to be in the album while the others are put on the shelf. After that, it could be another six months before the album is released.

Let's pretend that Lady Luck is really in your corner and your song has been chosen to be a single. It's played and gets into the Top 50; another eight or nine weeks go by and it gets into the Top 10 for a couple of weeks, or possibly becomes number one on the charts. You're in seventh heaven, and now you're wondering, how soon and from whom do I get my royalties for my song? Generally speaking, it would take anywhere from six months to approximately one year before you received any royalties, so hold onto your day job.

However, let me tell you the good news in order to keep your spirits up while you're waiting: you could be receiving a certain amount of money for the rest of your life if you've had a successful song(s). Once songs have been recorded and have known moderate success, I've always considered them to be a "musical insurance-policy dividend." You'll understand why when I get into more detail about these specific income sources later in this chapter.

Now, the first hypothetical example is predicated on the assumption that your song was recorded, was chosen as one of the final ten songs for the album, and was released as a single which found its way into the Top 10 of the national charts.

However, your song could have been on an album which didn't get on the national charts and, therefore, wasn't a hit. Any income you would receive would still take approximately six months to a year. And if your song did get on an album which didn't sell well and you received very little income from it, congratulations! Realize that something very important has happened here. Not only have you started your song track record, but your song has been recorded. It's now out there for any artist to hear and to re-record! Even a so-called little record can get your song on the road to becoming a monster hit! Naturally, I'm speaking from experience, and I fondly recall an incident where a small recording was the catalyst for a million-seller.

Years ago, I produced a four-track demo in my Central Songs recording studio in which I had Jim Alley do the vocal on Ivy "Jimmy" Bryant's song "The Only Daddy That'll Walk the Line." A very talented song man and good buddy of mine, George Richey, worked for me at that time and he took the demo to Dot Records. They liked it and it became a master record. Although it did get radio air play, it sold very little.

Somewhere down the line, Waylon Jennings heard it, liked it, recorded it and the rest is history. It was Waylon's first hit, which soon became a million-seller. And to show you how things can snowball, a female version of this song was recorded by Jody Miller called "The Only Mama That'll Walk the Line." It, too, became another hit that sold into the hundreds of thousands. So my little demo record released on Dot Records became a big hit for two other recording companies: Capitol and RCA Records.

It's amazing what can happen from any recording. So have patience and believe in your songs. In the meantime, hold onto your day job.

Here's another song scenario which could also happen to you. You've got a publisher for your song and he called you six months ago and told you that Conway Twitty is going to record it for his next album. You're totally thrilled and it inspires you to keep on writing songs. A year goes by and, although your song was never released as a single, you've noticed in the *Billboard* charts that the album was in the Top 10 country albums for about six months; therefore, it sold moderately well for a period of a year or so.

So when and where does the money come from to pay you, the writer, in all the above examples that I've given? There are four basic sources from which you can receive income from your song: mechanicals, performances, print, and synchronization rights. The first two are the major sources of income; you can make some money on the third source; and if you're lucky, you can make pretty good money on the fourth.

1. **Mechanicals:** This is one of the major sources of income for songs and, as a writer, you'll be hearing a lot about them. Mechanical royalties are any royalties which are earned from the sale of a manufactured reproduction of your song. This includes an album, a tape, a compact disc (CD), a music video or any form of reproduction vehicle that has not yet been invented. For instance, if they sold fifty thousand cassette tapes, thirty thousand CDs, five thousand albums, etc. then you would get a royalty percentage for each one sold. This is mechanicals. If your song is on an album, CD or tape, etc., the royalties earned will be prorated according to the number of song tracks in the album, and that amount is divided between the publisher and you, the writer.

However, if you have a song in an album and it's released as a single, you will receive separate royalties; and whatever the prevailing statutory rate is per unit, it will be divided between the publisher and the writer.

Both the record companies and publishers issue statements every six months — June and January. However, before a publisher can send out his statements along with royalty checks to the writers, he, obviously, has to receive statements from the record companies with whom he's doing business, which indicate the sales and income from mechanicals to date.

Then the publisher's accounting department calculates the appropriate royalty amount, not only for mechanicals, but also for any income earned from print and synchronization rights, which I'll soon be discussing. And once all these income sources have been determined, a detailed statement and royalty check is sent to the songwriter.

2. **Performances:** This is the other major source of income, and generally, it's the biggest source. As a matter of fact, you could generate performance income for life. As I've mentioned before, it's comparable to the dividend of an insurance policy.

"Performances" means exactly what the word implies: performing. If you have a hit, you will receive performance royalties on your song (as well as royalties from mechanicals). If it's a medium-sized hit, it will still generate royalties through performances. Should your song only be a turntable hit, that is, it was played on the air but it didn't sell a lot of tapes or compact discs (mechanicals), you would still receive performance royalties.

Even after the income from the mechanicals of a hit record has dwindled down to a precious few, a song can continue to be performed through these innumerable performing outlets which could, therefore, bring you an income for years. In other words, this could be your musical insurance-policy dividend.

The performance outlets or music users are many: radio stations, network and local television stations, concerts, nightclubs, amusement parks, hotels, dance schools, universities, and the list is endless. It's a big wide world out there, with millions of songs being performed through innumerable music users and performing outlets. How often is a song performed and where is it performed? These songs may be performed not only in the United States, but also in other countries. Who keeps track of all these performances?

All over the world, there are organizations called "performing rights societies." In many cases, these societies are also affiliated with foreign performing rights societies, and they all work together helping one another.

Basically, the performing rights societies acquire the right to perform from publishers and songwriters and, in turn, they will grant licenses to music users such as radio stations, television networks, nightclubs, etc. They are a collection agency, so to speak, for they collect fees from the music users and organizations to whom they've licensed their music repertoire. Then they distribute these fees directly to the writer and the publisher, after their operating expenses for their organization have been deducted.

The statement and payment schedule to the writers and publishers varies according to the particular society's accounting procedure. Regardless of the performing rights society to which you may belong, for the most part it's safe to assume that you'll be sent your royalty check on a quarterly or bi-annual basis. In the interim, hold onto your day job.

The three performing rights societies in the United States are: (1) ASCAP, which stands for the American Society of Composers, Authors and Publishers. It was established in 1914. (2) BMI was formed in 1940 and stands for Broadcast Music Incorporated. (3) SESAC, which stands for the Society for European Stage, Authors and Composers, was originally started and owned by the Heinecke family about sixty years ago.

In a nutshell, the performing rights societies basically grant licenses to their music-user customers, keep track of the performances of their affiliated members' musical works, protect their interests worldwide, and collect the fees and distribute the performance royalties to both writers and publishers. This is a monumental effort, which requires a lot of dedication, organization and business skill, and they do an incredible job for the writers and publishers.

As a beginning, aspiring songwriter, it's good for you to be aware of these societies, for the day may come when you'll be eligible to join one of them.

As of the writing of this book, you can write to any one of the United States' performing rights societies for more information at the following addresses:

▾ BMI, 320 West 57th Street, New York, New York 10019
▾ BMI, 8730 Sunset Boulevard, Third Floor West, Los Angeles, CA 90069
▾ BMI, 10 Music Square East, Nashville, TN 37203
▾ ASCAP, One Lincoln Plaza, New York, New York 10023
▾ ASCAP, 6430 Sunset Boulevard, Hollywood, CA 90028
▾ ASCAP, 66 Music Square West, Nashville, TN 37203
▾ SESAC, Inc., 55 Music Square East, Nashville, TN 37203

3. **Print:** A print is the reproduction of the melody and lyrics of your song in music-note form on paper, which is referred to as a music lead sheet, piano copy or folio and sold to the public. It's not the major source of income that it once was, for a variety of reasons. In the old days when there wasn't a radio or television to occupy our minds, families would gather around a piano in the living room and Mom, Dad, sister or someone would play it. They'd open up the piano bench, which would be full of piano copies, and they'd pull one out and entertain themselves by singing. So there was a big demand for print in those days which, of course, meant that money could be made from it.

Also around that time period, self-player-pianos were popular. Have you ever watched and heard an old-time self-player-piano play? I still get fascinated watching the keys moving on those pianos with no one sitting there. They were a big business for about a ten-year period. First of all, there was a market for them, so someone had to design and build them. Secondly, printed piano rolls had to be designed and printed, and people would have a collection of them, much like we have collections of albums, cassettes and CDs today. Thus, if they wanted to sing "You Are My Sunshine," they would put a roll in the piano, play it and sing along. Royalties were received by the songwriters on each piano roll sold as licensed by the publisher — just like the record companies today must be licensed by the publisher to release recordings of a song. Even today, some very posh restaurants have an old-time player-piano playing twenty-four hours a day, generating print and performance income.

Whenever you need sheet music, you go to the music store. If they don't have it in stock, they'll look it up in their sheet music catalogs; if there's a print available, you then place a special order for it. They don't have a wide variety on hand anymore because the demand just isn't there, except possibly in the gospel field.

Music folios, which are collections of songs, have always been popular. In most cases, you can find the sheet music you want in these folios, which are available in country, gospel, pop, folk, rock, etc.

A 21-Gun Salute to All Music Teachers: Of course, there always has been and always will be a print demand for beginners, intermediate and advanced musical instruction books for all types of musical instruments.

And when you have musical instruction books, you need music teachers. So I want to give a 21-gun salute to all the music teachers worldwide — past and present — who unceremoniously spend their time teaching the rudiments of music to students of all ages. What better gift can you give to anyone than to introduce them to the world of music and to patiently help them through all the stages of their musical development?

Print is still a major seller to high school and college marching bands, and to large and small choral groups, especially church choirs.

When I think of marching bands, I think of parades, and the one that immediately comes to mind is the world-famous Rose Parade, which has been taking place in Pasadena, California, on New Year's Day for years. The floats, decorated in a wide variety of flowers are magnificent! Of course, being a music man, I have always enjoyed the multitude of marching bands proudly doing their part in this classic event.

During football season, many of us have watched high school, college and professional football games either on television or in person. There's usually a marching band during half-time that plays a wide variety of popular songs, including standards.

Another vivid memory that comes to mind was the spectacular role that bands and music played in the opening and closing ceremonies of the Olympic games when Los Angeles was the host city in 1984.

In the events that I've just mentioned, all these bands had to have printed arrangements for each instrument in order to learn the songs. So money is earned by the writers and the publishers not only through print when this happens, but performances as well, because the song is being televised and/or performed somewhere in public.

As I have previously mentioned in this book, I was the director of the Country Music Division for the ATV Music Group in the 1980s under the supervision of Sam Trust, who was its president at that time, and who now has his own successful company, Primat America. Although it's difficult to find the appropriate words to express my deepest feelings, I want to say thank you to him. Down through the years that we've been close friends and associates, I have learned so much from him about the inner workings of the music publishing world at a high executive level. He was and still is my publishing mentor, and to this day, whenever I have intricate publishing questions and concerns, he is always there for me.

Since ATV had the Beatles' catalog and since their songs were and are loved worldwide, our company licensed many of them in a variety of ways.

I'll never forget the gentleman who called ATV and requested a license to manufacture and distribute marching band arrangements for some of the Beatles' biggest hit songs, such as "Help," "Hard Day's Night" and "Yellow Submarine." Sam had me fly from Nashville to the Midwest to visit this interesting man at his printing facilities. He was in the business of selling big marching band arrangements and had a mailing list of every high school and college in America. The printed arrangements were broken down into parts for every band instrument imaginable: the trombone, clarinet, trumpet, tuba, flute, etc.

Once his license request was granted by ATV, he then sold these Beatle instrumental arrangements to various schools for their marching bands. Come to think of it, he sort of looked and acted like Robert Preston in *The Music Man*. I wonder if...no, it couldn't be...

Greeting cards have become one of the newer print markets. One time, we negotiated a license agreement with a company to reproduce quite a few of the Beatles' hit lyrics on greeting cards, which were to be sold commercially throughout the world.

Comparatively speaking, print is not a major source of income like mechanicals or performances, since the popularity of recorded music has replaced the printed note. However, as you can see from my above print illustrations, it will always be important and there will always be a large demand for it in many areas. Therefore, money can be made from it, but not the amounts that it used to make. But then, nothing is like it used to be, is it?

4. **Synchronization Rights:** These are the rights a publisher grants a television or movie producer to use one of its published songs and/or music in a film.

Many times, songs that weren't hits became popular from their performance in a movie, which certainly doesn't hurt the writer's or the publisher's pocketbook. If your song is already a hit and is performed by a major star in a movie, than an additional fee is charged by the publisher. Depending on the popularity of the song in question, the amount could be anywhere from five thousand to fifty thousand dollars.

At one time or another, I'm sure that most of you have heard "Wind Beneath My Wings," which is rapidly on its way to becoming an all-time classic standard. It became number one on the pop charts from its movie exposure in *Beaches*, starring Bette Midler, who superbly sang this great song.

Did you know that Gary Morris had a big country hit with it? In 1983, it was chosen Song of the Year by the Academy of Country Music, and in 1984, it won the Country Music Association's Song of the Year award. I derive great pleasure from telling people these facts and many of them are so surprised when they find out. I guess a lot of people have preconceived ideas about country songs.

Since this song was extremely popular in the country field and did receive prestigious awards long before Bette Midler sang it in *Beaches*, can you imagine the money the writers (Jeffrey Silbar and Larry Henley) and their publishers received for the synchronization rights? Not to mention the musical insurance-policy dividend they've been receiving since 1984 from the other three sources — mechanicals, performance, and print? Who knows? Maybe your song will be in a movie someday, too!

There have been those instances when a song is a big hit first and becomes so popular that a movie is written and filmed around the song's title and theme.

Many years ago, this is what happened with Gene Autry's hit record "Down Mexico Way." Another movie that immediately comes to mind is *Love Me or Leave Me*, which starred Doris Day and James Cagney. In more recent times, two hit songs which later spawned movies with the same title were: *Ode to Billie Joe*, starring Robbie Benson and *The Night the Lights Went Out in Georgia*, starring Mark Hamill.

As a matter of fact, a song title can trigger off ideas for a television series. Tom T. Hall wrote a unique hit song called "Harper Valley P.T.A." Eventually, there was a television series with the same name, starring Barbara Eden.

Although commercials are in another category than motion pictures, I'd like to quickly add that the fee amount for using a song or a portion of it in a radio or television commercial is also determined by its popularity and whether or not it has been a big hit.

They are now pulling songs out of movies and making home videos out of them. This can happen with any song performed by any major star of any outstanding movie production such as *The Sound of Music* or *My Fair Lady*. For example, in the classic movie *Singin' in the Rain*, in which Gene Kelly danced and sang "Singin' in the Rain," they took this seven-minute performance out of the movie and released it as a home video. The various companies who release these videos have to establish a price for the use of the individual song in the film, and the future market for them is breaking wide open.

If you had written a song which was in a movie that was made over twenty years ago and they made a home video to be commercially available for the public, could you collect money on that song? Yes, you could. However, to my knowledge — as of the writing of this book — the exact royalty rate has not been determined.

But there's more to synchronization rights than having your song in a movie being performed by someone. There is also something called "source music." For instance, let's say you're watching James Garner and Sally Field in a Western film. Maybe in one of the scenes, Jim and Sally go into a country nightclub; and as they walk through the swinging doors, you hear the "Tennessee Waltz" or "Slowpoke" playing in the background. And as the music continues to play, they walk over to a table, sit down, order drinks. Maybe they get up and romantically dance to it for awhile.

This is source music, and the publisher collects money for the writer on that song's performance in the movie, too. The longer it plays, the bigger the paycheck. If it's ten seconds, it's a certain amount; if it's twenty seconds, you would receive more, and so on.

As long as we're on the subject of music and movies, there are numerous times when writers are commissioned by the producer to write a song or an instrumental theme for their movie. I'm sure you've heard theme songs and/ or instrumental themes in various pictures such as *Rocky, Chariots of Fire,* or *Love Story.* You'll hear a recurring theme weave in and out of different scenes as the movie progresses; and you'll think of this movie whenever you hear it. Many times, a motion picture and its theme song will have the same title; for instance, the movie *High Noon,* starring Gary Cooper and Grace Kelly.

Two very successful Hollywood writers, Ned Washington and Dimitri Tiomkin, were commissioned to write this song-made-for-movies, which requires special composing abilities. This is assignment writing at its finest. They either read the script or watched the movie (or both) and then wrote lyrics and music to fit the picture's story line and theme. Although I don't know the financial arrangements, you can be sure it was for big bucks! Tex Ritter sang the song, and I'm proud to say that I played bass and coproduced the music with Lee Gillette.

Another song that was commissioned for a motion picture in which I had some involvement was *River of No Return,* starring Marilyn Monroe. I received a call one day from Ken Darby, the musical director at 20th Century-Fox, who wanted Tennessee Ernie Ford to sing the title song. Since I was Ernie's manager at that time, I thought it would be an excellent opportunity for him, so I said, "Yes."

As usual, Ernie's singing performance turned out so great that we also released it on Capitol Records so it would coincide with the movie's release date. Although the song wasn't a smash hit, it did moderately well. This is a good example of how writers can make money when a song is commissioned to be written for a film which is simultaneously released as a single record for the public. Thus, the writers not only received their commission fee from the studio, but they received performance and mechanical royalties as well.

As you can see, synchronization rights can be an excellent source of money, depending on the song's individual situation. If it's a song which is a major hit, it's one fee; if it's source music, it's another fee, and this fee is determined by the popularity of each individual song. And it's here, too, like in all areas of publishing, that a knowledgeable publisher earns his keep; through his nego-tiating skills, he gets the highest fee possible and then pays his partner, the writer, 50 percent.

Now, let's take a perfect real-life song example that is currently happening as this book is being written, which will give you an overall time frame picture of the entire process that a successful song goes through.

For the past several years, my oldest son, Steve, has been an executive at Warner/Chappell Music, Inc. and currently holds the position of vice president, creative. In January of 1990, Ronnie Milsap and his producer, Rob Galbraith, flew in from Nashville to meet with Steve at his Hollywood office to discuss and listen to a variety of potential songs for his forthcoming album. This included a song that Steve and his good buddy, Johnny Cunningham, had cowritten six months prior to this meeting, called "Are You Loving Me Like I'm Loving You?" Rob and Ronnie loved the song and put a hold on it.

Ronnie began a six-month recording schedule that started in June, which included this song and twenty-two others that were also being considered for the album. To make a long story short and happy, their song made the final ten with flying colors.

In January of 1991, one year from the date the song was put on hold, to the ecstasy and agony of Johnny and Steve, they were informed that their song was scheduled as the album's first single to be released in mid-February.

Their agony turned to ecstasy ten weeks later when it went to number three in *Billboard* and number three in *Radio & Records*. And when any song and record reaches the Top 5 in any musical category, it's considered a major hit which, of course, means a significant amount of money will be earned from it.

Steve is due his first mechanical royalty check for this song from Warner/Chappell in August of 1991, which will be over a year and a half from the time it was put on hold for Ronnie Milsap's album. With regard to performances, he anticipates a substantial royalty check from BMI in the first quarter of 1992, which will be two years from the time the song was put on hold.

If all continues to go well, this song will earn Steve, Johnny Cunningham and Warner/Chappell a tidy sum of money, which should continue for a period of five years. This ain't too shabby, is it? And who knows what fate may have in store for this tune? Someday, there may be an r&b or pop cover on it or it could be chosen to be in a motion picture. Anything is possible.

Meanwhile, back at the ranch, Steve not only continues to write songs as he waits for his royalty checks, but he also holds onto his day job.

Can you imagine the income that is generated by the cream of the crop songwriters such as Irving Berlin, Sammy Cahn, Johnny Mercer, Hank Williams, Sr., Fred Rose, etc.? They, or anyone who becomes an heir to their classic songs, have no money worries for the next three lifetimes. But let's get back to the real world of the beginning, aspiring songwriter. I believe the important thing for you to do is to enjoy every step of the creative process of your song, whether or not you ever make any money from it. As with anything, it's all attitude and your attitude is in your power to develop.

I know a songwriter who has a perfect attitude about songwriting. She's like thousands of writers that I have met throughout my years in this business. She's invested a tremendous amount of her time, talent and money into her songs.

In one of our past conversations, she told me she would love to make a lot of money from her songs, and she would smile all the way to the bank as she deposited her royalty checks. However, money wasn't the primary objective or motivation which inspired her to compose songs all these years. She writes because she loves to write songs, and it fulfills her creative desire which is priceless to her. Monetarily speaking, she knows it's a gamble but she said she would rather take a chance in the music world than to go to Las Vegas and gamble away her money or to spend it frivolously on unimportant things.

I feel this kind of an attitude will free your mind and creative spirit, which will enable you to fully concentrate on your songwriting endeavors.

And don't be scared off by the negative echoes of disenchanted people who say songwriting is too competitive. Yes, it's competitive — just like every other business! So what! Just do your thing! Anything is possible if you believe.

It's possible that you could end up writing a wonderful song which will, someday, become some lucky publisher's product. And when you've got the product that people want, the money will take care of itself.

The reward for doing anything creative is the joy of doing it — so enjoy the here and now of writing your very own song(s). As I always tell people: Happiness is not at the end of the trail, but along the way.

In the meantime, hold onto your day job!

▼

CHAPTER SEVENTEEN

THE SONGWRITER WHO THINKS HE WANTS TO BE A PUBLISHER, OR ALICE IN WONDERLAND

Many beginning and aspiring writers at all levels of songwriting have heard so much about the money they can make by having their own publishing company. So why should they assign their copyright to a publisher and give him a 50 percent share of their song so that he can make all that money? Wouldn't it be better to start their own publishing company? And what does a publisher do anyway that would entitle him to get 50 percent of a song?

Hopefully, I'll be able to shed some light on this subject matter and dispel some of those *Alice in Wonderland* myths which are so prevalent.

I have worn and I'm still wearing both hats as a writer and a publisher. So, speaking from years of experience, it's very difficult to combine both of them. Sometimes I've wondered how on earth I've been able to handle both of them all these years. It must be my great love for songs and for people. It's important for you to understand that writing and publishing are two different worlds.

As a writer, you have to be very creative, which is very special in itself. I don't think there is anything more enjoyable or more fulfilling than creating something out of nothing; and after putting blood, sweat and tears into composing a song which becomes your baby, so to speak, it's not easy to get it recorded in the commercial music world. You must have music connections and a knowledge of what is happening on the music scene.

Unfortunately, your song may be rejected many times before someone likes it enough to record it; and rejections can be difficult to handle emotionally, especially if you've been turned down a number of times.

As a publisher, you've got to be a great salesperson, a promotion man and a top-flight businessperson because publishing is sales, marketing and administration.

Most publishers have developed a thick-skinned attitude about rejections and a "thanks but no thanks" is like water off a duck's back to them. Although they have to believe in the song in order to publish and promote it, they are not as emotionally attached to it as the writer, simply because they didn't write it. As I've said before when I discussed rejection, for every "yes" that a publisher gets, he's had a hundred "no's."

You are aware of some of the duties a publisher has because I've been giving you bits and pieces of his responsibilities throughout this book, especially in Chapters 15 and 16. Although I may be repeating myself in some instances, I'll succinctly outline the main priorities and tasks which comprise the publishing world, for there are numerous things to take into consideration.

First of all, without knowing anything about publishing companies, it's easy and inexpensive for anyone to legally start one in "name only." However, it may not be an active or credible company in the music business.

Will producers or artists return their telephone calls or listen to any of the songs that are sent to them? Do they have a working catalog? How many of their songs have been recorded and by whom?

Do they qualify and/or are they a performing rights society publisher? In order to be affiliated with one, they should have songs which are either being performed or are very likely to be performed in any one of the numerous performance outlets such as radio and television broadcasting.

Do they have the necessary knowledge to handle all the intricate administrative tasks which include granting licenses to record their songs, synchronization rights, print requests, royalty collections, foreign exploitation, etc.? Why start a publishing company or why tie up your song with a publisher who doesn't have the wherewithal to exploit your song in all areas of the business so that you can make the optimum income on your song product?

Let's step into the shoes of a professional publisher and take a walk down the yellow brick road.

The first thing to be considered is the innumerable overhead expenses that a publishing company incurs, which can be tremendous. Of course, it all depends on the size and prominence of the company. Regardless of the size, the expenses accelerate and accumulate at an unbelievable rate. The main overhead expenses include: monthly office rental, which can go into hundreds of dollars depending on the location and the size of the company; there are personnel salaries, workmen's compensation and insurance costs; accounting costs; legal fees in case of a lawsuit; enormous telephone bills and postage expenses; essential office supplies such as demo tapes and cases, letterhead stationery and envelopes; copyright fees; filing cabinets; music lead sheet transcription costs; indispensable office equipment such as computers, printers, typewriters, Xerox machine, calculators, fax machine — not to mention the costs incurred to maintain them; demo costs which range anywhere from four hundred to five hundred dollars a song; music-related luncheon and dinner meetings; airplane, car and/or travel expenses; and so it goes.

Then we have the time factor. I would estimate that a good publisher will spend 50 percent of his time listening to new material, meeting and working with songwriters, recording new demos, promoting his company's song catalog in a variety of ways, which include numerous telephone calls to his music contacts, and demo distribution for recording considerations. And when a recording company does decide to use one of his songs, the publisher grants the license and takes care of the necessary details.

The other 50 percent of his time is spent in a multitude of administrative duties which encompass the publishing world. For instance: various licenses have to be issued for print and for commercials on radio and television; there are synchronization rights for movies and home videos which he has to negotiate; he has to have a working knowledge of publishing worldwide because different copyright laws and regulations apply in different countries and he has to be aware of these constantly changing laws in both the United States and foreign countries; he has to deal with "subpublishers" on a regular basis, for he has to be sure to collect the royalties from them for the songs in his repertoire available for the public internationally.

Traveling is a big part of his job, for he has to attend meetings, conferences and award shows in the United States and all over the world in order to stay abreast with what's happening in the music field. Networking with producers, recording company executives, artists, managers and other publishers is extremely important for staying well connected in the ever-changing music industry.

Quite frankly, it takes years of hands-on experience to establish respect and credibility in this field and to gain the necessary knowledge to become successful. Two of my sons, Steve and Jonathan, will attest to this fact. Both paid their dues to reach their respective executive positions in the publishing world.

I've already talked about my successful songwriting son, Steve, who is also a vice president with Warner/Chappell Music, Inc. He's that rare type of person who can handle both worlds equally well, but he earned it.

So let's talk about Jonathan, who made the decision to solely concentrate on developing into a first-class publisher, although he is very capable of writing songs and has done so in the past. It was his singleness of purpose and hands-on experience that have taken him to the high-level executive position he enjoys in the publishing world today.

His career began over fifteen years ago when he spent four years at ATV Music in Nashville learning the country business. He came back to the West Coast and went to work for companies such as Filmways Publishing and the MCA Publishing Group before leaving them to work with Quincy Jones for three years. Today, he is the general manager of Windswept Pacific Entertainment Company, an exciting new publishing concept headed by Chuck Kaye, CEO, and Joel Sill, president. Jonathan will be the first to tell you that being a successful publisher is a full-time job!

Now comes the question, "Why does a publisher get 50 percent of my song?" Realize that from his 50 percent, he has to pay all his operating expenses, which include his salary; and as you know by now, it has taken years for a reputable publisher to acquire the skill and necessary knowledge to administer your songs. Whereas the writer doesn't have these operating costs nor the publisher's mind-boggling responsibilities and, therefore, gets his 50 percent free and clear.

Behind every successful song is a conscientious, hard-working publisher. Speaking from experience, a good publisher earns every cent of the royalties that he makes from any of the songs in his catalog.

Now, I can just hear some of you say that you've read somewhere that quite a few of the top artists or songwriters have their own publishing companies and the article said they're making all kinds of money from them. Yes, they are making money and deservedly so. These are established songwriters, artists and professional guys at the highest level of the music industry. They have been active in the business for a long time and they're well connected in the music world. Many of them have had hit songs and whatever songs they write will be listened to by producers and/or artists. With their successful track record, they are in a position to negotiate deals.

And when they do get a song recorded, many of them will do what we call in the music business "split-publishing" with another company. And one of the most important things to consider in a split-publishing situation is: Which company has the facilities, capabilities and music business knowledge to properly administer the multitude of details that will encompass their song (which I've previously mentioned in this chapter)?

Although I could do another twenty pages on this subject, I don't feel it's necessary because I've covered the salient points and have given you enough food for thought.

The first word in music business is music — the creative part; and the easiest part in the music business is writing a good song, and at times, that's not easy.

The second word in music business is business, and to make a success of any business takes time and commitment. The time that you spend as a publisher is time lost in creating a song, and it all begins with a song. Besides, the most difficult part in the music business is promoting a song and getting it recorded.

If you are motivated to do both, then possibly the day will come when you'll be able to handle the publishing and the songwriting worlds equally well. It's not that easy, but it can be done. The choice is yours.

At this point in time, however, I would suggest that you concentrate on developing your creative writing skills so that you can enjoy your own songwriting wonderland.

▼

CHAPTER EIGHTEEN

WHAT IS THIS THING CALLED PUBLIC DOMAIN? (OR, AS I CALL IT, "CORNFIELD HEAVEN")

When a song's registered copyright protection period has expired, it goes into "public domain" (p.d.), where anyone can use it. (I have always referred to it as "cornfield heaven", where anyone can go and pick the corn.) I think I just heard someone say, "What on earth is this guy talking about?" and, "What is this thing called public domain?"

This subject can get kind of complicated, and since I like to keep things simple, I'll give you just enough basic information which will be food for thought. I believe that it benefits not only the aspiring songwriter, but all songwriters to have some sort of working knowledge about this topic.

"Night and Day" might be the perfect song title to describe how a copyright and public domain differ from one another. Webster's Ninth New Collegiate Dictionary's definitions for both are very succinct. Copyright: "The exclusive legal right to reproduce, publish and sell the matter and form of a literary, musical, or artistic work." And the public domain definition which relates to songwriting:....."2: The realm embracing property rights that belong to the community at large, are unprotected by copyright or patent, and are subject to appropriation by anyone."

In the songwriting world, it means that once a song's registered copyright protection period is over, or if the copyright has not been renewed properly (if it was written before 1978), it becomes public property and it belongs to the world community at large.

This is quite a paradox, for the song belongs to no one and yet it belongs to everyone who desires to use it. In other words, anyone is free to make a new arrangement of p.d. material (see Chapter 19, "An Arrangement Is a Love Affair with Music"), and then register a copyright on their particular arrangement of that original p.d. source. Or they can write new lyrics to the p.d. music

132

if they wish, for it's usually the music or some part of the music that people copy or edit. By the same token, they are also free to write a new melody to p.d. lyrics. Consequently, after registering a copyright, they can collect royalties on the performance and/or mechanicals from their new version of an original p.d. source.

In country terms, your song is an ear of corn in an enormous government cornfield, and it's free for the pickin' to anyone who happens to like it.

I can hear some of you say, "But that's not right or fair!" Oh, but it is, dear songwriter/reader. Officially, it was given the blessing of the United States Constitution a long time ago, through the U. S. Copyright Act of 1790 and the Copyright Act of 1909. Most of the basic foundational principles still apply today, although there have been intermittent amendments, bills and revisions in copyright laws due to numerous changes in all areas of the music industry — especially with the advent of new mechanical reproduction inventions.

Some of you may ask, "What is the reasoning or purpose of this?" As I understand it, first and foremost and rightfully so, the copyright policy entitles the author protection of his creative endeavors during his lifetime and after his demise, a fifty-year protection period to his heirs if he has written a song after 1978. (If there was more than one author, this fifty-year protection period would apply after the demise of the last author.) As I mentioned at the beginning of this chapter, after the protection period expires, the song goes into public domain.

If a writer wrote a song before 1978, his registered copyright is good for a total of seventy-five years, considered to be the average lifetime of a person. (Two twenty-eight year intervals with an additional nineteen-year period added to the last twenty-eight years; see Chapter Fourteen, "Bashing the Mystery Out of Copyrights and Registration.")

After the registered copyright's protection period is over, or if it was not properly renewed for the second twenty-eight-year (plus nineteen-year) extension period, it becomes the world's inheritance, so to speak, which, in turn, benefits and contributes to the enrichment of our culture and our society in general.

Being right smack-dab in the middle of all facets of the music world all my life, I can certainly understand why. For instance, let's take some of the public domain compositions of the great classical masters like Beethoven or Chopin. If they were still protected by copyright, just the amount of time spent in trying to locate the heirs to these musical properties to obtain license fees for any type of potential recordings and/or performance material bookings would be next to impossible. Thus, many of the world's ears and souls would be deprived of these great classics.

Did you ever hear Freddie Martin's exquisite recording of "My Love"? He took a Tchaikovsky p.d. melody and arranged it with a new melodic and rhythmical beat; lyrics were written and his version became a million-seller. It's music and songs like this that indirectly expose people, in part, to classical music who might never have had the opportunity of hearing classical material. That's the glory of public domain, and we should be thankful for it.

One evening, I was looking at one of my granddaughter's piano instruction books, which was filled with p.d. melodies. In the print area, quite a few music-book publishing companies will publish public domain material in this way all the time. First of all, it's great for our youngsters to be exposed to the classics, for it gives them the solid foundation they need — no matter where their love of music may lead them! Secondly, since they are p.d. tunes, these companies don't have to pay royalties to anyone.

If you've read "About the Author," then you know that I was not only Tennessee Ernie Ford's manager but I also coproduced many of his albums and was the executive producer of his daily and weekly NBC television shows. We made up our own musical arrangements to many public domain gospels; they were copyrighted, published, and the majority of them were either sung on television or recorded and released in his gospel albums.

Because of limited budgets, many times high schools or colleges will use p.d. material for their stage performances. Did you know the operas of Gilbert and Sullivan are all in public domain? Anyone can perform them for absolutely no fee. As a matter of fact, we performed quite a few of their operas on Ernie's television show. By the same token, if one were to do *The Music Man* or *West Side Story* on stage or on television, one would be subject to fees as they are still in copyright. And this is why many areas of the music industry use public domain material. They have free access to the songs.

Do you remember any of the old songs that you or your folks sang at family sing-alongs with only a guitar or a piano? They were probably p.d. songs which were handed down from generation to generation. As a matter of fact, most of them were never registered in the first place, and no one really knows their origin except that they were from the Old Country. Most of the blues that came out of the South and out of Texas are all more or less public domain. They generally have the usual 16-bar chorus and it's one chorus after another — usually there are no verses.

Yesterday's and today's hit songwriters in all musical categories often refer to p.d. melodies either knowingly or unknowingly. In the country field, the melody to "I Didn't Know God Made Honky Tonk Angels" is public domain. Many country songs are written from old-time fiddlers' hoedown songs. "Faded Love" was a big hit for quite a few singers and it was based on an old fiddle tune, "The Maiden's Prayer." Although I can't specifically name them, there are several country songs which have basically the same melody and which were originally taken from p.d. material.

Folk songs are very much like country songs because they, too, generally tell a story. Many of them have a simple p.d. melody. There was a period during the late 1940s and early 1950s where folk songs enjoyed enormous popularity — folk singers had a field day with p.d. material. Merle Travis's "Nine Pound Hammer" and "John Henry" were both p.d. melodies; he wrote lyrics to them with his own arrangements and his copyrights were registered.

So now that I've got you interested, you may be wondering, "How do I know what songs are public domain and where do I go to find them?" Well, it's easier said than done. However, there are many avenues you can pursue if you have the time and patience.

If you want to take the time to investigate folk melodies (which would be time well spent), there are numerous books available at public libraries, and it only stands to reason that most of the songs are probably in public domain.

John Lomax did an in-depth study into the origin of folk music and some of his works are: *Folk Song U.S.A.*, *The Old Chisholm Trail*, *Cowboy Songs and Other Frontier Ballads*. His son, Alan, also wrote some books on the subject, which include: *American Folk Songs and Folklore* and *The Folk Songs of North America*.

Although I don't know for sure, I don't think public domain is under the aegis or authority of the United States Copyright Office. However, since a majority of the songs written after 1909 (especially if they've been published and/or recorded) have been registered, and since the copyright office handles copyright renewals, it's only common sense that they have deposit material and an application form on file. However, I don't know whether or not they keep a public record or a listing of all the songs whose copyrights have expired or simply haven't been renewed. If you want the status of a specific song, I suggest that you write to the United States Copyright Office.

At the various publishing companies for which I've worked in the past, whenever we wanted to know whether or not a song was in public domain we wrote to the copyright office and asked them to do a "search" on the song. They usually wrote back to us several weeks later with their findings. They might say something to the effect that to the best of their knowledge, the song was in public domain; or they might write that the original copyright was in 1904 and ran out in 1979, and therefore the song was in public domain.

And here's another suggestion which I would like to impart: I have always felt that it was good business practice to get a second "search" opinion with regard to p.d. material. It's equivalent to going to a doctor and he tells you that your time on planet earth is about to run out. Naturally, it's always best to go to another doctor to verify the first doctor's report. The same thing applies to p.d. material.

There are many "song detectives" that you could contact who specialize in the song search department, and one of them is Fulton Brylawski, whose office is located in Washington, D. C. Another avenue you could pursue is the performing rights societies like ASCAP, BMI or SESAC. Since they are performance collection agencies for publishers and writers, they should have some sort of composer/arranger status in their enormous song catalogs and files which indicate whether or not a song has had its roots from public domain material.

The primary function of the Harry Fox Agency is auditing record companies who are suspected of being evasive with their royalty payments to publishers/ writers. However, another one of their functions is the licensing of songs for various organizations. So it stands to reason that they, too, would be a good source for public domain information.

Down through the years, I've read a variety of articles with regard to all aspects of music, in a multitude of music magazines and/or books which are available. Along the way, I think I read somewhere that any sheet music published before September 1906 is a likely candidate to be public domain. So check out the dates on old sheet music.

Look at newspaper ads for estate sales and then go to some of them. It seems to me that all over America, there must be thousands of piano benches just chock-full of old sheet music which could be public domain.

136

Since I've been in the music business all my life, I have a private collection of old-time seventy-eight records, sheet music and music folios from which I have had some good leads on p.d. material. I'm sure there are many other music buffs out there who also have collections such as mine.

Almost every city has dealers or music stores which specialize in various music collections such as music antiques, seventy-eight records, old albums, old sheet music, etc. Even listening to songs on seventy-eights, or older albums, might give you a public domain song clue to check out.

Since there is absolutely nothing illegal or immoral about using p.d. melodies, making new arrangements and copyrighting them, start searching around and find yourself a public domain melody and put your own lyrics to it. One of the ingredients of a hit song is for people to go away humming or singing the melody upon first hearing it. Therefore, by adding words to an old p.d. melody, people will remember it easier, simply because they are already familiar with the music.

Dear songwriter/reader: Public domain material is available and free for all of us to embrace with our own individual creative abilities, and I have always thought of it as a potential gold mine from which anyone could hit pay dirt with a hit song if they persisted long enough. Other songwriters have done it, so why not you? Draw upon its gold mine of material by going out there and digging!

The corn is free for the pickin' in the public domain field. As I always say, if you wanna sell corn, you gotta go out into the cornfield.

CHAPTER NINETEEN

▼

AN ARRANGEMENT IS A LOVE AFFAIR WITH MUSIC

Since I have had a lifelong love affair with songs and music (coupled with the fact that I'm a romantic Pisces), naturally I would have a tendency to think of an arrangement as a love affair with music.

This thought really occurred to me the other day as I listened to Nat King Cole singing a few of his greatest hits, such as "Unforgettable" and "Mona Lisa" from an album that I have in my collection. I became totally immersed in the musical background, which is called an arrangement. Nat would sing a phrase, and then beautiful violins would come out of nowhere, complementing the lyrics and the melody. It seemed to me as if they were having a love affair with the song. (However, I don't get that feeling when I hear rock 'n' roll or heavy metal songs, although I'm sure their musical advocates do. It's simply a matter of different strokes for different folks.)

Occasionally, newcomers to music have asked me what the term arrangement means. In music, it means to put the lyrics and melody in proper order and sequence, and to add supportive background instrumental and/or vocal sounds. The person who does this is called an arranger.

Naturally, the first step in an arrangement is taken when a song is written in a particular key and then chords are added in the appropriate places, enhancing the song's melody and presentation. Another arranger could take this same song, change the chords and, thereby, give it a different sound and mood.

The sequence in which you put the chorus and verse is another aspect of arranging. First of all, there may be a 4 -, 8 - or 16-bar introduction which may be the best interpretation the arranger feels for that song at that moment. He may start with a verse and follow it by the chorus; or maybe the chorus will be scheduled first and the verses follow in the story-line sequence of your song. Many times, an instrumental of the chorus may be added, which is a common thing to do, especially if it's a dance tune.

This leads right into the tempo of a song which, naturally, is part of the arrangement. Some songs can either be played as a fox trot, which is 1, 2, 3, 4; or as a waltz, which is 1, 2, 3, 1, 2, 3; or maybe it's played with a tango or cha-cha-cha rhythm.

Almost any melody can be adapted to any rhythm the arranger wants to write. Maybe a song was originally written in a slow, ballad tempo. Another musician could come along and play it in a faster tempo and thereby completely change the song's presentation. For example, there have been those instances when Frank Sinatra has taken a slow ballad like "I've Got You Under My Skin," and has sung it with a swing beat, which completely changes the song.

Now we come to one of the most essential components of an arrangement, which are the musical sounds that accompany and surround the lyrics and melody. The next time you're playing one of your favorite songs, listen carefully to the accompanying "arrangement" of sounds. For instance, as a singer finishes the lyric phrase of a sad ballad, you'll hear other musical sounds such as guitar, violin or piano "licks" (as we call it in the trade) which stay and add to the mood of the song.

What I have always enjoyed most in well-arranged songs, especially up-tempo tunes, is how one instrument will seemingly appear to answer another instrument. The other day I was listening to a country song and I heard a steel guitar lick, which was immediately answered by a piano lick. You don't think those musicians aren't having fun! As a matter of fact, all the excellent musicians that I know (and have known) love playing their instruments — it's as if they're having a love affair with them! I got started in this business by playing bass and that's how I felt and still feel to this day. Just holding my bass in my arms and hearing the deep mellow tones that I can create from it takes me into a fantasy world of my own to which only other musicians can relate.

All of the above are part and parcel of the song's arrangement.

It's been said that a song's arrangement plays a dominant role in whether or not it's a success. Speaking from experience, I personally believe this to be true. Since most of you have heard Tennessee Ernie Ford's worldwide hit "Sixteen Tons" (which certainly played a big role in my life), let's use it as an example to show you how the arrangement played a major contributing factor in that song's success.

Very few people know that it was written and recorded by Merle Travis (for an album I produced called *Folk Songs of the Hills*) nine years before Tennessee

Ernie Ford recorded it. Merle's father was a coal miner and he was raised in that environment, so all the songs in this album dealt with that subject. The album was to be marketed in the folk music field, and since Merle was a great guitarist, I had him record all his songs with just his guitar.

He opened "Sixteen Tons" by talking about himself as a little boy. He went on to say how he remembered when his daddy would come out of the coal mine all dirty, and he would hear the whistle blow (the coal-mining term is "tipple"). Merle then started singing the song and playing his ever-faithful guitar. This was Merle's arrangement of his song "Sixteen Tons" in 1946.

In 1955, Tennessee Ernie Ford did the same song — the same words and melody. However, his arrangement was more country/pop. Jack Fascinato, our musical director and arranger, had written a very simple one for six musicians. There was a 4-bar intro, then Ernie started snapping his fingers to set the tempo which, incidentally, wasn't planned, but it was so effective that we left it in because it felt good. This was Ernie's treatment of the same song, which was different from Merle's, and it simply shows the difference in arrangements.

PUBLIC DOMAIN ARRANGEMENTS

In my public domain chapter, I briefly discussed the fact that once a song is in p.d., anyone is entitled to make an arrangement of it and then register their copyright on it. Thus, no one can use that exact same arrangement or treatment of it without paying royalties.

Again, let's use "Sixteen Tons" as the example. When its full copyright term expires, it will go into public domain, which means anyone can make an arrangement of it; then they can register their copyright and perform it without having to pay royalties to the writer's heirs or to the publishing company that published it.

To continue on with examples of p.d. material, Tennessee Ernie Ford is well known for his gospel albums, which are still selling today. As a matter of fact, we would always close his NBC television show with a gospel song. Many of these songs, such as "A Closer Walk with Thee" and "The Old Rugged Cross," were in public domain. Harry Geller or Jack Fascinato would write an arrangement; they were then registered with the Library of Congress in Washington, D. C., published, and Ernie would sing them on television or record them for his albums. This simply means we didn't have to pay royalties, and that no one could use the exact arrangements of Ernie's version without paying royalties. In other words, if one of Ernie's registered arrangements of a p.d. song were to be used on television or in a movie, then performance fees would have to be paid.

So a song's arrangement is everything! Sometimes I'll go into the recording studio and demo a song at a certain tempo, have an 8-bar introduction, open the song with the chorus, add voice harmonies in various parts of the song, etc. This is how I creatively feel the song should be done. Then I send it out and it's recorded by an artist who has an arrangement made, which is completely different from the demo arrangement I had sent him. It's his prerogative and his creative decision. Quite frankly, Scarlett, I don't really give a hoot. Speaking as a publisher, I'm just totally thrilled they're doing one of my songs because it means money for both the writer and myself.

With regard to the demo arrangement of your song, I suggest you keep it simple. Let the chords and the other musical instruments enhance your song as though they were having a love affair with one another. Should your song be published or recorded, let the top musicians and arrangers do what they do best, which is presenting your song in a commercial way as they feel it should be done.

A 21-Gun Salute to All Arrangers: I want to close this chapter by expressing my innermost feelings which I have had for arrangers all my life. They are among the most imaginative and creative musicians in the music business; they're highly respected and lauded for their contribution, which can make the difference between a song being a hit or a miss.

So to ALL arrangers — who include Billy May, Gordon Jenkins, Shorty Rogers, Don Costa, Billy Liebert, Herbie Alpert, Nelson Riddle, Jack Fascinato, Harry Geller, Bill Justice and the list goes on — a 21-gun salute to you! All of us live vicariously through your love affair with music!

CHAPTER TWENTY

SEX
AND THE SONGWRITER:
LEAD THEM TO
THE BEDROOM DOOR,
BUT DON'T TAKE THEM IN!

S E X — now that I have your attention! I am willing to bet a Stetson hat and a new pair of cowboy boots that this chapter will be one of the first ones you read in this book. You don't think I don't know how you lustful songwriter/musicians think out there! Well, it takes one to know one! After all, I'm a romantic Pisces.

As a relatively successful publisher, I'm absolutely amazed at some of the risqué and suggestive lyrics that supposedly nice older men and women bring into my office in the form of a song (probably just as surprised as you're going to be at what this nice older music man will be saying in this chapter).

All of us are fortunate to live in a country in which our Constitution grants us so many wonderful rights, especially the freedom of speech, which is relevant to the subject of this chapter. You are free to express any of your feelings in the lyrics of your song that you desire.

It's also very therapeutic to write down your thoughts and emotions. Afterward, you can throw them away or put them in a desk drawer somewhere. Should you pass on and your family finds your lyrics, they may shockingly say, "He or she wrote that!"

Or, if you find that your lyrics are on the borderline of being too sexually candid, you can say to anyone for whom you played it, "This didn't happen to me; it happened to someone else! I just heard and wrote about it because I thought it would make a good song!"

Naturally, I feel it's best to keep away from words which are too graphic or too provocative with regard to sex. Instead, use words that will "lead your listeners to the bedroom door, but don't take them in!" Otherwise, you'll find that your song won't be accepted by the majority of the publishers and the public.

I don't know whether or not you're aware of it, but there's considerable controversy about sexually explicit lyrics in the rock 'n' roll field. There have been songs which have been banned from being played on the radio because they've transcended the realm of good taste. In some instances, a few music videos have also been banned from television. I certainly understand why parents are concerned with their children hearing or seeing them.

As a matter of fact, there are lawsuits and protests about vulgar and profane lyrics currently taking place in the courts. The last I heard, Congress was considering a new law to stop the sale of recordings with obscene and lewd lyrics. Naturally, there are those who are protesting this action because of our constitutional rights.

Since I live in a semi-glass house (my rambling ranch home has a lot of picture windows), I'm not throwing stones (excuse the pun) or criticizing anyone. I once found myself in a little hot water for writing so-called suggestive lyrics with Stan Freberg even though they were written tongue-in-cheek and the song was promoted as a comedy record. I'm referring to the worldwide hit "John and Marsha," which Stan recorded for Capitol Records. No profanity was used and the lyrics consisted of two very acceptable words; in fact, they were two common names of a man and a woman, John and Marsha.

In his stage show, Stan was using these names in a one-minute comedy routine. We thought it would make an unusual and fun record, so we tried to expand this hilarious one-minute bit. As I recall, we stayed up all night trying to figure out different ways of saying these two words in order to fill a two-and-a-half-minute record. Stan would say, "Marsha" and then he'd change his voice so it would sound like a woman and say, "John." I had a lot of fun collaborating on it with Stan and Billy Liebert, who composed and played the background music.

At no time in the record did we say they were making love. They could have been painting the walls in their house, mending their fence or baking a cake. However, in the minds of many people, the song was a verbal picture of a couple making love.

Every song has its climactic high point and this song was no exception. We weren't responsible for the mental images or the reactions of the listeners who heard the song. These vocal intonations, as we soon found out, would turn on the world's imagination.

Even though this song was banned by churches and other organizations, it became a worldwide hit; it was especially popular in France and England and the rest of the European countries, where it's still popular today.

It's also interesting to note that since the release of this record, there have been many commercials in which a couple only used two words. For instance, in France it was Franz and Suzette; in Mexico, it was Juan and Juanita. To this day, I still see that same formula at work in various commercials on both radio and television. Many comedians have lip-synced to that record. Dick Van Dyke's brother, Jerry, did it with a man's and a woman's hat and it became an outrageous comedic presentation.

I recently listened to a Freberg comedy CD, which is now available in record stores. It was as funny to me now as when it was originally recorded. I'm proud to have been a part of it, and I recommend you buy it if you want to have a good laugh.

It's one thing to write something which is provocative but still within the bounds of good taste; it's another thing, however, to write something vulgar. There's no need for obscene lyrics which are definitely not acceptable to the majority of the public, and it certainly doesn't set a good example for the younger generation.

You have to be very careful if your song is about sex or making love because you're walking on thin ice. Once again, lead your listeners to the bedroom door, but don't take them in. If you want to get the song out into the music marketplace, you can always compose it in such a way as not to offend anyone. For example, if you were writing a song, it would be kind of crude to say the word nude. It's just as easy to be selective in your use of words. Let the listeners do the undressing in their own minds.

Doris Day was one of our biggest movie stars and singers of yesteryear. This good-looking, all-American, freckle-faced lady was the epitome of the girl next door, and the majority of her songs and motion pictures were as wholesome as apple pie, with happily-forever-after endings. Two of her numerous hits included "It's Magic" and "Secret Love." The lyrics in both songs are as romantically beautiful as the titles indicate; they conjure up images and feelings of love, flowers and romance with violins playing in the background, which were so typical of the songs she sang and the movies in which she starred.

On the other hand, there's a song called "Let's Get Drunk and Make Love."

(I have changed the latter part of the title for the mixed company reading this book.) This was a song that was produced and inexpensively recorded in a garage, and turned out to be a monster jukebox hit in the bars. The title alone indicates that the bedroom door is wide open, and it invokes the opposite effect in one's mind than the titles of "Secret Love" and "It's Magic."

At one time or another, most of you have probably heard the lyrics to Cole Porter's classic song, "Let's Do It." He selectively used words that tease his listener's imagination in a fun but very sensual way. The lyrics are about a few of God's creatures "who do it." What do they do? And by the time you get to the last lyric phrase, your imagination could be conjuring up all kinds of images, especially if you've never heard the song before. However, the last lyric phrase purifies the song's message because they fall in love. Even though I've heard that song a thousand times in my life, the lyrics still make me smile whenever I hear or think of them.

I'm sure you've heard the lyrics to the wonderful old standard "Makin' Whoopie." There's certainly no mistake as to what they're inferring with that title. This song is another perfect example of sensual but fun lyrics which were written with great taste.

Have you ever heard the lyrics to the great country classic "Behind Closed Doors"? The title alone is very seductive and stimulating to the imagination, yet it leads you to the door, but it doesn't take you in. It's very possible that they could be playing bridge behind these closed doors — isn't it?

Speaking of sex and songwriting, what comes to your mind when you hear the wonderful and sensuous Peggy Lee sing her classic song "Fever"? When you get the opportunity to hear it, just listen to her vocal intonations on the word "fever" alone. These provocative and timeless lyrics were written and sung with such great taste that they turned on the whole world then and they still do now.

About two years ago, I had the wonderful opportunity of having a music meeting at Peggy's beautiful home to discuss a potential country album. Since she has her own public address system and also had several of her musicians at the meeting, she proceeded to sing about eight or nine of her newly written songs for me and my associates, Joan Carol and Dale Sheets, Mel Tormé's manager. She's such an excellent songwriter. I gotta tell you, folks, this ageless lady still has that charismatic "it," and she can still sell a song in her inimitable, sensuous, sultry way which will whisk you off to never-never land and you don't care if you never come back! Peggy has that rare talent and ability to keep you wanting more when she's through singing.

When the meeting was over, we all had coffee and cake in her living room. During our conversation, I told her that I had always wanted to do a country album with her, for I believed it would be fantastic! She looked at me with her alluring Mona Lisa smile and said, "I've been thinking about doing a country album for years; you're an angel sent to me from heaven."

Now, folks...I've been a fan of hers for many years, and to have just listened to her sing in the privacy of her own home for over thirty minutes was almost too much for me. But to hear her call me "angel"...why...it was beyond my wildest Pisces dreams. I stammered, my heart starting racing, and I dropped a piece of chocolate cake on her living room floor. I was on cloud nine and I have no idea what I said for the next ten minutes. As a matter of fact, excuse me while I get an aspirin and some water. I think I'm running a slight "fever."

Can you imagine how many wonderful love songs have been written after love has been expressed in the most beautiful way possible? This has inspired many a songwriter to take pen in hand and write.

Joan and I cowrote the lyrics to a song in which we left the bedroom door slightly open. It's called "(Touched by) the Magic of You," and some of the lyrics are as follows: "Laying near you, watching you sleep/Feeling your breath soft on my cheek/Takes me back a memory or two/Touched by the magic of you...touched by the magic of you." See what simple and acceptable words can be used to write enticing lyrics which are still in good taste?

So the next time — after love has taken you to its ecstatic heights — instead of reaching for a cigarette (which the Surgeon General says is bad for your health), reach for a pen and paper and you just might score again! You could come up with a hit song! It's a lot healthier to do than smoke a cigarette, isn't it? Excuse me while I light my pipe and think about it.

Dear songwriter/reader: Realize the power of words! Your lyrics will conjure up mental pictures in the minds of your listeners and they, in turn, will react according to their own belief system, past experiences and attitudes on various subject matters.

Although you are not responsible for anyone else's thoughts, be aware of what you can and cannot write lyrically if you want to be a contender in the commercial music market place. There are many words from which to choose and so many different ways of expressing yourself which will get your message across without having to resort to words that border on the obscene.

Therefore, when you are writing a song about love, which may include the physical aspects of it, choose your words very carefully. The approval process of your song's lyrics first start with you — you will have to be your own censor!

The next step in this "censor process chain" will be the publisher, then the producer, the artist, the record company, the radio station until it finally reaches the public's ears. And it's a majority of the public who makes the final decision on whether or not your song will be a hit.

Therefore, when you write lyrics, simply remember to lead them to the bedroom door, but don't take them in.

▼

CHAPTER TWENTY-ONE

THE TRUE STORY ABOUT "SIXTEEN TONS"

There are several reasons why I decided to write this chapter about "Sixteen Tons" for my songwriting book.

First of all, "Sixteen Tons" will serve as an example and an inspiration to all writers that a song's subject matter can become ageless. Secondly, I am constantly asked how Tennessee Ernie Ford and I became associated with each other and how we came to record "Sixteen Tons." This may sound kind of strange, but as I look back in time, it seems to me as though it was all part of a divine plan. How we met in the first place was most unusual, to say the least. With regard to "Sixteen Tons," the meteoric characteristics between Ernie and the song were incredible. It's as if they were made for each other — both in a state of incubation until the timing was right.

And that leads into the third reason — timing. I want to briefly discuss the importance of this elusive phenomenon which seems to go hand in hand with a successful song — especially a worldwide hit.

THERE IS NOTHING MORE POWERFUL THAN AN IDEA
WHOSE TIME HAS COME — *Goethe*

Is it true that "Sixteen Tons" wasn't a hit in 1946 when it was first written and recorded by Merle Travis for Capitol Records? Is it also true that this same song became a worldwide hit for Tennessee Ernie Ford when he recorded it for the same label nine years later? Yes, it's true.

Why wasn't it a hit the first time around? Why are some songs written, published, released, promoted, played on the radio, and nothing happens with them? Then years later, a song is released by another artist and it's a smash!

This scenario is not uncommon in the music world. A more recent example that comes to mind is "The Greatest Love of All," which was a worldwide hit for Whitney Houston from her debut album around 1986. Yet the song had been written about ten years prior to that and had enjoyed moderate success when George Benson recorded it.

Down through the years, I have learned a little about a lot of things in my wonderful world of music. The longer I'm in it, the less I'm beginning to think I know. But experience has taught me that timing has everything to do with a song becoming successful — the timing of when a song is written, and especially when it's recorded and released for the public to hear.

I'm sure you have been inspired to write songs about subject matters which are currently happening; and it's good to do that because you're expressing your feelings — especially if they are about social issues. However, you must be careful that the song doesn't become dated. Regardless of the time period, the great songs are those which have been written in such a way that people can still relate and identify with them years later.

A lot of songs are currently being written about homeless people. We're all aware of this social issue because of the newspaper and television coverage. Although the homeless situation has been around for a long time (even before the Great Depression), it's suddenly a topical subject.

And so it goes with "Sixteen Tons", which became more topical in 1955 than in 1946 when it was first written and recorded by Merle.

Now, I don't profess to know a lot about timing, but it seems to me that it's a lot like electricity — I know it exists but I can't explain it. However, I am a great believer in following your own inner instinct — call it your sixth sense, a hunch, whatever. It's basically doing the right thing at the right time. That's positive timing!

I've certainly experienced timing, for I have been fortunate enough to have been in the right place at the right time. (I've also been in the right place at the wrong time, which I have always viewed with equanimity as just another of life's learning experiences.)

When anyone or anything enjoys super success — and this includes a worldwide hit song — myths and legends develop and the story of how they came to be are told as each individual remembers it. So sit back and relax while I step back into yesterday to relive all the relevant events encompassing the true success story of "Sixteen Tons" as I remember them.

In August of 1946, when most of you weren't born yet, I produced an album called *Folk Songs of the Hills* with Merle Travis, at the request of Capitol Records' president, Alan Livingston. At that time, I was not only in charge of the Country Music Division for Capitol, but I produced records as well.

I'll never forget the day when he called me into his office and said, "Cliffie, there's an artist who sings folk songs over at Decca Records (now MCA

Records) called Burl Ives, and he's selling a lot of records. Since we don't have a folk singer, maybe we should find one for ourselves."

I proceeded to tell Alan about a friend of mine, Merle Travis, who was a cast member of my band and worked with me on my radio shows and who I thought was in the folk-singer bag. Alan gave me the go-ahead to record him at fifty dollars a song. Merle would get four hundred dollars for eight songs for that album. In those days, that wasn't a bad deal. The song publishing aspect was taken care of, since Merle was signed as a staff writer to American Music.

I called Merle and told him about the deal offered by Capitol Records. I remember him calmly saying, "When did you want to record?" I told him as soon as possible because this guy, Burl Ives, was selling records like hot cakes and we needed to get in on the folk market action. Merle said, "How about tomorrow?" I said, "Have you got the songs?" He said, "No, but I'll have eight songs by ten tomorrow morning." I held my breath as I said okay, but I prayed that we could pull this album off in such a short period of time.

The next morning, I went to Radio Recorder's Studio, and soon Merle showed up sleepy-eyed and with all his songs fresh out of his heart and mind. The engineer, John Palladino, and myself were in the control room. Merle was in the studio with only two microphones — one for his voice and one for his guitar.

I can still visualize him sitting there with his guitar in hand, and singing his heart out about his early childhood in Kentucky where his daddy was a coal miner. The songs spoke about the hard times and lives of coal miners: songs like "John Henry," "Nine Pound Hammer," "Dark as a Dungeon," "I Am a Pilgrim" and, of course, the classic "Sixteen Tons" — all of which would eventually become hits. Although we didn't know it then, the timing wasn't right for those songs to be hits in 1946.

We finished recording all eight songs in about four hours. I thought the album turned out great! Merle played his usual wonderful guitar stuff on it. This was our bid at Capitol for the folk-music business. We released the album but, unfortunately, it didn't sell well.

I would like to take a moment to say that I have always been very proud of this album project which I produced with my dear friend, Merle Travis. Recently, Rhino Records released a CD with the original song track by Merle Travis with many of the aforementioned songs. As I listened to it the other day, I became overwhelmed with wonderful memories and the natural songwriting genius of Merle. It's such good stuff and I recommend that you buy it. Isn't it amazing? The album was not a success at that time. If anyone had told me back in 1946 that forty-five years later, many of those same songs would be released again as a classic album, I would not have believed them! Talk about timing!

To continue on with the story of "Sixteen Tons," nothing much happened with Merle's album, but a lot was happening with me. I switched hats; I left Capitol as a producer and signed as an artist with them myself. During my years as an artist, I'm proud to say that I had four hit singles that charted on *Billboard*: In March 1947, "Silver Stars, Purple Sage, Eyes of Blue" reached number four on the country charts; in March 1948, "Peepin' Through the Keyhole" also reached number four on the country charts; "When My Blue Moon Turns to Gold Again" reached number eleven on the country charts in August 1948; and "The Popcorn Song" hit number fourteen on the pop charts in August 1955. I owe a lot of my recording success to Ken Nelson, a man who would make a big dent in the country field for Capitol Records. When he became head of Capitol's Country Music Division, it started growing and flourishing under his guiding light and continued to do so for years. He oversaw the production of talented country artists such as Tex Ritter, Rose Maddox, Buck Owens, Merle Haggard, Hank Thompson, Freddie Hart, Roy Clark, Ferlin Husky, Linda Ronstadt, Glen Campbell and, of course, yours truly, Cliffie Stone. In my own private Country Music Hall of Fame, Ken's name stands out like a neon sign.

As I look back, I shake my head in amazement at all the musical hats I was wearing and I wonder where I got all the energy. (It makes me want to take a nap just thinking about it.) I was not only recording as an artist, but I also started "Hometown Jamboree" on the radio and eventually television, not to mention my band gigs. I had a talented group of cast members and musicians in my band and show, some of whom were Billy Liebert, Speedy West, Jimmy Bryant, Ray Merrill, Billy Strange, Roy Hart, Al Williams, Harold Hensley, Bucky Tibbs, the McQuaig twins — Jonell and Glenell, Joanie O'Brien, Molly Bee, Gene O'Quinn, Les Taylor and Herman "the Hermit," my beloved father. We performed in ballrooms, rodeos, picnics and clubs all over California. We gave them the music they wanted to hear, so we enjoyed a loyal following of fans that kept growing as the years went by.

As I entered the time period in which the paths of Tennessee Ernie Ford and mine were to cross, I had a regular Saturday-night dance at the American Legion Hall in Placentia, California. At the same time, I was producing and M.C.'ing a daily, one-hour, live radio show on KXLA called "Dinner Bell Roundup," later to be called "Hometown Jamboree."

One day, the general manager of the station, Mr. Loyal King, called me in and said he needed a newsman and wondered if I knew of anyone. I said, "Not offhand but I'll keep my eyes and ears open and if I find someone, I'll let you know."

A few weeks later, I had to attend an important music meeting in Palm Springs. As I was driving through San Bernardino, just by chance I happened to tune in my radio to KFXM. I became very impressed with the low, well-trained and modulated voice of the newsman. At the end of the newscast, he signed off with, "This is Ernest Jennings Ford."

Immediately following, another show came on, called the "Bar Nothing Ranch" which was M.C.'d by a backwoods, hillbilly personality called Tennessee Ernie. He played the current records of the day by Ernest Tubb, Red Foley and Roy Acuff. The unique thing that he did was to sing along with them in harmony. Then, during the chorus instrumental of the record, he would switch to the lead part. During the entire show, there were farm animal sounds: ducks quacking, pigs squealing, cows mooing, horses whinnying, dogs barking and so on. I thought this was the funniest country radio show that I had ever heard! As I look back, this show was actually the original radio version of the television show called "Hee Haw" which enjoyed enormous popularity for years.

However, I was basically interested in the newsman, since I thought he was just what Mr. King was looking for. So I stopped and called Ernest Jennings Ford at the radio station from a public telephone. We made an appointment to meet and approximately one hour later, two future country music Hall of Famers would come face to face at a coffee shop and both would have such an impact on each other that their lives would be changed forever.

I immediately liked Ernie. Who wouldn't like him? To this day, he still has that same unassuming, down-to-earth, country-boy charisma that has endeared him to his fans worldwide.

As we talked, he told me that he had recently been released from the Air Force in San Bernardino where he had met his wife, Betty, and decided to settle down there. I told him about the opening at KXLA and I suggested that he call Mr. King for an interview as soon as possible.

Out of curiosity, I also asked him about that hillbilly guy who came on right after the news with the "Bar Nothing Ranch" show. He looked at me, laughed and said, "That's me." He went on to say that he loved country music and loved to sing along with the country stars. He used his real-life "character" to do this show; and since his home town was Bristol, Tennessee, he called himself "Tennessee Ernie."

Needless to say, he was hired at KXLA. He was given the daily time slot from 10:00 a.m. to 11:00 a.m. as "Tennessee Ernie" for the "Bar Nothing Ranch." At 11:00 a.m., he would do the news as "Ernest Jennings Ford." At 11:30, he would introduce my live show, "Dinner Bell Roundup," and then come into our studio, sit down and listen to the music.

At that time, my cast included Merle Travis, Red Murrell, Tex Atchinson, a girl singer named Tex Ann, and Herman "the Hermit." I always ended my show with a gospel, and one day I asked Ernie to sing bass with our quartet.

A few days later, right on the radio airwaves, I spontaneously asked Ernie to sing a solo. After much protesting by him, he finally got up and sang Jimmie Rodgers's "Mule Skinner's Blues." The radio station switchboard lit up like a Christmas tree, and I knew that Tennessee Ernie Ford's light had just begun to shine.

As fate would have it, Ernie became a cast member of my "Hometown Jamboree" show and performed regularly at my Saturday-night dances at Placentia's little American Legion hall. Because of Ernie's growing popularity, we went from two hundred and fifty people every Saturday night to one thousand people in just a few month's time. Therefore, I had to find a larger location for my show, and soon the El Monte Legion Stadium in El Monte, California (which could hold over four thousand people) became our new home. (To this day, I'm proud to say, I'm still approached by fans who are so thankful for the wonderful memories of those family-oriented shows of yesterday.)

It was there that Ernie and I met a young man who would play an integral role in the musical tapestry of both of our lives — especially Ernie's. His name was Jim Loakes and he "came with the lease," since he was the general manager of the stadium. He was that rare type of person who goes the extra mile, for he was always there, day and night, giving his all by efficiently hand-ling the numerous details which occur when you're in the fast lane of show business, and we were preparing for the Indianapolis 500.

As my "Hometown Jamboree" show grew in popularity by leaps and bounds, he became my assistant and joined the payroll. He was a permanent member of our team when Ernie's star began to ascend, and we took him with us on our stratospheric flight to the moon to take care of all the essential, behind-the-scenes details. He turned out to be a jewel of a man who not only became a trustworthy partner to both Ernie and myself, but a valued friend as well.

Turning the next page of the "Sixteen Tons" story, eventually I took Ernie over to Capitol Records and introduced him to some people, since I was still under contract to them as an artist. To make a long story longer, on January 21, 1949, Ernie was given a recording contract at Capitol.

With every record release, such as "Shotgun Boogie," "Mule Train," and a wonderful duet with Kay Starr called "I'll Never Be Free," his star kept rising and growing brighter. Along the way, I had to make a major career decision when Ernie asked me to be his manager, which I accepted and I'm so glad I did. I turned my "Hometown Jamboree" radio show over to my good friend, Dick Haines, a country DJ, and never looked back.

I want to say something else which shows the depth and uniqueness of our friendship. Our contract was our word, cemented by a handshake, to which we both lived up to during the entire time I was Ernie's manager. A friendship like ours is almost unheard of — especially in the business world!

I wanted to make sure that I had a fairly accurate accounting of this classic-song legend, so after recalling my own memories of this phenomenon, I compared notes with Jim Loakes, who became Ernie's manager when I retired from that position thirty years ago. As we reminisced about this Camelot period of time in our lives, both of us became very emotional, to say the least, and we are still amazed at the happening, and it was a happening.

In January of 1955, Ernie started his daily, five-days-a-week, live NBC television show, which was on from noon to 12:30 p.m. We had a pretty tough schedule because we did four or five songs per show, five days a week, which means that we burned up one hundred songs a month. As we approached May or June, we were running out new material and, although we had Ernie sing some of these songs more than once, you can understand why we started looking for new tunes.

Now, Ernie and Merle Travis had worked side by side during my radio and television shows and somewhere down the line, Ernie had heard Merle's

"Sixteen Tons." As we were considering new songs in our music meetings for his daily television show, Ernie came up with the idea of doing "Sixteen Tons," since he had always liked it. So we had our music director and arranger, Jack Fascinato, create a very simple arrangement of the song. (Actually the arrangement was simple out of necessity because we had a very limited budget and we could only afford six musicians.)

We programmed it and Ernie sang it on television; within the next few days, over twelve hundred letters came into NBC about that song, which was my first clue that "Sixteen Tons" was very special. I was so impressed that I put the letters in a box and stashed them away. I don't know why — I just followed my instinct.

When our TV show took its summer hiatus, it was necessary that I travel with Ernie, since I was his manager. He performed at a number of fairs, one of them being the Indiana State Fair, which was one of the biggest. Included in Ernie's song repertoire was "Sixteen Tons" which, ironically, got the same emotional response as it had when he'd performed it on his daily TV show a few months back. Again, we were all impressed; however, we brushed it aside because we were on the run with the numerous commitments of Ernie's performance schedule.

During this period of time (as I've previously mentioned), Ernie also had a recording contract with Capitol Records which was conveniently located right across the street from the El Capitan Theater from where we were televising Ernie's show every day. (The El Capitan is one of the oldest theaters in Hollywood and to this day, it's still a treasured landmark. Many years ago, I performed there for three years with Gene Austin in Ken Murray's Blackouts. Later, Jerry Lewis would take it over and convert it to the Hollywood Palace.)

Because of our daily, hectic live television schedule and all the demands that go with the territory of being an entertainer, Ernie was overdue in getting another single released, even though the record company was right across the street. His producer, Lee Gillette (an exceptionally talented man who not only produced Nat King Cole's biggest hits, but other great artists such as Peggy Lee), began to call us regularly about recording. To satisfy him and to fulfill our commitment, we made a date to record two sides as soon as possible.

At this time, I want to say a few words about Lee Gillette, since he was so special to me. He was not only a dear friend of mine, but he was also my musical mentor who gave me my start, helped me along the way and influenced me more than any other person in the music business. He taught me to believe and to go with my innermost instincts about music. What greater gift can another human being give to someone? In my own way, I've tried to pass that gift along.

At this point in time, Ernie was not yet a major star, but he was rapidly on his way to becoming one. (On a scale from one to ten, he was probably a six or a seven, with a bullet, as they say in the trade.) Therefore, getting the right song for him was especially important. (It's important no matter what level of success an artist has attained, because no one maintains.)

After discussing song material, Lee decided the A side should be a cover tune, "You Don't Have to Be a Baby to Cry," which had originally been recorded by Ernest Tubb in the country field. All of us agreed that it was a great idea; however, we needed a B side for the single. It was then that I remembered the letters we had received when Ernie sang "Sixteen Tons" on his TV show. So I took them in a big cardboard box, walked across Vine Street, went up to the twelfth floor where the A&R Department of Capitol (Artist & Repertoire) was located and walked into Lee Gillette's office.

He looked up at me with such a surprised look on his face as I dropped this big box of letters alongside his desk. I remember saying, "Lee, here are twelve hundred letters that we received when Ernie sang 'Sixteen Tons' on his TV show six months ago. I think we ought to record it for the B side." Without a moment's hesitation, Lee said, "Let's do it!"

In October 1955, without fanfare, we went into Capitol's recording studio and recorded both sides. Lee immediately scheduled the single for release within the next two weeks.

Now, this may sound like it happened fast to you, and it did! But I want you to understand that the record business in 1955 was a different breed of cat than it is today. In those days, you went to your record producer and if he liked the song and the artist, he would give you the okay to record it, and it would be released in a couple of weeks.

So that you, as a beginning songwriter, will have an idea of how songs get on the national charts, I'll give you a thumbnail sketch by using "Sixteen Tons" as the example, since this is still how it's basically done in the music business today. The week that Ernie's record was released, we sent out approximately two hundred acetates to *Billboard* reporting stations. (An acetate is a very soft type of wax that can only be played approximately fifteen times, and then it's discarded. Today, they send out a CD single which can be played innumerable times.)

These *Billboard* reporting stations, obviously, report to *Billboard* magazine. They, in turn, make up the charts that show when a record is being played, where it's being played and how it's doing in those areas. Of course, to really make it a round robin, other program directors at other radio stations who also subscribe to *Billboard* will look to see what, where and how a song is doing. Then they'll include it in their programming schedule. It's a vicious circle — tough to get in and tough to stay in.

However, "Sixteen Tons" got in with a bang and stayed in because something very unusual happened at these *Billboard* reporting stations: the single turned itself over! Although Capitol was promoting the A side, "You Don't Have to Be a Baby to Cry," some of the DJ's started playing "Sixteen Tons," the B side, and it snowballed! Actually, I think a more descriptive term would be avalanche. We were in *Billboard* heaven because "Sixteen Tons" knew no boundaries. It crossed over into the pop field and soon became number one on all the *Billboard* charts!

"Sixteen Tons" sold faster and quicker and became the biggest record that Capitol had ever released. Within three weeks, it sold a million copies! Within nine weeks, three million copies!

Life magazine was a weekly publication at that time and they always had the current top stories or major news of anything that was hot. Selling one million records in three weeks made "Sixteen Tons" and Ernie the hottest! Therefore, they did a wonderful story on this unusual record event.

One of the lyric phrases in the song was "number-nine coal." In coal mining terminology, that's a lump of coal about the size of a man's fist. So imagine this if you will: *Life* magazine went through all the trouble of finding and gathering a mountain of number-nine coal. Then they took a picture of Ernie on top of it — in a suit and tie — wearing a coal miner's hat, and that great photo was in *Life* magazine that week! After that, there was no stopping the meteor-like career of the megatalented and lovable Ernie Ford. He could do nothing wrong. The Camelot days had arrived!

In 1956, he started his weekly NBC prime-time Thursday-night television show for the Ford Motor Company, which took off like a bolt of lightning and stayed in the Top 10 ratings for the next five years. Plus, we continued doing Ernie's daily TV show five days a week for one more year, which made for a very busy lifestyle for everyone involved with his career.

Although I don't know the exact figures, I think I either read or heard somewhere that Ernie's version of this song has sold in the neighborhood of ten to twelve million records worldwide.

However, I think it would be difficult for anyone to keep track of how many units have been purchased for sure, since there have been so many different commercial packages for which Capitol has granted licenses which, naturally, included that song—beginning from the time period when Ernie first recorded it up to the present day.

Why did it take nine years for that song to become a hit? Why not in 1946 when the song was originally written and recorded by Merle? Who really knows? When you have the right song and the right artist, and they're recorded and released at the right time, magical things can happen.

However, maybe some of the reasons why the timing was better in 1955 had to do with the up-and-coming 1960s decade. (For those of you who don't remember, the '60s proved to be a decade of tremendous change and confusion for so many people in so many ways.)

You aspiring songwriters, please take note at what I'm about to say: This was a song that had a "buzz line" or "cue line" in it — a lyric line which stood out above the rest and unconsciously made people remember that song: "I owe my soul to the company store."

This was a simple song about the life and times of coal miners back in the '40s. Instead of being paid by check or cash in the coal-mining business, they were issued "script." The coal mining company also owned a company store which was the only place the coal miners could spend it. They had to buy their food, clothes and other items at the company store and they paid towards their bill when they got their script. Talk about a round robin! The coal mining company would pay the miners for mining the coal in script. Then they made money on them when they went into the company store to buy the necessities of life. No money exchanged hands — just pieces of paper. Actually, when you think about it, this was probably the original version of the credit charge system that we have today.

So the lyric line, "I owe my soul to the company store" became a catch phrase not only in the United States, but all over the world. In fact, the record was more popular in European countries such as Wales, Scotland, England and Scandinavia. All those countries had the depressed, hard-working class of people who never got out of debt their whole life and they identified with this simple song and its simple arrangement.

Even today, people all over the world in some manner "owe their soul to the company store." Do you? You do if you're buying a car, a house, etc. and have borrowed the money from any type of credit union or a banking institution. You do if you use any one of a variety of charge-account credit cards available for charging all types of items and necessities.

Did you watch the Country Music Association's Award show on CBS-TV on October 8, 1990? Tennessee Ernie Ford was inducted into Nashville's Country Music Association's Hall of Fame on that day. The superb production and incredible singing style of the Oak Ridge Boys that led up to the surprise presentation of Ernie receiving his award were unforgettable.

They started by singing "Just a Closer Walk with Thee" and several other gospel songs and just before they stepped off the stage to walk over to Ernie's seat, they started snapping their fingers and singing "Sixteen Tons." As they urged Ernie to stand up and join them in singing this great song which people identify with him, the audience stood up together as a whole and gave both Ernie and the song a standing ovation. I don't think there was a dry eye at the Grand Ole Opry that night.

I was not only proud of Ernie that evening, but also proud that I had played a part in presenting that song to the world. I know that somewhere in the heavens above, both Merle Travis (who was probably strumming his ever-faithful guitar) and Lee Gillette were proudly standing tall with tears in their eyes, too.

And it was on this unforgettable day when Ernie received his Hall of Fame award before the world on national television, that the true story of "Sixteen Tons" came full circle and was finally completed.

In the music world, this elusive quality called timing is everything, and the longer I live, the more I realize that some things are just meant to be. We human beings have our own timetable which, many times, doesn't happen when we want it to happen.

Then there is God's timetable where the seemingly miraculous happens.

There is nothing more powerful than an idea whose time has come — *Goethe*

▼

CHAPTER TWENTY-TWO

THE OPPORTUNITIES ARE LIMITLESS FOR WOMEN IN THE MUSIC BUSINESS!

I n the past, it was traditionally a "man's world" in practically all fields of endeavor. Then, as more women moved into the business world to hold down a second job (the first one being one of the most responsible jobs of all, a housewife and/or mother), the women's equal rights movement became a dominant issue. (For the life of me, I've never understood why women would want to give up their superior status to be equal with men.) However, being a Pisces, I have always admired women and have been a "women's lib" advocate all my life.

Today, women play a vital and major role in all industries. This certainly includes songwriting and all areas of the music business where the opportunities are limitless. Whenever I think of highly successful women in the country music field, four charming "steel magnolias" immediately come to mind: Jo Walker-Meador, Dolly Parton, Frances Preston, and Tammy Wynette! In their individual ways, these Amelia Earharts of the music world became successful when it wasn't the vogue because the career choices in the 1950s were somewhat limited to being a housewife, secretary, teacher or nurse. However, all four of these ladies had a common bond that made them follow the beat of their own drum: a deep, uncompromising and dedicated love for country music.

I have known and worked with Jo Walker-Meador for years, and she's one of my favorite people in the whole wide world. This incredible lady is a behind-the-scenes star in country music. She's been the guiding light of Nashville's Country Music Association (CMA) ever since its inception. She has been associated with this organization for over thirty-two years and initially started out as its secretary. Through tireless devotion and hard work, she became one of its top-ranking officials and now reigns as executive director.

She exemplifies the charming, soft-spoken, Southern country princess who rules with an iron hand in a velvet glove. When the CMA was struggling hard to survive, she helped to guide it through its embryonic stages until it finally matured and prospered into the great music organization that it is today. All of us in country music — past, present and future — owe a debt of gratitude to her, which we'll never be able to repay.

Tammy Wynette is the definitive female voice of country music and every girl singer hopes they can sing just like her. When she sings "Stand by Your Man" (which she cowrote with Billy Sherrill), she makes me wish I were her man. She is my "queen of songs" and what she does to a lyric is awesome. Although other girl singers have had success and hit songs before her, she was the first to have monster hit recordings, one right after another. Not even Patsy Cline in her time had hits as big as Tammy.

As far as Dolly Parton goes — oh my, oh my! What a versatile, multitalented woman! She replaces the traditional rules and regulations that she breaks with new ones which become traditional. Country songs are known for their honest lyrics, but she broke new ground in this area with her simply written but "tell it like it is" songs. As far as I can remember, she was one of the first women (outside of Loretta Lynn) to pioneer the trend of female singers writing and singing their own songs. However, she's not only a great country singer and songwriter, but she has also carved out a unique place for herself in the motion picture industry with wonderful performances in films such as *Steel Magnolias*, *The Best Little Whore House in Texas*, and *Nine to Five* in which she wrote the title song which became a big hit.

I left Frances Preston for last because she's accomplished so many "firsts" in her lifetime which, therefore, makes her a hard act to follow, regardless of gender. This dynamic lady has it all: beauty, brains, an unquenchable thirst for success, and most important of all, she cares so much about people that she makes everyone she meets feel special with that Midas touch of hers.

In 1958, she coordinated the Southern regional office of BMI (Broadcast Music Incorporated) at the request of Judge Robert Burton, who, at the time, was a senior vice president. Seven years later, she herself became a vice president, which made her the first female corporate executive in Tennessee. Through her innate business acumen and people skills, she climbed the executive ladder of success by organizing and building BMI into one of the elite performing rights societies in the world. Today, she is its president and CEO. Not a bad track record for a young lady who started out as a receptionist at WSM-AM-TV in Nashville, is it?

I first met her in Nashville years ago when my company, Central Songs, became an affiliated member of BMI. We became good friends through the years when my company's songs, and also ATV's songs (the company for whom I worked after I sold Central), garnered their share of BMI awards — I am proud to say!

Her accomplishments and awards would fill a book, and I hope she writes one someday because it would be inspirational to all women regardless of their field of endeavor.

In 1990, the *Ladies' Home Journal* listed her as one of the 50 Most Powerful Women in America. I love her succinct advice to women who want a business career: "Forget that you're a woman, and go to work."

At the 1987 CMA Awards in Nashville, Frances received the Irving Waugh Award of Excellence, which is a prestigious award given for contributions which have "dramatically broadened and improved country music's influence." When it was presented, the CMA board said of Frances Preston: "Her intelligence, her incredible administrative talents and her boundless energy have helped shape not only country music, but the entire music industry." I feel these words succinctly express this dedicated woman's enormous contribution to music.

From the very beginning and, as I'm writing these accolades, she has fervently protected and championed the rights for all songwriters and publishers so they will be compensated for their works, which, in turn, will enable them to continue to earn a living in their chosen profession.

If I sound as though I'm a big fan of hers, it's because I am — myself and one hundred thousand other songwriters and publishers! She is the "wind beneath my wings" to all of us who are affiliated with her and BMI.

All the above ladies have set high standards and have become role models for other women in music to emulate. They have wholeheartedly given the very best of themselves in their particular area of the music industry, and country music has been elevated to the exalted position that it enjoys today because of women like them.

And a few more of these "country class" women of yesterday and today include (in alphabetical order): Sherry Bond, who successfully manages her late father's publishing company, Johnny Bond Music; Fran Boyd, executive secretary of the Academy of Country Music in Los Angeles — whose steadfast love and respect for country music has immensely contributed to the academy's growth, importance and success; Connie Bradley, Southern executive director of ASCAP, located in Nashville — whose beauty is Hollywood's loss and Nashville's gain; Felice Bryant, songwriter-publisher — together, Felice and her husband, Boudleaux, wrote over 1,500 recorded songs and she made the difficult transition from successful songwriter to successful publisher; Maggie Cavander, the vivacious director emeritus, Nashville Songwriters Association International; Patsy Cline, whose country voice, to this day, has never been equaled; Helen Farmer, the dedicated director of special projects, Country Music Association; Lib Hatcher, the lady who discovered, believed and manages the talent of Randy Travis; Wynonna and Naomi Judd — the delightful, multi-award-winning mother-and-daughter duet team; Betty Kaye, one of the largest talent bookers on the West Coast; Loretta Lynn — the songs she wrote and sang were a country-flavored version of the women's movement before it came to be. The wonderful movie of her life, *Coal Miner's Daughter*, is a country classic. Rose Maddox, daughter of a California migratory worker, whose wild, untrained voice will never be forgotten; Barbara Mandrell, who proves that big talent comes in small packages and she's my Entertainer of the Year forever; Kathy Mattea, whose new traditional musical sounds bring back old traditional memories; Reba McEntire, who sings with a touch of traditional class; Patsy Montana, the first girl singer to yodel her way to the top; K. T. Oslin, the songwriter/singer of "80's Ladies," which won CMA's Song of the Year, and who proves that age is only a number; Bonnie Owens, award-winning singer/songwriter — the Academy of Country Music honored her and Merle Haggard with the Top Vocal Duet award in 1965, 1966, and 1967; Minnie Pearl — comedienne and country music's priceless treasure; C. Diane Petty, vice president of SESAC — who has helped to expand and elevate it to its present position in the performing rights societies arena and still growing; Martha Sharp, vice president of Artist & Repertoire, Warner Bros. — who has the sharpest (and prettiest) ears in Nashville; Dinah Shore — this charming, talented, ageless Southern belle has been and continues to be successful in all her career endeavors, and will always be a country girl at heart, and I'm proud to say we share the same Pisces birthday. Paige Sober, senior director of Writer/Publisher Relations, BMI-Los Angeles; Cindy Walker, songwriter — Texas's gift to country/western music in its early years; Kitty Wells, one of the first country female singers whose records inspired all the rest; Dottie West, singer/songwriter — whose sultry voice and songs inspired the saying, go West young man, go West; Theodora Zavin, senior vice president, Special Counsel, BMI

— although this unique lady is far from the spotlight of country music, she has had a powerful effect on its growth and success. And the list is endless. Please forgive me if your name isn't mentioned. You know who you are!

Since I admire and respect each one of you, I want to collectively thank all of you, through my book, for doing your part in making country music what it is today! A 21-gun salute to all you lovely ladies of country.

THE ASPIRING FEMALE SONGWRITER

As an aspiring female songwriter, where do you fit into the scheme of things, be it country, pop, etc.?

Although men have basically dominated the scene, women songwriters have always been an integral part of the musical tapestry — more so today than ever before! By becoming a songwriter, you're at the very creative core of music — because it all begins with a song.

There was a wonderful article in *Billboard*'s November 10, 1990 issue, "Nashville Scene" written by Edward Morris. Boldly emblazoned across the page was the caption: "Female Writers Set High Lyrical Standard." Basically, the article was about the current country crop of women songwriters whose lyrical contents are very candid and truthful about the human condition, which basically revolves around love and relationships.

And if this is true of women writers in the country field, then it's also true of women songwriters in the categories of pop, contemporary, r&b, etc. A few of these talented ladies include: Cynthia Weil, Linda Creed, Carole Bayer Sager, Marilyn Bergman, Melissa Manchester, Diane Warren, Tracy Chapman and the list goes on.

EQUAL PAY FOR EQUAL WORK

I am aware that there have been many salary injustices when men and women have had the same job classification in the business world. This is one of the main issues for which the women's movement has been fighting and rightfully so — equal pay for equal work!

Now here's the good news: There is no sexual discrimination when it comes to royalties. You, as an aspiring female songwriter, have the same potential of making as much money as a male songwriter. If that doesn't add motivation to your writing desire, I don't know what else will.

I feel that housewives are in a very advantageous position. By becoming songwriters, not only do they have a creative outlet to express themselves while doing all the million-and-one things a wife and mother has to do, but there's a chance they'll earn an income from their creative endeavors.

If you're a housewife, stop and think about it for a moment. Your subject matter is unlimited. What could be more important than love of home and family? Also, you can write anywhere you feel like it and on your own time. That's one of the great things about writing songs — you don't have to be in a certain room or place. You can write while you're at the laundromat, cooking dinner, driving your car, changing diapers, on vacation — anywhere. All you need is a pen and paper or a tape recorder and then tune in to your creative thoughts.

During the day, how many of you watch the numerous talk shows on television like "Phil Donahue," "Oprah Winfrey," "Joan Rivers," "Sally Jessy Raphael" or "Geraldo"? Whenever I'm home, I love to watch them myself and, in doing so, I've noticed that the majority of the audiences at these shows are women. As a matter of fact, I would venture to say that 80 percent of them (not to mention the television viewing audience) are women, which only goes to prove that a man should consider a woman's opinions because they play a large role in all issues.

The current topics and events which make up our daily lives are uninhibitedly discussed on these talk shows. A thousand different song ideas can be gleaned from watching them. The variety of subjects and their subsequent problems are presented on these shows with regularity, such as sex or divorce which many times lead to the topic of the "other person." Your song will certainly be commercial, since the majority of the women will be able to relate to and identify with it. After all, they've been watching the same show from which you got your song idea. By the same token, men are also given a chance to express their viewpoints, since these talk show hosts generally present and discuss all aspects of an issue. Consequently, both men and women will not only get song ideas from these shows, but if they listen to these discussions with an open mind, they'll learn how the other sex thinks and feels about certain subject matters. Therefore, both sexes will become more sensitive and understanding to the viewpoint of the opposite sex.

I once had a great idea for a wonderful one-hour television special called

"Stand by Your Man," which I didn't pursue. The entire concept of the show would have been built around ten country girl singers and their songs about the men in their lives. Of course, the perfect sequel to my elusive dream show would have been to have ten country male singers sing about the women in their lives. Maybe someday...

WOMEN VERSUS MEN SONGWRITERS

Why should men and women compete with each other? Each of us has our own God-given talent, brains, intuition and imaginative powers at various degrees.

Being a peace-loving man, the last thing I want to do is get into a battle of the sexes discussion. However, I'm sure all of us, at one time or another, have said, "I can't live with him/her and I can't live without him/her." It seems to me that the big difference between a man and a woman is their emotional makeup, which probably has to do with genes, hormones and the environment in which they were raised.

Of course, a lot has to do with attitude, which is in our power to change if we have an open mind. Without getting into a big analytical discussion about all these things which are only my personal opinion, I'd like to briefly discuss what each sex brings to their songs from their own emotional point of view.

I've heard it said that women generally express their emotions more than men do. However, I've never believed that because, speaking from experience, most of the men I have known, including yours truly, have always been emotional and expressive in their feelings. Of course, maybe that's because I've been associated with musicians all my life, and in order to be a good one, you have to be uninhibitedly expressive. After all, we make our living by wearing our hearts on our sleeves. Maybe that's why male singers and musicians have always been so popular with women and have always had a large following. For the most part, it's the women who buy the records and drag their boyfriends or husbands to the concerts of their favorite male performers. Look at the popularity of the inimitable Frank Sinatra all these years!

It's my belief that it all depends on how aware and attuned a man is to his inner feelings. Of course, at one time society said it wasn't manly for a man to cry or to express his emotions outwardly, which I've always believed was hogwash! Unfortunately, that kind of belief or attitude, which causes men to keep their emotions in check, has brought about many physical illnesses like ulcers, asthma, and heart attacks.

Nowadays, thank goodness, men from all walks of life are getting in touch with their sensitive, innermost feelings and are expressing them without being embarrassed about it. A lot can be learned from European men, especially the Italians, who are outwardly demonstrative and certainly don't hold back when it comes to love and romance.

The great songs are the ones whose lyrics are filled with strong emotional feelings. That's why music is so therapeutic for the soul; it irresistibly sweeps aside all self-made blocks and barriers of even the most emotionally hardened people and gets them in touch with their innermost feelings and thoughts.

I believe a woman can put emotions into a song that most men can't, simply because there are certain feelings which men will never experience and vice versa.

Actually, I think it would be an interesting experiment to give the same title to both a man and a woman songwriter, and have each one of them write from their emotional point of view on that song's particular subject matter — be it love, sex, children, divorce, loneliness, etc. Wouldn't it be fascinating to see what each one came up with? You would get two totally different songs because they would approach it from two different emotional points of view. A woman will usually see it through different eyes than a man and vice versa.

However, when either a man or a woman songwriter can objectively open up their mind and become more aware and sensitive to the various viewpoints of the opposite sex, they will be able to write great lyrics in which both sexes will be able to relate and identify.

K. T. Oslin did a fine job of candidly writing and singing "Hold Me," which won a Grammy in 1988 as Best Country Song of the Year. She really hits the mark with regard to how couples can sometimes become tired and discouraged by the routine of daily life. Her astute but simply written lyrics in one verse were from a man's point of view; in the other, a woman's. Each of them tried to leave each other but in the process, they realized how much they cared which, of course, gave their love a new meaning and a new beginning. For this song to be such a huge success means that a lot of men and women identified with those lyrics.

One of the all-time great country singer-songwriter-actor legends, Johnny Cash, and his lovely wife, June Carter, sang a duet called "Jackson," which became a big hit for them. The lyrics were written in a teasing, fun-loving way, and in the song, Johnny tells June that he's going to Jackson to fool around. She, in turn, tells him what she thinks about him doing so. Most men are very much aware of women's attitudes with regard to playing around, and Billy Wheeler and Gaby Rogers did a great job on those lyrics. I listened to it the other day. It never fails to bring a smile to my face. I can still recall the times I've watched Johnny and June perform this song. They have such fun singing it together!

I get very sentimental when I think about Johnny Cash because country music and I have known him for a long time. On April 24, 1991, the Academy of Country Music honored Johnny with its Pioneer Award. As I sat in the audience watching the film clips which were part of this magnificent tribute to him, I realized that I had vicariously lived most of those moments with him. How lucky I am to have been on the country music scene when this one-of-a-kind man — fearlessly and historically — did things his way.

A MAN-WOMAN WRITING TEAM IS THE
BEST OF BOTH WORLDS

One of the best ways for a man and a woman to become more aware, sensitive and understanding of each other is to write together. By harmoniously combining their respective emotions, insights and talents, they will be able to create an excellent song that will be the best of both worlds. Some of the biggest hits have been those in which a man and a woman collaborated.

In the pop field, Barry Mann and Cynthia Weil have certainly had their share of hits. "You've Lost That Lovin' Feeling" still knocks me out every time I hear it. Another big hit for them was "Make Your Own Kind of Music," and this title itself is the underlying theme of my songwriting book!

Some time ago, I remember seeing a television special on the wonderful songwriting team of Adolph Green and Betty Comden, who have not only co-written some of the most classic songs in pop, but have been involved with numerous Broadway shows. Three of my favorite songs which they cowrote with Jule Styne are: "Just in Time," "Make Someone Happy" and "The Party's Over."

One of my very favorite songs is "The Greatest Love of All," which was written by Linda Creed and Michael Masser. It's a very deep and philosophical song about the importance of loving yourself, which is the greatest love of all and it's the very foundation of self-esteem. It took the combined insights, sensitivity and talents of a man and a woman to create such an important song whose timeless theme is relevant to all human beings throughout the world. However, let's not forget the magical singing talents of Whitney Houston, whose interpretation made the true meaning of those lyrics come alive to create a worldwide hit.

Who doesn't become sentimental when they hear Barbra Streisand sing "The Way We Were"? This was written by an extremely successful husband-wife songwriting team in the pop field, Alan and Marilyn Bergman, who have written numerous songs for motion pictures. Another one of their wonderful hit songs is "The Windmills of Your Mind."

The fabulous Patti LaBelle and Michael McDonald had a hit duet in 1986 called "On My Own," which was written by the megatalented husband-wife songwriting team, Burt Bacharach and Carole Bayer Sager. As I recall, the song was about being on your own once again after breaking up with someone; the lyrics are from both a man and woman's viewpoints, which came out of the minds and hearts of Burt and Carole. The passionate performances of both Patti and Michael added immensely to the song's lyrical content.

Burt and Carole wrote another song whose title says it all: "That's What Friends Are For." It was originally written by them in 1982 for a film called *Night Shift*. Somewhere down the line, it was heard by Dionne Warwick and she recorded it with Elton John, Stevie Wonder and Gladys Knight. All the proceeds from that record went to the American Foundation for AIDS Research. This was a wonderful gesture by all four of these top artists, which exemplified love for your fellow man.

As a matter of fact, I remember seeing a dynamic television special that Dionne put together so that donations could be sent in for this deadly disease so prevalent in our society. It certainly brought tears to my eyes and I'd like to commend Dionne for all her humanitarian efforts.

If my next inspirational example doesn't prove to you that the combined talents and harmonious writing efforts of a man and a woman has within it the possibilities of fame and fortune, I don't know what else will!

One of the most famous and successful husband-wife songwriting teams is country music's Boudleaux and Felice Bryant. Their songs knew no boundaries, for many of them were either pop hits or country hits or both. They wrote most of the early Everly Brothers' hits, which include, "Bye Bye Love," "Wake Up Little Susie" and "Bird Dog." This best of both worlds writing combination resulted in the creation of fifteen hundred recorded songs — copies of which have sold over two hundred million records. This incredible song track record has taken them to an elite and exclusive nomination in the country field: as of the completion of this book, which is May of 1991, they have become one of the Country Music Association's Hall of Fame nominees. (As far as I'm concerned, when anyone is nominated, they are automatically a winner because it's an honor to even be considered.) Whether or not they are the final choice for this prestigious award in October is beside the point. Both Boudleaux (who passed on to songwriter's heaven in 1987) and his lovely wife, Felice, have made a special place for themselves in country music history, for they have reached a pinnacle of success which is known to very few people.

IT DOESN'T MATTER WHO WROTE IT — IS IT COMMERCIAL?

Speaking as a music publisher, whenever I listen to a new song (or any song for that matter), I never wonder whether or not a man or a woman wrote it. It's totally irrelevant and I'm sure most publishers feel this way, too. Quite frankly, all I listen for is whether or not the song has a feeling which has emotionally hooked me in some way and, therefore, would have commercial possibilities.

Although both sexes are coming from different emotional points of view, all of us human beings have basically the same desires and needs. Love is the greatest and most important emotional need of all. It's the golden thread which connects us to one another and makes all of us one.

One last thought to all the ladies reading this book: You are an integral and major part of the music business and the opportunities are limitless. The brass ring belongs to anyone daring enough to climb aboard the musical carousel — so start writing your songs.

As Frances Preston, BMI's President and CEO, has been quoted as saying: "Forget that you're a woman and go to work!"

And never forget the good news: "Equal pay for equal work."

CHAPTER TWENTY-THREE

A 21-GUN SALUTE TO TALENT NIGHT SHOWS!

Lord, how I love music and people! I suppose you could say I've had a love affair with them all my life. This is why I've always enjoyed being a master of ceremonies at talent night shows — they are so near and dear to my heart! I'm such a people person, and nothing thrills me more than to see potential new talent get up on the stage and courageously sing, dance, play an instrument or perform in some manner.

In the past, only a certain percentage of singers in all musical categories wrote their own songs. Today, however, most of the recording companies in the country, pop and rock fields look for and sign artists who can write and sing their own songs.

Dear aspiring songwriter/singer: What if you not only wanted to write your own songs, but wanted to sing them as well? Where would you go to get this invaluable experience in performing your songs before an audience?

In this day and age, I can only think of two places where new talent can get this initial beginner's experience. One is church choirs and church events; the other is talent night shows, which many nightclubs and other sponsoring organizations have on a regular basis all over the country and, in fact, all over the world.

Aretha Franklin, the great r&b and pop singer, started singing in choirs at a very early age. When my son, Steve, was in his teens and early twenties, he wrote religious songs which were, and still are, performed regularly at the church he has attended all these years.

I cannot say enough good things about talent nights. I don't think many people are aware of the importance of this first step on the ladder to success. I believe that performing and participating in these talent nights is vitally important for all songwriter/singers at all levels of writing and singing development. Everyone has to start somewhere, and it's places like these where you can learn to overcome stage fright, be free to make mistakes and become seasoned. It's the very first stage that beginners can step on and get a feel for what it might be like to be a performer. There's no rehearsal — you simply sign up and when it's your turn, you get up on stage and do your thing.

And this is a good time to bring up the subject of stage fright and/or nerves. I always tell people to substitute these words with another one — excitement. You are merely excited about getting up on stage. By doing this, your attitude will change and, in turn, your stage presence will improve substantially. Never forget what I'm about to say: Anyone who gets up before an audience, whether they are a performer or a speaker, will be excited and/or nervous to some degree; it doesn't matter how much experience they may have or how calm and cool they may appear to be! It's this flow of adrenalin which makes speeches, performances and songs come alive. In fact, welcome it and never lose it! It's just a matter of learning how to channel this nervous energy in a positive way and merely experiencing yourself being successful at it.

I have been credited for discovering quite a few big-name talents, and I'm proud to say that many of them (like Merle Travis, Tennessee Ernie Ford and Molly Bee) broke in their act on my local radio shows, on my Saturday-night shows and dances at El Monte and on my local "Hometown Jamboree" television shows, which eventually became syndicated on numerous television stations throughout the country.

When I tried to retire from the music business over ten years ago, I didn't realize how important music, people and new talent were to me in my life. So to fill the void, I became the talent night master of ceremonies at various country nightclubs like the late Tommy Thomas's famous Palomino club in North Hollywood, California. I guess it was reminiscent of my early days when I introduced new personalities at my Saturday-night dances and on my television shows. For many years, the Palomino club had its famous talent night shows on Thursday evenings and people would come from all over the world just to perform there. Many big-name artists have climbed up on that stage to perform at one time or another: Willie Nelson, Hoyt Axton, Linda Ronstadt, Bobby Bare, Dwight Yoakam...just to mention a few.

Many of the new talent participants at these shows where I was master of ceremonies would come back regularly every week. As a matter of fact, a number of them would participate at other talent nights at other clubs in the Southern California area. They had their own circuit going and the experience that many of them accumulated was unbelievable; I was so pleased to see them became so relaxed and professional in front of an audience.

I could write a book about all the acts that I've seen at these talent shows.

Usually, a club will program one night a week for them. There are no auditions and they are allowed approximately four minutes for one song or whatever. Rarely do we have any idea what they're going to do and, in some cases, neither do they. I have always found it fascinating to see what twenty or thirty people will do once they're on stage their first time around.

Every week, there would usually be some sort of strange or unusual performance. I'll never forget how surprised I was when these two guys got on stage and did a strip — the women sure loved it! I found out later that they were rehearsing for a tryout at some men's strip club in Los Angeles.

I recall how this one shy housewife gathered up all her courage to get on stage and read a poem she had written. She was so nervous that she broke into tears and ran off the stage crying.

Countless numbers of people would get on the stage and be so nervous that they would either sing in the wrong key or forget the lyrics — even to songs they had written themselves. This might come as a surprise to some of you, but that's common among the best of professionals, too. However, a pro has learned to stay up there, ad-lib and go on with the show.

One time I was performing at a country club dance and this one gentleman (who appeared to have reached his quota of alcohol intake) kept on requesting the "Tennessee Waltz." None of us knew the lyrics, but he became so insistent that I finally said, "Okay, I'll sing it." All I did was repeat the first two lines of the song all the way through and nobody knew the difference. Afterwards, the dancers and the audience all clapped and the man gave me a twenty-dollar tip and went happily on his way. So if you ever forget the lyrics, don't panic. Ad-lib and more than likely, the audience will think you're terrific.

Cupid has been known to make an appearance more than once at talent nights. I remember this one guy and gal who met there and decided to sing a duet together. Eventually, they put a band together, got married, and to this day, they are making a good living performing in clubs all around Southern California. As a matter of fact, this is where I first heard a couple of Joan Carol's songs.

I believe that everyone has the "ham" in them to some degree and these talent nights are an excellent outlet for their fantasies. I've also seen many folks get the show-business bug out of their systems; they'll perform three or four times at these shows, decide it's not for them and then go off into another direction with their lives.

I very rarely get upset on the stage but the one time I do is when someone puts down or pokes fun at the brave souls who try their best to perform at these shows. I have always made it a top priority to make sure they are treated with dignity and respect.

Because my feelings were (and are) so strong about the importance of new talent getting up on stage for the experience of performing, I would make it a point to tell all of them at the outset that only one person was going to win tonight; and, therefore, I advised them not to be overly concerned about winning the big prize or even being a runner-up.

Since all of us human beings live on hope, I also tried to give them hope by telling them that they could be a diamond in the rough, and there could be someone in the audience who might see their potential and help them in some way. (In the past, I've discovered some fresh new talent and given them a helping hand. Several are now doing well in the music business. As I always say: If you want to sell corn, you gotta get out in the cornfield.)

And to further elaborate on this subject, I feel it's important to understand that talent nights in Southern California, especially in the Los Angeles and Hollywood areas, are important because this is where aspiring new talent from all over the country comes to live, and hopes to be discovered. Some of them have nowhere else to go to present their talent and many times there will be agents and record people in the audience.

Now, I'm not only talking about the importance of talent nights for the country field, but also for the budding new talent in pop, folk, rock and all musical categories, including comedians. As I said before, oftentimes this is the only avenue open for many aspiring, talented people to try their wings.

When the big band era was prominent, pop singers like Frank Sinatra, Peggy Lee, Doris Day, etc. all became seasoned by traveling with these big bands and performing in ballrooms and clubs all over the country.

As far as radio exposure was concerned, to my knowledge, the "Major Bowes' Radio Amateur Hour" was one of the first to really commercialize amateur entertainment. The aspiring artists would perform and the listening audience would then vote through the mail. After counting the votes they received via these letters, they would bring the winner back the next week. Performers would come from coast to coast to take that first step on the stairway to the stars. Since the list of superstars who got started on Major Bowes' radio show is long, I'll mention only one familiar name who started there many years ago:

174

the great Frank Sinatra, who is in a class all by himself.

When television came along, the "Arthur Godfrey's Talent Scouts" show became a great vehicle for artists. However, the performers who appeared on this show or shows of this type were past the initial beginner's stage. Today, we have Ed McMahon's "Star Search" on network television. On the Nashville Network, there's a show called "You Could Be a Star."

And if you watch these shows, you'll see great staging, great wardrobe and great song arrangements. Yes, these are wonderful stages for our stars of tomorrow because they help to shape, season and hone their acts. But they, like the "Arthur Godfrey's Talent Scouts" show are for those past the beginner's stage, which is what I'm initially expounding upon in this chapter. However, I'm sure that many of these performers have had several years of experience at local talent night shows before taking the next step up and appearing on network television programs.

As I sit here talking into the tape recorder and smoking my pipe, I recall the time I had a great idea for a one-hour television special which would honor and showcase the importance of talent nights. The video opened with a shot of the Palomino club's sign. Then we slowly panned the participants who were waiting in line to sign up. We filmed three separate talent nights and selected about eight of the best acts. We would get a close-up of the singer singing for about sixteen bars, and then slowly fade away from them with a long shot while I simultaneously interviewed them. I would ask questions like, "Have you been here before on talent night?" They would say, "Yes, I've been coming here for a year; and two weeks ago, I won third place so I thought I'd come back and try again." I would say something like, "You're very talented — keep on trying and never give up. Folks, remember that name...Vivian Rae." For an added attraction, we interviewed several famous entertainers who had performed at talent nights at the beginning of their own careers.

Although I believed that television audiences would truly find this show exciting and unique, apparently the timing wasn't right for a network to take a chance on televising a one-hour special on talent nights. Yours truly certainly knows what it's like to get his share of "thanks but no thanks." However, I still believe it would make a very entertaining show! Maybe someday...

Today, talent nights are becoming a big business. On the West Coast, the popular Howard & Phils Western Wear organization has sponsored many talent nights, and it's the proof of the pudding when major corporations such as Marlboro and True Value Hardware sponsor them.

You can go anywhere in the world where there is a gathering of people and there will usually be some local talent ready, willing and able to entertain the crowd. I remember taking several cruises between London and New York. One of the most popular nights aboard ship was talent night, when many of the passengers entertained the rest of the people and the crew.

Public Speaking Classes: When producing an album, I really work with my singers to "speak-sing" their songs, since singing is so much like everyday speaking. I know an innovative songwriter/singer who told me her stage fright and nerves were so bad before an audience that in order to get over it without having to take a drink or a tranquilizer, she attended public speaking classes. It was there she learned not only to speak in front of audiences, but to properly write three-minute speeches which, in turn, helped her to write songs. Since most songs are no longer than three minutes, she simply applied many of the principles she had learned about writing speeches to her songs. She is one of my favorite songwriters and she consistently writes good songs. So give this avenue of audience exposure some thought, too.

Highway 101: Let me share with you an inspirational success story about my middle son, Curtis, who has followed in my bass-playing, songwriting and entertainer footsteps. These footsteps, however, consisted of a twenty-year journey in order to get honed and seasoned before he made the big time with the award-winning Highway 101 group, one of the most exciting and vibrant bands in the country music business today.

As a teenager, he started out playing guitar, writing songs and singing in a folk trio called the Folk Swingers, which lasted for a couple of years. Soon he seriously started learning and playing the bass. Then rock 'n' roll made its dynamic entrance onto the musical scene and stole his heart for awhile. He became a member of several different rock 'n' roll groups, one of which was called the Lounge Lizards. (That name still sends shivers down my spine.) He and the different groups that he played with during those years performed at countless free showcases and talent nights throughout the Southern California area — hoping to be discovered and signed by a record company.

During this period of time, he lived at the ranch, and soon the barn was turned into a four-track recording studio and a rehearsal hall in which their rock 'n' roll sound could be heard for miles around the Santa Clarita Valley area.

And when things seemed to be the darkest for him and his band, from out of nowhere, a potential manager or agent would show up and "dangle a carrot" in front of them. This would never fully materialize, but it gave them hope to keep on keeping on — and, as I said before, we all live on hope. While he struggled and strived and pursued his seemingly elusive musical dream, he also held onto a day job in order to supplement his music income.

And because of my diversified career in the country field, I'm happy to say that during Curtis's formative musical years, he was exposed twenty-four hours a day to country, cowboy, hillbilly and bluegrass music.

This osmosis exposure finally broke through and he saw the light of day. He began working with great local country bands during the urban cowboy era and met Jack Daniels along the way. Their group, the Electric Cowboy Band, performed in my "Showdown U.S.A." gig, which ran three consecutive summers at Alpine Village in Torrance, California. And for the first time, it seemed to me as if Curtis had found a musical direction to work toward.

Somewhere in this time frame, they hooked up with Cactus Moser, who came from Denver, Colorado, where he (like Curtis and Jack) worked with local rock 'n' roll groups, country groups and big bands to get honed and seasoned. It was the beginning of a very special friendship, which would hold the three of them together through the lean years while they worked to build and become a tight rhythm section.

They played for scale (and sometimes less) at many small clubs and honky tonks in Southern California just to keep themselves together as a unit on a stage in front of people and to put bread on the table for their supportive wives and families. Finally, one of the dangling carrots (which all aspiring artists have experienced while pursuing their pot of gold at the end of the rainbow) came to pass and turned their elusive dream into a reality.

One day, Cactus got a call from Chuck Morris, a friend of his from Denver, who told him that he wanted to form a country band and he was looking for several musicians to put together with lead singer Paulette Carlson. After hearing and seeing the magical musical chemistry between Curtis, Jack, Cactus and Paulette, he had the foresight to courageously put all his marbles on the table to back them. The rest is country music history: Highway 101 was born, and they started rolling down the interstate at a rate which would accelerate with every single record release.

To see their growth as musicians and performers in the last four years has been mind-boggling. Jack Daniels, who played in all the rock 'n' roll bands, is now rated as one of the most "dangerous" guitar pickers in Nashville, in that he plays such outrageously original guitar licks. The third original band member, Cactus Moser, is, without a doubt, one of the most charismatic, high-energy, percussionist-drummers ever to work on stage.

It's difficult to be objective about my son, Curtis, but speaking as a man who made his living playing bass, which turned out to be the key that opened new doors of opportunity for me, Curtis's bass playing is the driving force and the foundation for Highway 101's great rhythm sound.

As of the writing of this book, they now have a new lead singer, a beautiful redhead by the name of Nikki Nelson, whose powerful country voice is equally at ease with ballads or up-tempo tunes.

I can't begin to tell you how proud I was as I watched them perform at the opulent Bally's Hotel in Las Vegas this past April. What a pleasure it was to watch this dynamic group appreciating and having fun with their "overnight" success — it couldn't happen to a nicer group of guys and gal. They have come a long way in a seemingly short period of time but, as you can see, their "overnight" success really didn't happen overnight.

Dear aspiring songwriter/singer: I encourage you to perform your songs wherever and whenever you can — especially at talent night shows, choirs and other church-related events, or some other public environment where you can get experience in front of an audience.

Remember: A singer is not a singer unless he/she sings; a musician is not a musician unless he/she plays; a writer is not a writer unless he/she writes; a dancer is not a dancer unless he/she dances, and a comedian is not a comedian until he makes people laugh. No one maintains. The more you perform, the better you will be; the less you perform, the worse you'll become. You have to work at it. This is what all the band members of Highway 101 did individually and together as a unit — and look where the road took them!

So get out on the stage of life! Don't hide your talent under a bushel. Come to the talent night cabaret and let your light shine!

CHAPTER TWENTY-FOUR

YOU ARE YOUR OWN ORCHESTRA AND YOUR OWN MUSIC MAN OR MUSIC WOMAN

I was taking some antibiotics for a bad cold and was sort of spaced out — possibly hallucinating — when the idea for this chapter occurred to me. So please indulge me as I share my insight and my fantasies with you.

I got to thinking about people who have such a deep inner urgency and desire to write music but who have no musical education, who don't know one note from another, one chord from another and can't play an instrument. What could they use as a musical base from which to write?

THE DOMINANT CHORD

As I mentioned elsewhere in this book, I heard a sermon by Dr. Fletcher Harding entitled, "The Dominant Chord," which made a deep impression on me and it's certainly worth repeating. He was speaking about the God-Spirit that dwells in each of us which is dominant over everything else in our lives, regardless of whether or not we are aware of it. To illustrate his sermon's theme, he went over to the organist, had him play a chord and then play a melody and other chords around it. Like a homing pigeon, the other chords and notes always came back to that initial dominant chord.

Being a music man, I've never forgotten this analogy which automatically came to mind when I thought about the musically untrained people who have a desire to express themselves through music. Then the thought occurred to me that our whole body is an orchestra and has all the sounds and rhythms of this universal orchestra.

Look at what the good Lord has given us: Fingers to snap with, hands to clap with, feet to tap with, lips to whistle with, a voice to sing with — and this wonderful mind with its vivid imagination and visualization powers that conducts our individual innate orchestra from which all the feelings and emotions within our souls are expressed.

Let your imagination run wild with me as I take them individually and expound upon them further.

Fingers with which to snap: I'll never forget when we were in the recording studio about to record "Sixteen Tons" with Tennessee Ernie Ford. Just as we rolled the tape for take one, we heard this loud, sharp finger snapping. Ernie had unconsciously started snapping his fingers to get the beat going within himself. It was so effective that we kept it in the record. The other song that comes to mind which was so effective with finger snapping is Peggy Lee's recording of "Fever."

Hands with which to clap: One of the greatest traditional sounds in America is the spiritual gospel sound of the South where the clapping of hands dominates. How many times have you been at a concert or nightclub and the entertainer has asked you to clap your hands in rhythm along with him? This is one of the greatest ways to have the audience participate in a song.

Feet with which to tap: Today, like yesterday, foot tapping is how most musicians and singers establish the right beat and rhythm for their songs. Watch someone who is either playing an instrument or listening to music. Usually, their foot is automatically keeping time with the music.

Do you realize the first real talk shows in America were the minstrel shows? There was an interlocutor (known today as the master of ceremonies as in Johnny Carson, Jay Leno, Arsenio Hall, whomever), who sat on a chair in the middle of the stage and called different members of the organization out to do their act one at a time. Each show usually ended with the creative tap dancing done by almost every member of the cast.

I recall a wonderful movie that I saw last year called *Tap* which starred Gregory Hines and the late great Sammy Davis, Jr. The movie was about tap dancers who, naturally, expressed their music through their feet. It's amazing to me how many different sound beats they can make by tap dancing and hitting the sides of their bodies for different sounds.

Vocal chords, mouth and lips: Our mouths could be equated with a horn section that can make all the sounds of the brass — trombone, trumpet, clarinet, etc. Just listen to great jazz singers like Ella Fitzgerald and Mel Tormé and you'll hear how they imitate jazz instruments. Vocal chords that vibrate and cause sound which we use to talk and sing. I believe everyone can sing! Some just better than others. You can hum, can't you? You also have lips with which to whistle and which help you to form sounds.

Ears with which to hear the miracle of sound! What a joy it is to hear the wonderful symphony of mother nature: the sounds of birds singing; the ocean's roar; the evening serenade of crickets; and so it goes. With these ears, we can hear all kinds of sounds: romantic, sad, and happy sounds — sounds which have inspired songwriters so they can express the entire spectrum of human emotions.

Musical sounds: All the composers of the world have had thirteen notes with which to work; music which is composed into hundreds of different packages and forms for us to enjoy with our ears. I was always amazed at the classical masters who would hear all the various parts of the orchestra inside their heads first before they wrote it down on paper.

Eyes to view the world's constant glory. Stop for a moment to think about the whole spectrum of colors that we physically see: red, white, blue, yellow, green, etc. The dark shadows, the bright sunlight, the multitude of ever-changing colors of sunrises, sunsets and all the colors of the rainbow. Look how colors influence our songs in country, pop, rock 'n' roll, folk, r&b, classical — you name it. So many songs have been written describing these colors: "Don't It Make My Brown Eyes Blue," "The Yellow Rose of Texas," "Red Roses for a Blue Lady," "Blue Skies," "Silver Stars, Purple Sage, Eyes of Blue," "Silver Bells," "The Green, Green Grass of Home," "I Forgot What the Blues Was Like," and the list is endless.

Down through the years, I've noticed that there is usually a song in the Top 100 which has the word "blue" in it. So keep this in mind when you're searching for a new song title.

Our eyes are one of our most priceless senses. However, you don't have to have sight to enjoy music. You can still see the music through your mind's miraculous visualization powers. Look at some of the world's greatest singers who see in their mind's eye: Ray Charles, Ronnie Milsap, Stevie Wonder, Jose Feliciano.

Feelings and emotions: To me, emotions are kind of a string section with violins, cello, viola — all playing together and yet each playing its solo part in celebrating the entire emotional spectrum which is within each of us, ranging from happiness to sadness. It's this energy force, this soul within us that is the basic inspirational foundation of our very being and which motivates us in all we do.

Our mental capabilities: Since we have now established the fact that you are your own instrument or orchestra, who is the conductor? Your brain — with its incredible intuition, imagination and visualization powers — is the greatest conductor in the world! And we use our mind's capabilities unconsciously when we compose music or lyrics and when we perform. Look at how our "computer" brain takes words and forms them into mental pictures. Did you ever stop to realize that when we dream, we dream in mental images — not words?

I love to listen to all types of music. Recently, I read the biography of one of the greatest composers of all time in the classical field: Ludwig van Beethoven. He was born in Bonn, Germany, on December 16, 1770. Some of the world's greatest musical compositions were created by this musical genius. He had a very difficult childhood and his life story illustrates how this innate, indefinable spirit and soul, which is within all of us, can help us triumph over any tragedies or hard times that may befall us.

At the age of thirty-one, he began to notice that he was growing deaf which, naturally, brought anguish and despair to him, since he lived to compose and play music. However, his progressive deafness only inspired him to create with more passion than ever before. Can you imagine what a difficult task that must have been? He brought to life, in the physical realm as we know it, the music that he could only hear inside his head! Some of his masterpieces include: the *Appassionata, Waldstein,* and *Moonlight* sonatas for the piano; and the *Eroica* Symphony.

Around 1818, he started composing the *Ninth* Symphony, the *Missa Solemnis,* and the final quartets. It's my understanding that the last symphony he ever wrote broke all the rules and regulations of structured music previously known to the world at that time; they were new dimensions of musical expression which had never been imagined or created before! This wonderful Sagittarius is a man after my own heart!

The last time Beethoven appeared before the public was in 1824. The audience didn't know he was deaf as he introduced and conducted his newest creative effort — the *Ninth* Symphony.

I want you to imagine with me, if you will, the scenario that took place and which will probably pull at your heartstrings as it did mine: After the symphony ended, the audience started to enthusiastically applaud, but Beethoven, who couldn't hear their applause, continued conducting because he was several measures off the actual, physical performance of the symphony. It wasn't until one of the performers walked over to him and turned him around to face his fervently cheering and appreciative audience, that they realized he was actually deaf! Apparently the applause and standing ovations for him were endless — and rightfully so!

The point that I'm trying to convey to you, which illustrates the miracle of this chapter's subject matter, is that although Beethoven was deaf to the actual sounds of music, he could still write the majestic and eloquent sounds that he heard within his soul.

The inability to hear and the miraculous power of music hits close to home because my daughter, Linda, is a dedicated speech therapist at the Oralingua School in Whittier, California, which specializes in teaching hearing-impaired children from two through twelve years of age. These devoted teachers patiently teach them to become independent and to live in the world of people who can hear and speak.

Once a child learns sign language, he has a tendency to stop trying to hear. Therefore, the basis of this school's teaching is "listening" and "hearing aids." By using listening, they teach the communication skills of language and speech which open a whole new world to the children in every way.

Music plays a big part in their curriculum. The children can feel musical vibrations and learning songs is a great teaching tool because there is something about a song's cadence — its rhythms and melodies — which helps these children to use and improve their speaking skills.

Since they believe that hearing-impaired children should have the opportunity to be on stage to dance, sing and talk to an audience, Linda produces an hour-long show once a year in which the children perform. This, in turn, motivates them to explore their creativity and innate musical talents.

Since this unique, one-of-a-kind school is a small, private, nonprofit organization, they have several fund-raising events a year in which I have been honored to participate as a guest celebrity.

Last year, one of the events was a celebrity basketball game in which many of the Los Angeles Rams played various celebrities who were coached by one of basketball's "winningest" coaches in the nation, Jerry Tarkanian, who is from the University of Nevada at Las Vegas.

Before the game, Linda took her children out on the basketball court and they sang "God Bless America." Just seeing those sweet, innocent little faces courageously singing the song they hear in their hearts is a tear-jerker. They received a standing ovation from the crowd as they always do at these events.

I was particularly moved when I received my star on the Hollywood Walk of Fame two years ago, because Linda's entire school came to Hollywood for this special occasion. As I listened to all the accolades which were being bestowed upon me this memorable day, none was greater than the gift of song which these little Oralingua children had learned especially for me and which they proudly sang as they stood on the corner of Sunset and Vine.

Although these children cannot hear the actual sounds of music, they, like Beethoven, can still hear, feel and communicate the musical vibrations in their souls which are life itself, and connect all of us to one another.

So much can be learned through biographies, books, plays and movies which can uplift and inspire you in your own individual life. There was a wonderful Broadway play which was made into a movie called *The Music Man*, starring Robert Preston and Shirley Jones. If you haven't seen it and want to be thoroughly entertained, I suggest you rent a home video or watch it on television when they run it again. Robert Preston plays a silver-tongued salesman who goes from town to town with various schemes, collects the money and then leaves without delivering the goods.

His Waterloo occurs when he goes into the town of Gary, Indiana, and sells its townspeople the idea of a young people's marching band. Naturally, they would need new instruments and uniforms, and he would be more than happy to supply them with these items.

None of the youngsters can read music or play an instrument very well, much less play together as a band. As a matter of fact, Robert Preston knows very little about music himself. However, he instills the belief in them that they can do it. He gets the whole town involved and excited about this project. He says that if they would just listen to the music inside their heads and imagine themselves playing their instruments, they could do it. Naturally, he falls in love with Shirley Jones, who is the town's librarian and music teacher. However, she can see through his scam and she tries to tell the people that he's an imposter. However, no one listens because for the first time in their lives, they are excited! They start hearing the music inside themselves. Their unwavering blind belief makes it possible for them to actually play! Not as a great John Philip Sousa marching band, of course, but as a Gary, Indiana youth band.

The upshot of this wonderful play and movie is that the magic of believing creates musical miracles — to the surprise of Robert Preston. And the story ends happily as he changes his ways, settles down and marries Shirley Jones.

Joan Carol and I recently had dinner with several teachers who are good friends of ours: Ann Fisher, a dedicated Los Angeles elementary schoolteacher who uses music to teach English to her non-English speaking students (she, like my daughter, Linda, has discovered that the mystical magic of a song's cadence motivates children to learn and improve their speaking skills); Lois Erickson, who is one of the top music teachers in the Los Angeles City School District; and Dr. Donald Dossey, an author and lecturer on phobias, who encouraged and shared with us his book-publishing experiences.

As we were discussing our book with them, I was delightfully surprised when Lois corroborated what I had instinctively written in this chapter. She went on to say that one of the first things she teaches children who have no prior musical knowledge or skills, is to clap, snap, tap, and use mouth sounds which are a rhythmical introduction to music.

You Are Your Own Orchestra
And Your Own Music Man or Music Woman!

So what if you can't play an instrument, read musical notes or don't have any musical knowledge! You are born with your very own built-in orchestra, and you are your very own music man or music woman!

So play your dominant chord and have fun with your orchestra for all you are worth!

CHAPTER TWENTY-FIVE

THE END IS ONLY THE BEGINNING

D ear songwriter/reader: As the last mile of this musical book journey comes into view, I want you to think of it as the beginning of your very own musical odyssey. Maybe you'll be having a meeting with me or another publisher someday with a song you've written that may have been inspired, hopefully, by something I've said in this book.

If I were to condense all the songwriting suggestions that I've given you, it would be the succinct writing formula which has always worked for me: Tell them what you're going to say, say it, and then tell them what you said. And if you're writing a sensuous love song, add the following statement to the above formula: Lead them to the bedroom door, but don't take them in.

We are all part of the vibrational rhythm that beats throughout the universe. Learn to listen, believe and march to the musical beat of your own heart. Mozart, Beethoven, Bach, Chopin and other creative geniuses did, and look at the music they gave to the world — as all the creative souls have done, are doing, and will continue to do in the future.

When you have given your all by reaching deep down inside yourself and have completed whatever creative endeavor in which you are participating, there is a sense of pride and a feeling of accomplishment that money can't buy and no one can ever take away from you. These are the feelings that both Joan Carol and I have as this musical book journey of a thousand words comes to an end.

However, there were those times when both of us were in an "idea gridlock" and we needed inspiration to keep on keeping on. It was during one of those times that my daughter, Linda, shared with us an "accomplishment poem-prayer" that she wrote many years ago, which I will share with you at the close of this chapter.

What she wrote says it all. It's what I have always believed and have tried to do all my life. Since all of us are in this thing called life together, I have always felt that we should give to one another what is alive in each of us to give. What is alive in me are these songwriting suggestions that I've given you throughout this book, which could be the beginning of an exciting new life.

Thank you for spending this time with me. I hope you've not only learned something, but that you've had as much fun and enjoyment reading this book as I have had writing it and sharing my thoughts with you.

If any of my suggestions have sparked a flame of belief or planted a seed of hope in your mind which, in turn, will help you to grow and develop your songwriting desire, then this book has accomplished what it set out to do: to inspire and to help you write your song(s) which I know is within you to write!

Your talent is God's gift to you, and the way you use it is your gift to God. Welcome to the wonderful world of creative songwriting!

"Today"
By Linda Stone-Hyde

Help me to make this day...a day of Accomplishment:

> *Help me to fill one heart with a new joy.*
> *Help me to quench one thirsty mind with*
> *a swallow of wisdom.*
> *Help me to stir one soul with the knowledge*
> *of my love.*
> *Let my ear be patient and understanding as*
> *it listens for one new truth.*
> *Let my voice blend with another in harmony.*
> *Let my hand be steady as it reaches out to*
> *touch one other hand in tenderness.*
> *Help me to take just one more step along*
> *the path you have chosen as mine.*

Above all, Lord, let my own heart be full, my spirit be whole, because through your guidance, I have Today done these things.

Amen

AWARD-WINNING SONGS

"Beautiful Lies"	by Jack Rhodes
"Behind the Tear"	by Ned Miller & Sue Miller
"Blackberry Boogie"	by Tennessee Ernie Ford
"Bright Lights and Blonde Haired Women"	by Eddie Kirk
"Conscience, I'm Guilty"	by Jack Rhodes
"Dime a Dozen"	by Harlan Howard
"Do What You Do Do Well"	by Ned Miller
"Don't You Remember?"	by Ace Dinning
"Five Hundred Miles"	by Bobby Bare, Charlie Williams & Hedy West
"Foolin' Around"	by Harlan Howard & Buck Owens
"Goin' Steady"	by Faron Young
"Happy to Be Unhappy"	by Bobby Bare
"He'll Have to Go"	by Joe Allison & Audrey Allison
"He'll Have to Stay"	by Joe & Audrey Allison & Charles Grean
"I Don't Believe I'll Fall in Love Today"	by Harlan Howard
"I Never Picked Cotton"	by Charlie Williams & Bobby George
"If That's the Fashion"	by Tommy Collins
"If You Ain't Lovin', You Ain't Livin' "	by Tommy Collins
"I'm a Truck"	by Robert Stanton
"Invisible Tears"	by Ned Miller & Sue Miller
"It's Such a Pretty World Today"	by Dale Noe
"Kicking Our Hearts Around"	by Wanda Jackson
"Live Fast, Love Hard, Die Young"	by Joe Allison
"Loose Talk"	by Freddie Hart & Ann Lucas
"May the Bird of Paradise Fly Up Your Nose"	by Neal Merritt
"Milk 'Em in the Morning, Feed 'Em...Evening Blues"	by Tennessee Ernie Ford
"My Baby's Gone"	by Hazel Houser
"Next Time I Fall in Love"	by Ned Miller
"Odds and Ends"	by Harlan Howard

"Only Daddy That'll Walk the Line"	by Ivy "Jimmy" Bryant
"Put Your Hand in the Hand"	by Gene MacLellan
"She Called Me Baby"	by Harlan Howard
"Shot Gun Boogie"	by Cliffie Stone & Tennessee Ernie Ford
"Silver Threads and Golden Needles"	by Jack Rhodes & Dick Reynolds
"Snowbird"	by Gene MacLellan
"Teen Age Crush"	by Joe Allison & Audrey Allison
"The Gods Were Angry with Me"	by Bill Mackintosh & Roma Wilkinson
"The Popcorn Song"	by Bob Roubian
"This Song Is Just for You"	by Cecil Harris & Perk Williams
"Together Again"	by Buck Owens
"Try a Little Kindness"	by Curt Sapaugh & Bobby Austin
"Under the Influence of Love"	by Harlan Howard & Buck Owens
"Under Your Spell Again"	by Buck Owens & Dusty Rhodes
"Wait a Little Longer Please, Jesus"	by Hazel Houser
"Waitin' in Your Welfare Line"	by Harlan Howard & Buck Owens
"Whatcha Gonna Do Now?"	by Tommy Collins
"You Better Not Do That"	by Tommy Collins
"You Took Her Off My Hands"	by H. Howard, W. Stewart & S. McDonald

PUBLISHED SONGS

INCLUDE:

TITLE	RECORDING ARTIST
"Blanket on the Ground"	Jeanne Pruett
"Bless Your Pea-Pickin' Heart"	Tennessee Ernie Ford
"Dear John"	Ferlin Husky & Jean Shepard
"Do What You Do Do Well"	Ned Miller
"Don't Go Courtin' in a Hot Rod"	Tennessee Ernie Ford & Molly Bee
"Foolin' Around"	Buck Owens
"Girl's Night Out"	The Judds
"I'm a Truck"	Red Simpson
"I'm Just an Old Chuck of Coal"	John Anderson
"John and Marsha"	Stan Freberg with Cliffie Stone Band
"Just Beyond the Moon"	Tex Ritter
"Maggie"	Stan Freberg
"Mama, He's Crazy"	The Judds
"New Steel Guitar Rag"	Bob Wills; Bill Boyd
"Only Daddy That'll Walk the Line"	Waylon Jennings
"Put Your Hand in the Hand"	Anne Murray
"Shot Gun Boogie"	Tennessee Ernie Ford
"Silver Threads and Golden Needles"	Linda Ronstadt
"Smokey Mountain Boogie"	Tennessee Ernie Ford
"Snowbird"	Anne Murray
"Take it Any Way You Can Get It"	Cliffie Stone
"That's My Boy"	Stan Freberg
"The Gods Were Angry with Me"	Tex Ritter & Eddie Kirk
"The Lord's Lariat"	Tennessee Ernie Ford
"The Popcorn Song"	Bob Roubian with Cliffie Stone Band
"Together Again"	Buck Owens (20 other artists)
"Try"	Stan Freberg
"Try a Little Kindness"	Glen Campbell
"Under Your Spell Again"	Buck Owens & Dusty Rhodes
"Watch It Neighbor, Watch It Friend"	Eddie Kirk with Cliffie Stone Band
"Wrong Time to Leave Me, Lucille"	Kenny Rogers
"You Gotta Have a License"	Tommy Collins

SONGS WRITTEN AND/OR COWRITTEN

INCLUDE:

TITLE	WRITERS
"Anticipation Blues"	Cliffie Stone & T. Ernie Ford
"B. One Baby"	Cliffie Stone & Stan Freberg
"Black-Eyed Peas & Cornbread"	Cliffie Stone & Herman "the Hermit"
"Blue Butterfly"	Cliffie Stone & Joan Carol Stone
"Chopstick Boogie"	Cliffie Stone & Steve Stone
"Country Junction"	Cliffie Stone & T. Ernie Ford
"Country Rap"	Cliffie Stone & Jonathan Stone
"Deja Vu (All Over Again)"	Cliffie Stone & Joan Carol Stone
"Divorce Me C.O.D."	Cliffie Stone & Merle Travis
"Famous Last Words"	Cliffie Stone & Joan Carol Stone
"Gas Station Blues Boogie"	Cliffie Stone
"He's Left the Building"	Cliffie Stone & Ginny Peters
"I Forgot What the Blues Was Like"	Cliffie & Joan Stone, John Hobbs
"I'm Here Darlin' and I'm Real"	Cliffie & Joan Stone, Mark Burnes
"I'm Just a Memory You Left Behind"	Cliffie Stone & Georgia Yates
"John and Marsha"	C. Stone, S. Freberg & Billy Liebert
"Jump Rope Boogie"	Cliffie Stone & Linda Stone-Hyde
"Lawdy What a Gal"	Cliffie Stone & Merle Travis
"Looking at You Looking at Me"	Cliffie Stone & Vivian Rae
"Lord, I Thank You"	Cliffie Stone & Joan Carol Stone
"My Life Began"	Cliffie Stone & Joan Carol Stone
"New Steel Guitar Rag"	C. Stone, L. McCalliuffe, M. Travis
"No Vacancy"	Cliffie Stone & Merle Travis
"Riding Through the Purple Sage"	Cliffie Stone & Darrell Rice
"So Round, So Firm, So Fully Packed"	C. Stone, Merle Travis & Eddie Kirk
"Spanish Bells"	C. Stone, Porky Freeman, Jimmy Dolan
"Storeroom of Memories"	Cliffie & Joan Stone, Larry Keyes
"Such a Pretty Picture"	Cliffie Stone & Joan Carol Stone
"Sunday Morning Tears For a Saturday Girl"	Cliffie Stone & Ned Miller
"Sweet Baby"	Cliffie Stone & Mark Burnes
"T N Teasin' Me"	C. Stone, Frances Kane, Claude James
"The Electric Cowboy Band"	Cliffie Stone & Curtis Stone
"The Right to Remain Silent"	Cliffie Stone & Gary Murray
"They Said It Wouldn't Last"	Cliffie & Joan Stone, Larry Keyes
"Think About It Boogie"	Cliffie & Joan Stone, Mark Burnes
"Touched by the Magic of You"	Cliffie & Joan Stone, Mark Burnes
"Yellow Roses, Summer Sunshine"	Cliffie Stone & Joan Carol Stone

BIBLIOGRAPHY

Lomax, John. *Folk Song U.S.A.* New York: Duel, Sloane & Pearce, 1947.

Lomax, John. *The Old Chisholm Trail.* New York: Fischer, 1924.

Lomax, John. *Cowboy Songs and Other Frontier Ballads.* New York: MacMillan, 1938.

Lomax, Alan. *American Folk Songs and Folklore.* New York: Progressive Education, 1942.

Lomax, Alan. *The Folk Songs of North America.* New York: Doubleday, 1960.

Leshan, E. *It's Better to Be Over the Hill than Under It.* Newmarket Press, 1990.

Tormé, Mel. *It Wasn't All Velvet.* New York: Penguin Group (Viking), 1988.

RECOMMENDED READING

Braheny, John. *The Craft and Business of Songwriting.* Ohio: Writer's Digest Books, div. of F&W Publications, Inc., 1988.

Shemel, Sidney and Krasilovsky, M. William. *This Business of Music.* New York: Billboard Publications, Inc., 1971.

Theroux, Gary and Gilbert, Bob. *The Top Ten: 1956 to Present.* New York: Fireside/ Simon & Schuster, 1982.

Dossey, Donald, Ph.D. *Keying: The Power of Positive Feelings.* California: Outcomes Unlimited Press, Inc., 1990.

Hay, Louise L. *You Can Heal Your Life.* California: Hay House, 1984.

Buscaglia, Leo, Ph.D. *Living, Loving and Learning.* New York: Ballantine Books, 1982.

Lee, Peggy. *Miss Peggy Lee.* New York: Donald I. Fine, Inc., 1989.

A SPECIAL ACKNOWLEDGMENT

A special acknowledgment to the multitude of people who have made up the integral tapestry of my fifty years in the entertainment and music business. Each one of them colored my life with their expertise and special talents in some way. If I inadvertently have left anyone out, please forgive me. I know that you know who you are. In alphabetical order, they are:

Adams, Berle

Adams, Michael and Andrea

Allison, Joe

Arnold, Danny

Arnold, Eddy

Austin, Gene

Autry, Gene

Autry, Jackie (Mrs. Gene)

Bare, Jeannie and Bobby

Bee, (Sotzsky) Allen

Bee, Molly

Blankenship, Johnny

Bodine, Maritza

Bond, Johnny and Sherry

Boyd, Fran and Bill

Bradley, Connie

Bradley, Harold

Bradley, Owen

Bryant, Jimmy

Buttram, Pat

Clapper, Sherry

Corbin, Paul and Marless

Cox, Paula and Clem

Daniels, Jack and Alicia

Darling, Peaches

Davidson, Cheryl and Lindsey

Dean, Eddie and Dearest

Devord, John

Dickerson, Diane

Donavan, Carol

Dossey, Donald

Douds, David

Einsel, Debbie

Elmendorf, Seth

Erickson, Lois

Fisher, Ann

Ford, Brion

Ford, Buck

Ford, Tennessee Ernie and Beverly

Freberg, Stan

Friedman, Brian

Frizzell, Lefty

Fuller, Jerry and Annette

Gillette, Lee

Grandpa Jones and Ramona

Grant, Johnny

Hall, Susan

Hamblen, Stuart and Suzy

Hansen, Maxine

Harding, Fletcher

Hart, Freddie

Hicks, Judy

Hobbs, John and Doni

Hobson, Jim

Hoffman, Milt

Huffine, Charlotte

Hyde, Harvey

Hyde, Katy

Hyde, Susan
Johnson, Nettie and Porky
Keltgen, Cory
Kenny, Mary
Keyes, Melva and Larry
Kiczenski, Conrad J.
Kiczenski, Daisy and Leo
Kiczenski, Keely
Kiczenski, Kristine
Kiczenski, Ronald
Kiczenski, Ronald, Jr.
King, Loyal
King, Bob and Laurie
Kraeger, Cathy and Steve
Landis, Joe
Lear, Norman
Levine, Marc
Levy, Leeds
Levy, Lou
Liebert, Billy
Linn, Roberta
Loakes, Jim
Louvello, Sam
Marquez, Sabina
Michaels, Danny
Monroe, Smiley
Morgan, Denise and Pete
Moser, Cactus and Ellen
Murray, Ken
Nelson, Ken
Nichols, Alice
Palmer, Edith
Palmer, Karen
Parker, Michelle
Peacock, Eloise
Petty, Diane C.
Phillips, Garth and Connie
Phillips, Kay and Gregg
Pierce, Alvin

Powell, Hope
Preston, Frances
Ramsey, Astrid
Reeves, Jim
Rhodes, Dusty
Riccobono, Rick
Riggins, Pug and Rig
Roark, Marie
Rowe, Debbie
Salamone, Mary
Sands, Tommy
Sheets, Dale and Joan
Sill, Lester
Silver, Betty Jo
Singer, Linda
Smith, Dolly D.
Sovine, Roger
Stone, Amy
Stone, Cathy
Stone, Devonne
Stone, Ina
Stone, Jonathan, Jr.
Stone, Missy
Stone, Rachael
Stone-Elmendorf, Mandy
Tauber, Selwyn
Tharp, Steve
Trust, Sam and Joan
Tuttle, Wesley and Marilyn
Vescovo, Al
Walker, Harvey
Walker-Meador, Jo
Ward, Bill
Weed, Gene
West, Speedy
Whitehouse, Dick
Williams, Charlie
Yorkin, Bud
Zettel, Virginia and Dick

INDEX

198

199

Los Angeles Songwriters Showcase, 106
Lounge Lizards, 176
Love Me or Leave Me, 123
Love Story, 52, 53, 124
"Love's Freedom," 83
Lowe, Ruth, 112
"Lucille," 94, 95
Lynn, Loretta, 161, 163
MacGraw, Ali, 52
"Macho Man," 40
MacLellan, Gene, 4, 73
Maddox, Rose, 151, 163
"Major Bowes' Radio Amateur Hour," 174
"Make a Move on Me," 45
"Make Someone Happy," 168
"Make Your Own Kind of Music," 168
"Makin' Whoopie," 145
"Mama Tried," 40
Manchester, Melissa, 164
Mandrell, Barbara, 163
Mann, Barry, 168
"Mansion on the Hill," 34
"Marie Lavaux," 69
Marks, Johnny, 26
Marlboro, 176
Martin, Freddie, 134
Masser, Michael, 168
Mattea, Kathy, 37, 163
Matthew 7:7, 113
May, Billy, 141
MCA Publishing Group, 130
MCA Records, 149
McDonald, Michael, 169
McEntire, Reba, 37, 163
McKuen, Rod, 86
McMahon, Ed, 175
McQuaig, Glenell, 151
McQuaig, Jonell, 151
"Me and Bobby McGee," 47
Melody, 89
Mercer, Johnny, 112, 126
Merrill, Ray, 151
Michelangelo, 44
Midler, Bette, 38, 122
Miller, Jody, 116
Miller, Ned, 15
Miller, Roger, 16, 108
Milsap, Ronnie, 125, 181
Missa Solemnis, 182
"Mona Lisa," 138
Monroe, Marilyn, 124
Montana, Patsy, 163
Moonlight Sonata, 182
Morris, Chuck, 177
Morris, Edward, 164
Morris, Gary, 122
Moser, Cactus, 177, 178

Motown, 31
Mozart, 186
"Mule Skinner's Blues," 153
"Mule Train," 154
Murray, Anne, 4
Murray, Ken, 155
Murrell, Red, 153
Music Row magazine, 105
My Fair Lady, 123
"My Grandfather's Clock," 12
"My Love," 134
"My Venus DeMilo," 85
Nashville Network, 175
"Nashville Scene," 164
Nashville Songwriters Association International's Hall of Fame, 60, 95, 163
National Songwriters Guild, 69
NBC, 134, 140, 154, 155, 157
Nelson, Ken, 151
Nelson, Nikki, 178
Nelson, Willie, 69, 172
Newton-John, Olivia, 45
"Night and Day," 132
Night Shift, 169
"Night Watch," 71
"Nine Pound Hammer," 135, 150
Nine to Five, 161
Ninth Symphony, 182
"No Vacancy," 5, 38
O'Brien, Joanie, 151
O'Neal, Ryan, 52
O'Quinn, Gene, 151
Oak Ridge Boys, 159
Ode to Billie Joe, 123
"Okie From Muskogee," 40
"On My Own," 169
"On the Other Hand," 10, 19
Oralingua School, 183, 184
Oslin, K.T., 163, 167
Overstreet, Paul, 10
Owens, Bonnie, 40, 163
Owens, Buck, 13, 30, 35, 151
Palladino, John, 150
Palmer, Karen, 108
Palomino, 172, 175
Parton, Dolly, 12, 25, 160, 161
Pearl, Minnie, 163
"Peepin' Through the Keyhole," 151
Peters, Ginny, 72
Petty, C. Diane, 163
"Pillow Talk," 14
Pitchford, Dean, 45
Plummer, Christopher, 46
Pointer Sisters, 45
"Popeye, the Sailor Man," 18
Porter, Cole, 145
Potter, Peter, 62
Presley, Elvis, 31
Preston, Frances, 160, 161, 162, 170

Preston, Robert, 121, 184, 185
Primat America, 121
Pruett, Jeanne, 14
"Put Your Hand In the Hand," 4, 73
Radio & Records, 105, 125
Radio Recorder's Studio, 150
Rae, Vivian, 72, 175
Rambo, 40
Raphael, Sally Jessy, 165
RCA Records, 116
RCA Victor, 111
"Red Roses for a Blue Lady," 181
Redford, Robert, 39
Register of Copyrights, 99
Return Music, 111
Rhino Records, 68, 150
Richey, George, 72, 116
Riddle, Nelson, 141
Ritter, Tex, 15, 124, 151
River of No Return, 124
Rivers, Joan, 165
Robbins, Marty, 29
Robinson, Julius, 45
Rocky, 124
Rodgers and Hammerstein, 46, 71
Rodgers and Hart, 71
Rodgers, Jimmie, 153
Rogers, Gaby, 168
Rogers, Kenny, 15, 94, 95, 104, 115
Rogers, Roy, 53
Rogers, Shorty, 141
Ronstadt, Linda, 151, 172
Rose, Charlie, 71
Rose, Fred, 34, 46, 126
"Rudolph, the Red-Nosed Reindeer," 26
Sager, Carole Bayer, 164, 169
"Satin Doll," 14
"Satin Sheets," 14
"Saturday Night Shuffle," 16
Schlitz, Don, 10
"Secret Love," 144, 145
Selleck, Tom, 17, 40
"Send Me the Pillow You Dream On," 14
SESAC, 103, 104, 119, 136, 163
"Seven of Clubs" 15
Shafer, Sanger D. ("Whitey"), 95
Shanley, John Patrick, 78
Sharp, Martha, 163
Shaver, Billy Joe, 111
Sheets, Dale, 75, 145
"Sheila," 69
Sherrill, Billy, 161
Shore, Dinah, 163
"Shotgun Boogie," 154
"Showdown U.S.A.," 177
Silbar, Jeffrey, 38, 70, 122
Sill, Joel, 130
"Silver Bells," 181

201